T0290195

THE NATIVE VOICE

Caitlin Press Inc.
8100 Alderwood Road,
Halfmoon Bay, BC V0N 1Y1
www.caitlin-press.com

Text and cover design by Vici Johnstone
Printed in Canada

Caitlin Press Inc. acknowledges financial support from the Government of Canada and the Canada Council for the Arts, and from the Province of British Columbia through the British Columbia Arts Council and the Book Publisher's Tax Credit.

Canada Council
for the Arts

Conseil des Arts
du Canada

BRITISH COLUMBIA
ARTS COUNCIL

Library and Archives Canada Cataloguing in Publication

Jamieson, Eric, 1949-, author
        The native voice : the story of how Maisie Hurley and Canada's first Aboriginal newspaper changed a nation / Eric Jamieson.

Includes bibliographical references and index.
ISBN 978-1-987915-17-4 (paperback)

        1. Hurley, Maisie—Influence. 2. Native voice. 3. Indian newspapers—British Columbia—History. 4. Newspaper publishing—British Columbia—History. 5. Native Brotherhood of British Columbia—History. 6. Native peoples—British Columbia—History. I. Title.

PN4914.I553J34 2016   071'.108997   C2015-908120-3

THE NATIVE VOICE

THE HISTORY OF CANADA'S FIRST ABORIGINAL NEWSPAPER
AND ITS FOUNDER MAISIE HURLEY

ERIC JAMIESON

CAITLIN PRESS

*This book is dedicated to Canada's First Peoples;
we have much to learn from them.*

CONTENTS

ACKNOWLEDGEMENTS

As with any book, it takes many more people than the writer to see his or her efforts turned into print. My case was no different and below you will find the people who assisted me in making *The Native Voice* possible.

First, I must thank Nancy Kirkpatrick and Shirley Sutherland, director and assistant director of the North Vancouver Museum and Archives (NVMA) for suggesting that Maisie would make an interesting book subject. Nancy introduced me to Moira Movanna, Maisie's granddaughter, whom I especially thank for her memories of her Nana. The same goes for another granddaughter, Maureen Woodcock, who offered invaluable help in understanding her complex grandmother and her family. Other grandchildren—Maisie McKinnon, Bill Bell, Marge Neilsen, Jack Hill and Valerie Murphy—furthered my understanding of their grandmother. Great-grandchildren such as Kerrie Haynes and Aran Murphy also offered support.

There would be no book were it not for the kindness and support extended to me by Bill Duncan (Gilakas'la), the business agent for the Native Brotherhood of British Columbia (NBBC or the Brotherhood), who provided me with surplus copies of the *Native Voice* newspaper and kept me enthralled over many lunch meetings with information on the *Voice* as well as the NBBC.

I owe a huge debt of gratitude to Chief Dr. Robert Joseph (OBC), hereditary chief of the Gwawaenuk First Nation and ambassador of the Truth and Reconciliation Commission, for agreeing to write the Foreword to the book. As well, a great deal of thanks to Tom Berger (OC, OBC), who read a first draft and offered invaluable help. I would also like to thank Buffy Sainte-Marie for her insightful comments about Maisie.

There would be no book at all were it not for Vici Johnstone, owner and publisher of Caitlin Press. Thanks also to her competent staff, namely Betty Keller, noted author, educator and editor and Catherine Edwards, copy editor, for turning my scribbles into this book.

The following acknowledgements are alphabetical, each no less important than the other:

Earl Anderson, author of *Hard Place to Do Time: The Story of Oakalla Prison 1912–1991,* for his knowledge of the infamous prison; John Bennett for sharing his experiences as a boat builder and his knowledge of the early fishing days on the northern coast; Robin Brown, formerly of Masset, for his recollections of Alfred Adams; Carol and Natasha at the NBBC office in West

Vancouver for their help; Alissa Cherry, librarian with the Union of BC Indian Chiefs for her help locating commissions and amendments to the Indian Act and other documents; Delores Churchill, daughter of Alfred Adams, for her recollections of her father; Helen Clifton, from Hartley Bay, for her recollections of her father-in-law, Bobb Clark, Communications and Program Manager for the Nisga'a Lisims Government; the late Heber Clifton, one of the NBBC founders, and her late brother-in-law, Robert Clifton, former NBBC president; Tracy Cogan for permission to use her wonderful portrait of Dick Patrick; Hugh Dempsey, author and former director of the Glenbow Museum, for his recollections of Maisie; the late Alvin Dixon for his recollections of residential school life and the *Native Voice*; Andy Everson (Nagedzi), talented First Nations artist, for the significance of naming ceremonies; Dr. Sharon Fortney for her scholarly article and knowledge of the Maisie Hurley Collection; the late Peter Grauer, author, for his research on Bill Miner and his blogged information on Maisie; Kevin Griffin for his *Vancouver Sun* Maisie stories and his assistance; Joan Hall for her recollections of Maisie; Patrick Hayes, University of Saskatchewan; Jennifer Hill, related to Big White Owl; Daien Ide, NVMA, for her assistance with archival material; Sasha Jacobs, Haisla Nation; Arlene John, for her recollections of her brother, Dick Patrick; Gene Joseph, author of *A Brief History of the Native Brotherhood of British Columbia*, for her knowledge of the NBBC; Jane Kristovich, daughter of Alfred Adams, for her recollections of her father; Jamie E. Lamb, former newspaper columnist, for his insightful column on Maisie; Janet Nicol, journalist, for her research on Tom and Maisie Hurley; Dr. Phil Nuytten, author, for his knowledge of First Nations culture and his recollections of Maisie; Kathy Plett, head librarian at the College of New Caledonia for her knowledge of Dick Patrick; Phil Rankin, lawyer, for his knowledge of Tom Hurley; the late Ron Rose, former *Vancouver Sun* reporter, for his recollections of Maisie and Tom; the late Judge Alfred Scow for his recollections of Maisie, the *Native Voice* and the NBBC; Darryl Stonefish, relative of Big White Owl and historian at the Delaware Nation Moravian Thames Band, for his recollections of Big White Owl; the late author, Paul St. Pierre, for his recollections of Maisie; Ron M. Strickland of Perth, Australia, for his knowledge of the Merry family; Janet Turner, archivist at the NVMA, for help with text and photographs in their collection; Dr. Robert Ward, author, for his recollections of his wife's relative, John Reginald Rowallane Armytage-Moore; Laura Williams, Haisla Nation; Chief Bill Wilson (Hemads-Kla-Lee-Lee-Kla), for his recollections of Maisie; Michael Nicoll Yaghulanaas, author and visual artist, for his knowledge of Alfred Adams.

I would also like to thank my many friends for their support and encouragement. My wife, Joan, my daughter, Amanda, my son, Ian, my daughter-in-law, Carlie, and my ever-inquisitive, sweet granddaughter, Jessica Jean, offered me unconditional love and an environment conducive to work. My late father, John Vernon Jamieson, was oblivious to the inspiration he provided, but from him I inherited a small totem pole carved by the famous Kwakwa-ka'wakw carver, Charlie James, and among the many books I received from his estate was *The Roar of the Breakers*, by Alan Morley, about the life of Peter Kelly, whose advocacy frequents these pages.

My apologizes for having missed anyone; it is certainly not intentional. Any errors or omissions contained in the text are mine alone.

FOREWORD

I applaud Eric Jamieson for bringing to light the valiant and relentless effort by one "white woman," Maisie Hurley, to seek justice for Aboriginal people.

She created the *Native Voice* newspaper, launched in 1946, that gave profile to the early political, socio-economic, and Aboriginal rights struggles that go on today. She created awareness and advocated fiercely for equality for Aboriginal people. This bold, courageous and outspoken woman is an unsung hero.

Jamieson's book, *The Native Voice*, is compelling, startling and sometimes disturbing as it shines a light on Canada's brutal dismissal and treatment of Aboriginal people throughout the colonial period.

The Native Voice is a timely publication following the release of the Truth and Reconciliation Commission of Canada report in June 2015.

The dark side of our collective history is once again revealed as successive provincial and federal governments demonstrate discriminatory attitudes and actions by way of legislation and policy. It lays bare the rampant and systematic racism that set the stage for the conditions now existing in far too many communities.

There are so many poignant moments in this book.

"In the fall of 1944, Haida Elder Alfred Adams bumped into his old friend Maisie Hurley on a Vancouver street."

Adams was dying of cancer but was still preoccupied with his people. At the same time, Maisie Hurley was deeply distressed over the well-being of her two sons who were overseas in the war.

"You are worried over your sons, but service to others will help you and bring you happiness. I want you to give your life to my people by telling the white people about them."

She took this to heart and mind and launched the *Voice* as the official organ of the Native Brotherhood of BC, one of the oldest organizations in the country.

As the pages unfold, you will meet other incredible and visionary leaders like Alfred Adams. You will get to know Joe Capilano, Basil David, Charlie Isipaymilt, Reverend Peter Kelly, Chief Andrew Paull, Heber Clifton, Edward Gamble, Bill Scow, Reginald Cook, Dan Assu, Oscar Peters, William Pascal and others... all giants and legendary. We owe them much; they are all a part of our rich history and lay a foundation for our current times and the future.

While it is a challenging history, it will and has contributed to the vibrance and hope for our country.

Canadians everywhere are in a mood to seek a new way forward and to right relations with Aboriginal people. This additional story as told in *The Native Voice* will further enlighten and create a deeper understanding among us, which will lead to transformative relationships.

—Chief Dr. Robert Joseph

INTRODUCTION

In the winter of 2010 I visited the North Vancouver Museum for an exhibition called *Entwined History,* which presented a selection of art and ceremonial objects from the museum's Maisie Hurley Collection. It had been curated by Dr. Sharon Fortney and Damara Jacobs, director of education for the Squamish Nation, and the title referred to a unique and first-time collaboration between the museum and the Squamish Nation. Prior to that visit I had never heard of Maisie Hurley. I learned that she was born in Wales, but arrived in BC as a small child and devoted much of her life to advocating for First Nations people in the courts and as the publisher and editor of the *Native Voice* newspaper.

After viewing the show, I approached the director of the museum, Nancy Kirkpatrick, to offer my congratulations. It was then she suggested Maisie would make an interesting subject for a book. The idea excited me. A few of the courses I had taken for my Bachelor of Arts degree at the University of British Columbia had been anthropological and archaeological in nature, and I had developed a deep interest in BC's First Nations people and their struggle for justice. Later I had served a total of eighteen years on the boards of three community museums—Campbell River, Prince George and North Vancouver—where I had learned more about Canada's First Peoples.

My preliminary research into Maisie's life and story was disappointing. She appeared to have written no diaries, and I soon discovered that her personal filing cabinets had disappeared from her home after her death in 1964. However, after a meeting with Moira Movanna and later with Maureen Woodcock, two of Maisie's granddaughters, my prospects improved considerably. They improved again when I met Bill Duncan, the business agent for the Native Brotherhood of British Columbia, who offered me surplus copies of the *Native Voice* newspaper as well as an education on the history of the Brotherhood. It was only then that I felt I could write Maisie's story.

Once I began to read the copies of the *Native Voice* Bill had given me, her life slowly materialized before me because in her editorials and articles, she would occasionally let slip some personal fact that I had to store away until I could find the right place for it. And as I read of her frustrations, her anger and her love for her First Nations friends, something curious happened. I began to channel her voice as I moved along the road to justice with her, becoming angry when she was angry, sad when she was sad and hopeful when she was hopeful.

As with any reconstruction of a life, my book is bound to present a lesser characterization than the subject deserves, but what can't help but shine through in her life and story is her selfless devotion to the cause of First Nations justice.

1—SPIRITED YOUTH

In the fall of 1944, Haida Elder Alfred Adams bumped into his old friend Maisie Hurley on a Vancouver street. He was on his way to visit his doctor, and although he had cancer and would soon join his ancestors "in the Great Beyond,"[1] he was still focussed on the welfare of his people. After consoling Maisie, who was worried about her sons who were overseas in the war, he said, "You have always loved our people and have been a friend to them. You are worried over your sons, but service to others will help you and will bring you happiness. I want you to give your life to my people by telling the white people about them." He added that BC's Aboriginal population needed a voice to tell of their work and activities, to speak of their grievances, of their wish to educate their children—a voice that would be heard all over North America.[2]

Maisie was so moved by Adams' faith in her that she took his request to both heart and mind, and she determined to finance and publish a small newspaper for British Columbia First Nations people, a paper that her first editor, Jack Beynon, a World War I veteran, suggested she call *The Native Voice*. Her daughter, Kitty Bell, recalled her mother's simple rationale for this venture: "The Indian's voice is a voice in the wilderness, and it's not being heard."[3] The *Voice* was launched in December 1946 as the official organ of the Native Brotherhood of BC. "I have worked with the Indians and then the Native Brotherhood for many years," she later wrote to journalist Hugh Dempsey, one of her frequent contributors, and "seeing they needed a paper, I founded this paper on a shoestring (my own) in 1946 and it is growing in spite of many setbacks—run purely to help the Indian cause."[4]

It was not the first newspaper in North America for Aboriginal people. The Cherokee people had started the *Cherokee Phoenix* on February 1, 1828; however, two years later the US government passed the Indian Removal Act, and government troops smashed the Cherokees' presses, uprooted the people and drove them as well as other tribes on a forced march, infamously known as "the Trail of Tears," to a new home in Oklahoma. There, in 1843, they began a new publication called the *Phoenix Advocate* and operated it until 1906. In BC, a small paper called *Hagaga* was started by the Anglican missionary J. B. McCullagh in the Nass River area in Nisga'a territory in 1891. It was first published in the Nisga'a language in phonetic script, but by the late 1890s it had been renamed *North British Columbia News* and published in English. It had a wide circulation in the Nass River region.

Maisie's first editorial in the *Native Voice* left no doubt about the tone and direction she intended for the paper:

> In this initial presentation of the *Native Voice* to the people of British Columbia, we intend that the voice of the original Canadians will open a new era for our people who have striven to keep in step with all ranks of the march of time. An era in this atomic age where progress is measured for mankind the world over by scientific discoveries of learned people who, by their individual and co-operative methods, have the power to make this so-called Christian world a haven of consent for every human being in existence.
>
> *The Native Voice* will assert at the beginning the firm objectives at which we aim and hope to achieve in the not too distant future. An objective which will mean an honest guarantee of equality for the original inhabitants and owners of Canada. A Canada where under the Indian Act we suffer as a minority race and as wards or minors without a voice in regard to our own welfare. We are prisoners of a controlling power in our own country—a country that has stood up under the chaos of two world wars, beneath the guise of democracy and freedom, yet keeping enslaved a Native people in their own home land.
>
> Charity begins at home and it is up to those in control to sweep the steps of Parliament clean and bring into being a real democratic Canada, with freedom for all races—a Canada of which we can be proud. At this time, our Dominion is not in a position to point a finger of scorn at the treatment meted out by other countries toward their people until she liberates her own original and subjected race.[5]

The woman who would come to be known as Maisie Hurley was born at Bryn Heulog, a wealthy estate in the upscale Swansea suburb of Sketty, County of Glamorganshire in Wales, on Sunday, November 27, 1887. That day the wind had see-sawed between a moderate to strong gale, sweeping the clouds from the storm-tossed North Atlantic across the Bristol Channel and onto the mainland. Some might say that the driving rain, the thunder and lightning presaged the life that the child would lead, and they would be not too far wrong.

The 11.5-pound baby girl, born that day to 24-year-old Ronald Campbell Campbell-Johnston and his 27-year-old bride, Amy Ellen Chadwick (née Merry) Campbell-Johnston, would be christened Amy Campbell Campbell-Johnston, but she would soon be known simply and less pretentiously as Maisie. This was probably to differentiate her from her mother, but the less formal name would later help her straddle the barriers that the class system placed in her way. On the other hand, whenever it benefited her, she also had no reservations about trotting out the full authority of her hyphenated name and its provenance.

Maisie's mother came from an old Birmingham family of steel merchants. Her father, Alfred Senior Merry, was the managing director of a nickel and cobalt refining works at Hafod Isha, Swansea, having amalgamated his own father's failing metal-works firm with that of Henry Hussey Vivian in Birmingham in 1855. His household was not only busy—he and his wife, Eliza Mary Merry, had three sons and five daughters—but influential as well. Alfred Senior was friends with such notables as Charles Darwin and Professor Thomas Huxley of the Royal School of Mines, the latter having famously supported the former when his controversial theories on evolution collided with the creationist view of the church.

Maisie's mother, Amy Ellen Chadwick Campbell-Johnston (née Merry), came from a prominent English family. Friends of the family included such notables as Charles Darwin and Thomas Huxley. Photo from the family collection.

Amy (Merry) Campbell-Johnston was inclined to paint a much more glamorous picture of her forebears, however, claiming direct lineage to the pharaohs of Egypt and the ancient kings of England, including King Arthur, "although he is foolishly supposed by many to be but a myth."[6] She also claimed to have inherited the role of family seer, and wrote that earlier generations of Merrys (or Meris) had the duty to arrange the marriage of each family member at birth to keep the pedigree pure Anglo—with no taint of Saxon. And she believed that the ghost of the Merrys would appear to the head of the family in the form of an owl before each important occasion such as a birth, death or marriage.

Maisie's father, Ronald, an impressive-looking Scot with a lofty brow, sweeping moustache and imperial countenance, had deep family connections to a long line of royal and titled Scots, some of whom had acquitted themselves admirably in the administration of Britain's colonial interests. He was born at Oban, Argyleshire, Scotland, in 1863, educated at the elite Sherborne School for Boys in Dorset (established in 1550) and then the Royal School of Mines, London, from which he graduated in 1881. After serving an apprenticeship with the London engineering firm of John Taylor & Sons, he spent his next few years managing the company's mining assets in India.

Maisie's father, Ronald Campbell Campbell-Johnston, was a Scottish-born mining engineer and related to both the regal houses of Argyll and Montrose. Photo from the family collection.

Following Maisie's birth in Wales, Ronald moved his family back to Madras (now Chennai), India, to resume managing his employer's mines. There, in the manner of their ilk, Maisie's parents hired amahs and nannies to take care of their youngster. When she didn't pick up her native tongue as quickly as expected, it was discovered that her progress had been merely diverted; she was conversing very well in the languages of her caregivers.

By the time Alfred Senior Merry was in his mid-70s, he had dispatched the boys in his family, as well as son-in-law Ronald Campbell-Johnston, who had returned to Swansea with his family, to the four corners of the globe to take care of the family mining interests. Thus, in 1888 Ronald was sent to Joplin, Missouri, to take care of the family's zinc mines there, and upon returning to Swansea two

Maisie's great-great-grandfather, Lord William Campbell, was the last Royal Governor of South Carolina, but his tenure there ended after only three months when he was forced to flee for his life. Photo from the family collection.

years later, was reassigned to the Murray Mine near present-day Sudbury in northern Ontario. He quit the family firm in 1891, returning to Swansea long enough to collect his family before emigrating again, this time to British Columbia, a province rich in mineral exploration, though more importantly, adventure. At Swansea the family had its last gathering at Bryn Heulog before Ronald and Amy, along with their two children, Maisie and baby Ronald Junior, boarded the SS *Labrador* at Liverpool to begin the long journey to British Columbia.

Ronald Campbell-Johnston was not the first of his family to set foot on the North American continent. His great-grandfather, Lord William Campbell, a Scot with loyal ties to Britain, had been the tenth governor of Nova Scotia, serving from November 1766 until October 1773. He served as the last royal governor of South Carolina, arriving at his post in June 1775 with a mandate to quell the growing revolutionary unrest, but his tenure ended abruptly three months later when he escaped a horde of demonstrators and climbed aboard HMS *Temar*, never to return. It was one of Lord William Campbell's daughters, Louisa, who began the Campbell-Johnston lineage by marrying Sir Alexander Johnston in 1799. He would eventually become the chief justice of Sri Lanka (at that time called Ceylon).

Approximately one hundred years later, another related Campbell visited these shores. Sir John George Edward Henry Douglas Sutherland Campbell, Marquis of Lorne, 9th Duke of Argyll, and husband to Princess Louise, Queen Victoria's fourth daughter, became the fourth Governor General of Canada on October 7, 1878. He and his wife were interested in the arts, the duke being an amateur artist himself, and he and the princess encouraged the establishment of the Royal Society of Canada, the Royal Canadian Academy of Arts and the National Gallery of Canada, even selecting some of its first paintings.

In the spring of 1891 when the Campbell-Johnston family stepped from the Canadian Pacific Railway (CPR) coach to the station platform at the foot of Granville Street, the City of Vancouver was only a year older than Maisie. As she gazed about her, she saw a group of Chinese men with "their long queues and their different coloured coats... they looked so clean... pinks and blues and mauves, you know, and the funny Chinese shoes..."[7] They stared down at the passengers, captivated by the flurry of activity on the platform. She probably wouldn't have heard their voices over the jingle of cart, carriage and coach harnesses, the whinnying of horses, the shouts of passengers and the barks of cabbies competing to be heard over the general din of the saw-mills and other waterfront industries pushing roughly up against the city's downtown core.

The emerging city, though almost completely recovered from the devastating fire of June 1886, was still a haphazard assembly of sturdy commercial buildings and houses, wooden shacks and vacant lots. But on the "Bluff" just above the station, as if to advertise how lucrative the railway business was, the CPR bosses had built their palatial residences. A couple of blocks farther up the hill, at the corner of Georgia and Granville, was the CPR's first Hotel Vancouver, which Maisie recalled was complete with tennis courts and a cricket pitch. Just south of it was the city's new opera house, also built by the CPR, which boasted a capacity of 2,000, although the city's population was a mere 13,709 persons. It had opened on February 9, 1891, with a grand performance of Richard Wagner's romantic opera *Lohengrin*, starring the Austrian soprano, Emma Juch. That September, Madame Sarah Bernhardt arrived aboard a private train with her forty-three-person theatrical company to perform in *Fedora* and *La Tosca*, and the city fathers and retailers of women's fashions could not have been happier.

Just below the train station, the white-hulled Canadian Pacific Steamships' *Empress of India*, one of three *Empress* ships plying the Pacific from Hong Kong to Vancouver harbour, sat regally at her berth. This impressive liner carried wealthy tourists, businessmen, freight and mail from East Asia to Vancouver, where they transferred to the CPR train for Halifax and then embarked on another CP steamship bound for England. While there was no question that Vancouver was still a rough diamond hovering on the edge of the western frontier, the CPR in its wisdom was betting firmly on its potential to be something more.

Maisie recalled travelling from the train station to the hotel on that first day—"I think we went up by cab"—where Harriett Evans, the family nurse-maid, marshalled her young charges through the front door and past the doorman, Smith. "I'm a Welshman, too," he said, his black face creasing into a broad smile that delighted the child. Maisie also recalled dining there with Rena and Flora Oppenheimer, whose impossibly curly hair impressed her enough to remember it seventy years later. Their father, David Oppenheimer, one of the city's most prominent businessmen, also happened to be its mayor. At the tender age of four, and even in this outpost on the edge of nowhere, Maisie was already mingling with Vancouver's elite.

Soon after their arrival, Ronald Campbell-Johnston opened an assay and consulting office on Granville Street and settled his family into rental housing west of the city centre. The wilds of the nascent city were still as close as a few city blocks away, and on daily walks Harriet would push Ronald along in his buggy, Maisie trudging determinedly behind, the goal being to reach the sandy beach at English Bay for a picnic. Often they were accompanied by Sedley Campbell "Bimbo" Sweeny in his pram, jostled through the muck by his own nursemaid. (Bimbo, who was the son of Campbell Sweeny, manager of the Bank of Montreal for BC and the Yukon, would grow up to become the head of the Vancouver Stock Exchange as well as a noted sportsman.) For Maisie, the all-day excursion to the protected waters of the bay was an opportunity to learn to swim, but she found the water far too chilly to entice her in for a lesson with the ubiquitous Joe Seraphim Fortes, the unpaid Trinidadian who had made it his life's work to assiduously patrol the beach looking for errant bathers while instructing the city's youth in the fine art of the crawl.

In 1896, since much of Ronald Campbell-Johnston's consulting, prospecting and preparation of assay reports was conducted in the Interior of the province, he relocated the family to the town of Nelson on Kootenay Lake—although this would prove to be only the first stop of many in the next ten years. From Nelson, Ronald would often travel fifty miles by horseback with his young daughter to Rossland in order to inspect the rich placer deposits in the area. They would stay at the Hotel Allan, whose hostess, Mrs. Allan, had considerable mining interests herself. In a book titled *The First History of Rossland* written in 1897, the author, Harold Kingsmill, described her as "a lady of education and culture, of graceful manners, with the ready and tender sympathies of a mother and a tact and judgement in business affairs unusual in her sex."[8] In later years Maisie recalled the proprietress as "quite a character... blond and generously built, and I forget now whether she had six or

Maisie and her father at a Slocan mining camp. It was in the province's rugged Interior that Maisie learned to love the western style of life and where she first encountered the province's First Peoples. Photo from the family collection.

nine husbands, something like that... and one would be a bartender, another would be swabbing the decks and she had them all employed around the hotel... One day she walked into the bar and heard them all comparing notes... and she bawled them out... She said, 'I wouldn't give the whole bunch of you change for the dirt [under] Allan's toe nails!' So Allan was the one she loved most of all."[9] And Allan was the surname she chose to keep, despite being born a McLaughlin.

The years in BC's Interior would prove to be a pivotal time for Maisie. It was when and where she would first encounter the province's First Nations people, and it would astound her that these people, who had occupied this land long before Europeans had claimed it as their own, had yet to be granted citizenship. Her interest was also influenced by her parents' attitude to the Aboriginal peoples. Amy Campbell-Johnston often accompanied her husband on his geological expeditions to these isolated locations and she especially enjoyed the four visits she made to the remote Groundhog coal deposit in the far northwestern corner of the province between 1908 and 1912. While there, she took the opportunity to write down the stories she heard from local First Nations residents when she was lodged in their camps and villages while awaiting her husband's return from his more rigorous forays.

The relationship the Campbell-Johnstons developed with the First Nations people they encountered, however, was not a one-way street, and occasionally they stretched their pocket books and influence to assist someone in need. During these northern expeditions, the Campbell-Johnstons also collected First Nations objects and art with a view to preserving them, later donating them to the Vancouver Museum, where they remain today.

In the winter of 1905, Ronald was hired by the CPR to inspect some coal deposits near Spences Bridge, and he closed his office in Nelson and moved his family there. "There was no railway in those days," Maisie recalled, "although construction camps had been started on the CPR main line [actually a branch line]. Spences Bridge was a wild hooting, tooting western camp; they say there was a shooting a week there."[10] A few days after they arrived, the family took the stage to Lower Nicola where they mounted horses and rode into Aspen Grove. According to Maisie, at that time it consisted of "the Dodd Ranch, with a one-room shack built for store and post office. The mail was brought in by pony express... I can see Johnny Clapperton now, coming around the long stretch on the dead run, the old stage rocking from side to side. Johnny always came that way, the few passengers—generally a commercial traveller among them— would have a strained, shaken look on their faces. Johnny, his horses steaming, would pull up with a flourish. He was a handsome, lean, dark cow-puncher with a tilted Stetson hat and high-heeled boots."[11]

Being the only white girl in the vicinity could be lonely, but it had its advantages. Maisie befriended a young girl of mixed heritage by the name of Lena Voght who taught her that life on the land was far removed from the silver and servants of her privileged upbringing. "We'd ride out to some lonely place and she'd ask me to find something to eat," Maisie recalled. "When I couldn't, she'd get down and show me some roots or little plants and call me a 'stupid white girl.'"[12] Maisie was not only a popular playmate of the local First Nations children, but she also had time to explore and observe. Gathered at Dodd's were a cast of characters whom she described as "a great bunch of men. Scattered for miles through the hills and valleys, those men of the old west [were] from Texas, Colorado, California, Nevada and other parts, drifting from camp to camp as civilisation caught up with them."[13] There was "Smokey" Chisholm, "that little dark crippled gunman, the son of a Presbyterian minister in Nova Scotia," whose horse, "Mowich, a chestnut streak of lightning,"[14] Maisie was allowed to ride. Then there were Long Jack Bud and Bill Augsted, the Pennsylvania Dutchman, and J. P. "Dad" Allen, whom Maisie had first met at Slocan City in 1897 when she was just 10 years old and living in Nelson. Allen had been running a livery stable there complete with a pack train service to the local mines. That he was kind and of Scottish descent, despite being born in New York City, was not lost on her. By then

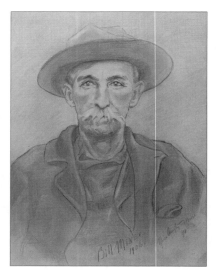

Bill Miner, known to Maisie as George Edwards, was a notorious American train robber who reputedly originated the phrase "Hands Up" for his nefarious activities. Pastel portrait by Maisie Hurley. Photo (1986 19 107) courtesy of the North Vancouver Museum and Archives.

in his 80s, he rode a raw-boned, three-year-old grey stallion called Turk, and he was contemptuous of the English style of riding, calling those who practised it "limejuicers." Having learned to ride and break horses in the southern United States, he rode high in the saddle with no bend to his knee like a Mexican vaquero. Teaching Maisie the finer points of sitting astride a horse, he interjected his instructions with great streams of "black strap" tobacco juice, which he squirted, steaming, from pursed lips with predictable accuracy.

Also quietly observing, but for much more sinister reasons, was one George Edwards, whom Maisie remembered would often ride in from Quilchena: "quiet, well-educated, grizzled, with keen steel blue eyes, gentle and kindly of manner with women and children; a dead shot and a fine horseman." What Maisie didn't know about her new friend, who wore a nondescript "blue mackinaw and an old battered Stetson," was that he was not who he said he was. His real name was Bill Miner. No matter. To Maisie he was just a kindly old gentleman. Watching her struggling to skate on the small ice rink she had built, he cleared a much larger level spot in the field next to Dodd's and diverted a small stream to flood the area. He also taught her a lesson that perhaps became one of the guiding principles of her life:

> We had many talks; one I remember particularly was on bigotry. It seems that Bill had two fine old grandmothers, both good Christian women, one was Roman Catholic and the other Protestant; they used to argue and fight over religion, sometimes not speaking for weeks, which worried Bill as a little boy because he loved both and knew how kindly and sweet they were. So Bill said to me, "Little'un—Dad's name for me—never let them make a bigot out of you; always be tolerant of the other fellow's religious views no matter what they are. So long as he prays, be thankful that he prays.[15]

The following spring Ronald moved his family to Lower Nicola, and one evening Maisie and her mother were walking through the Shulus Reserve when they came upon George Edwards and a companion, both on foot with packs on their backs. After explaining that they were on their way to Kamloops and that their horses were farther down the trail towards Spences Bridge, they carried on their way. Several days later the news broke that the CPR train had been robbed at gunpoint at Ducks Station near Kamloops on May 8, 1906, and that it looked like the work of the infamous American bandit, Bill Miner. His subsequent arrest at Douglas Lake, together with his partners, Lewis Colquhoun and William "Shorty" Dunn, for that robbery as well as one at Silverdale near Mission on September 10, 1904, shocked the impressionable Maisie.

Maisie and her friend, Fleda, riding in Madera County, California. Photo from the family collection.

Later when Dad Allen rode in from his mining claims at Aspen Grove to the Woodward's Halfway House at Lower Nicola where Maisie and her family were staying, he consoled his young friend and cautioned her "not to judge our old friend too harshly... because, Little'un, he never killed anyone nor robbed the poor. He was just one of those socialist fellows who took from the rich and gave to the poor."[16] Beuregard Roberts and his wife mirrored Allen's comments when they recalled that: "He stayed a whole winter with us one year... but we didn't know of his depredations then. He was always a gentleman and he helped many a poor family with money and labor."[17] But Bill Miner was not always such a philanthropist, according to the late Peter Grauer, who wrote that Miner "never was above taking from the poor when the occasion demanded."[18] "In spite of this," wrote Maisie, "these wild men of the mountains and plains were finer men with a greater sense of honour than many of our respected business men of today; at least I would rather have them for pals."[19]

It was this attitude combined with her general wilful behaviour that began to concern her parents. Riding and roping became frequent pastimes, and on the occasional visit to the ranch owned by her uncles at San Rafael, California, where she had first learned to ride, she was not above trying to break the odd bug-eyed cayuse. Dad Allen was concerned that Maisie's habit of breaking in wild horses bareback would cause her harm, but her mother assured him that she had been doing it without injury for some time. Even riding astride a horse western-style would have been enough perhaps to cause most of her contemporaries in England to whisper their disapproval, but had they known of her other activities, they would have been aghast. This was not the way a lady behaved, especially one as highly placed in the social order as Maisie, and especially not if one wanted to snag a respectable mate.

It all came to a head when she fell for the local Anglican preacher,[20] and whether it was out of love or to spite her disapproving mother, she and her lover made the decision to elope on November 27, 1906, her nineteenth birthday. Breaking trail on horseback through deep snow, they skirted jack pine copses and struggled across heavily drifted bunch grass meadows towards Lower Nicola where they had planned to marry. However, they didn't have much of a head start, and after Maisie's nag began to tire, she turned in her saddle and caught a glimpse of riders chasing after them. Maisie would later tell this story at parties as part of her repertoire, and the reporter, author and politician Paul St. Pierre recalled that she had often told him how "they [had] opened the corral gates and stampeded all the camp's horses except the two they were on, so they figured they couldn't be followed… but the father and his crew rounded up enough horses to follow them and seize them."[21]

To rein Maisie in, her parents shipped her off to boarding school in England to complete her education and attend elocution training. Maisie complied, but she must have yearned for the rough-and-tumble life of BC's wide-open spaces. When she graduated a couple of years later, she rejoined her family, who by that time had returned to Vancouver. At the age of 21, she had completed all the formal education that she would ever receive, but despite this abbreviated tutelage, she had the outward appearance of a perfectly cultured, educated young woman. And at five feet, eight inches with dark brown hair and blue eyes, she turned heads. She was now ready for the next step for young women of her age: marriage. It is believed that it was her mother who found a gem for her right in Vancouver.

John Reginald Rowallane Armytage-Moore (known as Reginald or Reggie to his family), who was born at Arnmore, County Cavan, Northern Ireland, on March 25, 1876, had arrived in Vancouver via New York in January 1907. He had all the earmarks of the perfect mate for Maisie. He had a profession (estate agent), he was the right age (33) and height (six feet), and he was devilishly handsome with a dark complexion, brown hair and blue eyes. As well, he had a pedigree. Close relatives included his aunt, Priscilla Cecilia, Countess of Annesley (wife of the third earl); his sister, another Priscilla Cecilia, Countess of Annesley (wife of the fifth earl); and her daughter, Constance Malleson, writer and long-time lover of the philosopher Bertrand Russell. His family moved in the highest circles of London and Dublin society."[22]

Although Maisie was a Roman Catholic, on September 29, 1909, she married Reginald Armytage-Moore in an Episcopalian ceremony to accommodate

Maisie, seated in the lower left, poses for a group photo with her fellow actors of her high school play. Photo from the family collection.

his Church of England upbringing. Their union, however, was short-lived, and his family hint that the marriage may have been a convenient mask for his preference for men, the likely cause of the abbreviated nuptials: safer to be unhappy in marriage than ostracized in life. But his new wife was a vibrant, rebellious young woman, tantalizingly attractive and most definitely not willing to settle for the charade that characterized her marriage. Although Maisie had been constantly reminded of her heritage by her mother, she eschewed all that it stood for when she abandoned Armytage-Moore in favour of a slightly younger man, Martin Joseph Murphy, a "Liverpool Mick"—the name given to Irish Catholic immigrants to Liverpool—and amateur pugilist whom she had met in Vancouver and whose child she was soon carrying. Martin Murphy wasn't every woman's dream, but he was smart, self-taught and well-read, and he represented two of the things that were missing in Maisie's life: risk and adventure. In addition, he was everything that Maisie's mother, Amy, would have rejected as being far too common, which perhaps made him even more attractive. To friends Amy would explain Maisie's odd behaviour in decamping with Murphy with the derisive comment that "she was kicked in the head as a child."

Murphy had transferred his survival skills from the mean streets of Liverpool to the sport of boxing in the British army, and later, as a semi-professional lightweight class boxer, he began chasing a withering dream throughout

Maisie met Martin Joseph Murphy (left) in Vancouver. Murphy began boxing in the British Army and later became a semi-professional lightweight-class boxer chasing a withering dream throughout the Pacific Northwest. Photo from the family collection.

the Pacific Northwest. However, he was far more content reading Jung, Freud and the great philosophers than sparring, and against Maisie's wishes, he soon wrapped up his boxing career. The two of them spent the next few years knocking about the West Coast on both sides of the border, Murphy labouring in logging and mining camps and taking on the odd amateur boxing match for prize money. Always in tow was his old friend and sometime sparring partner, Harry Bailey. Maisie, however, couldn't shake her love of boxing. "I had a stable of boxers in the US," she recalled. "They had ferocious names like Tiger Sealeaf, who had a wild disposition and was famous for his glass jaw. My big ambition was to get a white hope who'd be able to win the world title."[23]

The trio's progress up and down the coast was officially registered by the birth of Maisie and Martin's five children: Michael Martin Murphy, born April 14, 1914, in Portland, Oregon; Kathleen "Kitty" Murphy, born January 3, 1917, in San Francisco; Ronald Alexander Murphy, born April 1, 1919, in San Francisco; Miriam Murphy, born October 26, 1921, at the Guylard Logging Camp in Myrtle Point, Oregon; and Terrence Patrick Murphy, born September 5, 1923, in Kerry Line, Oregon.

In San Francisco they lived in a rented house at 475 Mississippi Street near Potrero Hill from 1916 to 1920, subletting a room to Harry Bailey. Martin got a job as a helper with the Union Iron Works and later as a marine fireman with the Pacific Steamship Company while Maisie was kept busy with their first two children. Although not legally married—Maisie's Catholic faith prohibited her from divorcing Armytage-Moore, who by that time had relocated to New Zealand—she now called herself May Murphy, possibly to avoid embarrassment but possibly to dodge discovery by her mother, who may have had no idea where she was or that she had already given birth to two children.

On May 18, 1917, when the United States passed the Selective Service Act to assemble an army to enter the war in Europe, Martin, who had already served in the British army, wasted no time registering for duty. Although he

Maisie's two brothers served in the Canadian Infantry in WWI. The family was heart-broken when the brothers were killed in battle within a day of each other. Left: Private Ronald Campbell-Johnston; right: Lieutenant Alexander Campbell-Johnston. Photo from the family collection.

was not called up and therefore avoided the mud and blood of the war in Europe, the Campbell-Johnston family was not so lucky. Maisie's two brothers, Lieutenant Alex Campbell Campbell-Johnston of the Canadian Infantry (Manitoba Regiment), 16th Battalion, and his older brother, Private Ronald Alfred Campbell-Johnston of the Canadian Infantry (British Columbia Regiment), No. 3 Company, 7th Battalion, were felled within one day of one another in the same battle, Alex on September 2 and Ronald on September 3, 1918, just two months before the armistice that ended the war. For the longest time their mother, Amy Campbell-Johnston, refused to believe that her precious sons were gone, and the loss likely hastened their father's death eleven years later.

Maisie too was inconsolable because she had been close to both of her brothers, but she now had responsibilities to her own young family, despite handling them poorly. She always had somewhat of an air of entitlement about her, and having grown up in households with servants who had done everything for her, she had few domestic skills to rely on and disdained the drudgery associated with common housework. Her children remember being dressed virtually in rags, living in a ramshackle cabin near some logging or mining camp and being fed some horrible soup concoction for dinner, but in Maisie's defence, they did receive more than mere broth in ancestral education. Maisie's granddaughter Maureen Woodcock recalls that "they didn't get through a day when they didn't get a complete breakdown of what their lineage was—who the Duke of Argyll was and who was, you know, Lord William Campbell and Lord Johnston, the chief justice of Ceylon, so they knew all these things, and so they had a very high opinion of themselves."[24]

Later in life, Maisie's daughter Kitty would recall that her mother had been "a fairy princess, exquisitely dressed, beautifully groomed. When I was a child, I lived in a complete fairy-tale world. A most magic fairy princess, that's what my mother was. She had this lovely out-of-this-world manner. I've never known anybody so fearless as my mother and my grandmother."[25] Bob Bouchette, who was Maisie's friend and an occasional boarder with the family, told her daughter, "Kitty, after they made your mother, they broke the mould. So don't try to understand her. Just love her."[26]

As well as having few domestic skills, Maisie also had no discernable employable skills, but she found satisfying work organizing for the International Workers of the World (IWW), generally known as the Wobblies, a radical group that promoted the concept of "One Big Union" and sought to unite all workers under a new social order that rejected capitalism and wage labour. Maisie had always been firmly on the side of the working class, but it was perhaps her time with the Wobblies that matured her already keen sense of social justice. Martin and Harry found their niche there too, coaxing prospective members with not-so-subtle persuasion.

Maisie's less heavy-handed tactics were no less effective, especially when it came to dealing with recalcitrant labour bosses. It was the all too common practice of logging outfits in the Pacific Northwest to cut timber and then move on in the dark of night to avoid paying their workers the wages they were due. Maisie got wind of this practice in 1923 when Martin and Harry were working on the Kerry Line in Coos Bay, Oregon, and she rushed to their employer's office with all her children in tow, admonishing the bosses with, "I know you scoundrels are going to skip out and you're going to leave the rest of these guys... But you're not going to leave my guys," she said.[27] Their fervent denial was not enough for Maisie, who demanded that the wages due Martin and Harry be paid forthwith. The bosses, probably somewhat bemused by the tactics of this seemingly harmless young mother, cut her a cheque, which she promptly tore up, demanding cash. She refused to leave the office without it and soon had a diaper line set up and was settling in for a long sit-in with her squally children when her demands were met.

It was about this time that Maisie and Martin's common-law union began to disintegrate. Martin's addiction to alcohol, his sporadic employment and the pressure of raising five children on an itinerant labourer's wage were taking their toll. So sometime in 1924 Maisie, Martin, Harry Bailey and the children returned to Vancouver where Maisie moved in with her parents in their West End home while Martin, Harry and the children rented a rambling old house in East Vancouver. When Maisie's parents, Ronald and Amy, discovered they were grandparents five times over, they were understandably shocked, but were warm towards their grandchildren. Maisie, meanwhile, was almost estranged from her offspring and only visited them on Sundays to do what cleaning she considered necessary and bring them either cash or groceries. It appears that Harry Bailey was the children's principal caregiver during this period, which, given his affection for Maisie, he was happy to do, but when both men were otherwise occupied, the children would be shuttled back to Maisie's care. She had once again assumed her married name of Armytage-Moore and was referring to herself as Amy, although she would eventually revert back to Maisie. It appeared that she had now run the gamut of her wild side and was ready to settle down to experience the life that destiny had in store for her.

During this period Martin was finding work either in the shipyards or as a boxing instructor at various athletic clubs where he felt most at home. Maisie also continued to frequent athletic clubs to satisfy her own love of boxing, and she could often be seen ringside, the occasional cigar clamped firmly between her teeth. "I smoke too many cigarettes," she once remarked of her vice. "I'd rather smoke a cigar any day—I think they have much better taste."[28] It was at the Vancouver Athletic Club, which she was helping to revitalize, that she met another boxing enthusiast, Thomas Francis Hurley, who would eventually become her boss, her soul mate and her comrade-in-arms. The two couldn't have been more ideologically suited, and at 5 feet 8 inches, the brown-haired, blue-eyed, silver-tongued Irishman was a natural fit for the feisty Maisie Armytage-Moore.

Tom Hurley was born at County Cork, Ireland, on December 15, 1885, almost two years to the day before Maisie was born in Swansea, Wales, albeit she had begun life in a more privileged neighbourhood than his working-class father could afford. Tom, the only boy among four girls, was the second-born. When his father, Cornelius Hurley, was young and single, he had left Ireland due to lack of employment and landed in the civil parish of Canton just outside Cardiff's old town boundaries. This was a second home to hundreds of immigrant families at that time, many of whom were Irish, and it is where he met Tom's mother, Elizabeth Donovan, another Irish immigrant. They eventually relocated to Ireland where Cornelius became a commission agent's clerk. Tom completed his university there, subsequently returning to Cardiff to work in a law office.

He was granted his registrar's certificate by the secretary of the Law Society at Cardiff on September 18, 1908, and after working for a time in Cardiff, shipped to British Columbia by way of San Francisco, surfacing in Vancouver in 1911. He was taken on as an articling student by the law firm of MacNeill, Bird,

McDonald and Bayfield and admitted to the BC bar on July 3, 1911.[29] (He did not actually sit his BC bar exams until July 6, 1925, but such was the state of the law in British Columbia at that time that this was not considered unusual.) [30]

Doing one's articles in Vancouver was haphazard at best. Although the BC bar had set the standards high, local law firms often treated their articling students as clerks and in some cases actually deterred them from practising law or appearing in court. Justice Denis Murphy, writing in the *Vancouver Law Students' Annual* under the pseudonym "Quill," argued that "if students were to be forced (as was required) both to article and to demonstrate advanced legal knowledge as a precondition to practising law, then it followed as a sort of *quid pro quo* that they were entitled to have a properly formal education made available to them."[31]

And Vancouver certainly did need lawyers. The city's population had grown from about 14,000 in 1891 when Maisie arrived to just over 100,000 by the time Tom arrived two decades later. But he had turned up when student action was getting underway to demand an adequate legal education, although it would continue to consist of invitations to benchers to lecture on various aspects of the law until the opening of a local law school in 1914. By then Tom was already experientially qualified, calling himself a barrister after he became employed by the criminal defence lawyer Charles S. Arnold. Shortly thereafter he added "notary" to his qualifications and began practising on his own in the Province Building on West Hastings Street.

That Tom Hurley thrived was in part because of his love of the law, but also because of his entertaining and legendary courtroom theatrics—an opposing counsel once said that "if Hurley ever tired of the law, he could make a fortune playing Hamlet"[32]—and the beneficence and compassion that he exhibited towards the unfortunate and impecunious, traits that became the hallmarks of his career. His compassion was honest, learned in the working-class neighbourhoods of his simple upbringing and translated into affirmative action once he had the wherewithal to accomplish this. With a total lack of hubris, he balanced his many achievements with the comment that he was just "a simple Irish boy."[33] He seldom sought money and his proclivity to defend those on the lowest rung of the economic ladder on a "pay if you can" basis meant that, although he was talented, he would never make a very lucrative partner. In fact, before the days of Legal Aid, he defended most of his First Nations clients free of charge and once he successfully defended a Tsimshian man held on a charge of murder for the grand sum of four beaver teeth. Thus, he would practise alone for most of his career, but his poorest clients received the same level of defence that he gave to those with more substantial means.

In 1934 Tom hired Maisie's 20-year-old son, Michael, as a clerk. A year later, Maisie, who had been employed as the manager of the Police Book

Publishers, joined Tom's law practice as his secretary, where she became privy to the one-sided justice meted out to the First Nations people of the province. At this time she was once again domiciled with Martin and her children in East Vancouver, a necessity given that her father had passed away in October 1929, forcing her mother to move from her large West End home into smaller quarters. Martin, however, soon departed for his old haunts in the United States, leaving Maisie to take care of her youngest children alone.

In 1937 Michael left Tom's employ just as Tom took on a legal partner, Angelo Branca. Although the partnership dissolved a year later, Branca, who would become known as the "Gladiator of the Courts," remained a life-long friend of the equally combative Tom Hurley. That same year Tom relocated his law practice to a one-room office in the Standard Building on West Hastings, and although Maisie had no formal legal training, she began taking on clients of her own. She frequented the courts with such regularity, either representing her own clients before a magistrate or seeking Tom out to remind him of "forgotten appointments or upcoming cases," that she became well-known to all and sundry, and those who mattered closed their eyes to what Tom called Maisie's "bootleg law." In 1964 she estimated that she had defended "nearly 80 cases and never lost one." She added, "I've come to the conclusion that they let me win to get me out of there."[34] During one case where she was defending a First Nations woman accused of stealing a hotel clerk's wallet, she seared the hapless plaintiff with such a withering cross-examination that he responded with an off-colour remark, earning him a citation from the magistrate for contempt of court; when he refused to pay the fine, he spent a night in jail.

2—THE BROTHERHOOD

One evening in the summer of 1931, a group of First Nations fishermen hunkered down to wait out a storm on a long crescent of sand at Egeria Bay on the east coast of North Island (now called Langara Island) in Haida Gwaii, which were then called the Queen Charlotte Islands. That year salmon prices offered by the local canneries had been too low to support the operation of their motor vessels, let alone feed and clothe their families, and to make ends meet, they had resorted to hand-trolling salmon from small rowboats. These double-ended, fifteen-foot, clinker-built craft were ideal for this purpose, and the fleet that summer numbered about 200 to 300 boats. Drawn up on the beach at night, tipped over and covered with tarps, they also served as ideal shelters. It was a hardscrabble life, broken only occasionally by brief trips to Masset to visit family and friends.

But the storm that summer day had prevented them from launching even these seaworthy little craft, and now as night came on, the group of Haida and Tsimshian fishermen sat resignedly before a raging driftwood fire, straining to hear each other over the roar of the great rollers crashing onto the beach. It had not been too many decades since these two groups had been living as they had for millennia—sometimes trading but more often than not warring with each other in the pursuit of wealth and slaves. Now they were united against a common but more intangible enemy, a faltering economy that was destroying their way of life.

As they talked, the flickering light of the fire danced over their weathered faces as they sifted warm sand through their calloused fingers. But they looked up when a middle-aged man materialized out of the darkness and took a seat among them. It was obvious that he wasn't a fisherman. He had tried fishing—gillnetting on the Skeena River—but his brother, an experienced fisherman, had been forced to bail him out, fix his torn and tangled nets and spend valuable fishing time instructing him. But some among the fishermen on that beach knew him because he operated a small satellite general store on the island, and in his capacity as a lay minister he had always blessed the boats and fishermen at the beginning of the fishing season.

His name was Alfred Adams and he was already in his early 50s, twice as old as many of the men around him. He was an Elder of the Haida Nation, and his people called him Nangiitlagadaa,[35] meaning "one who is rich and respected," the word "rich" referring to experience, not material wealth. When he spoke, people were inclined to listen.

Adams straddled both white and Aboriginal worlds; he was firmly Haida—in fact, he was a member of the Raven Clan with the high-class name of Skildaadwaans,[36] meaning "much loved fairy"—but he had been educated at an Anglican residential school, the Ridley School for Boys at Metlakatla, where he not only had a glimpse of the white man's world, but had been indoctrinated into the school's system of "acculturation"[37] as well. Metlakatla had been established on the North Coast near Port Simpson in 1862 by the first Anglican missionary to the area, William Duncan, and if ever there was a model of assimilation, this unique settlement was it. Duncan had been convinced that if he was ever to achieve "his aims and purposes, it could be accomplished more quickly and more perfectly if he had his converts in a community by themselves, rather than for them to be scattered among neighbours with unregenerate natures, still clinging to their sinful customs." The rules for living in his "Christian" community were: "(1) to give up their 'Hallied' or Indian deviltry; (2) to cease gambling; (3) to cease drinking liquor; (4) to rest on the Sabbath; (5) to attend religious instruction; (6) to be clean; (7) to be industrious; (8) to be peaceful; (9) to build neat houses; (10) to be liberal and honest in trade."[38]

Duncan's radical methods were not always viewed with favour by his sponsor, the Church of England, because he was not ordained and he went against the church's wishes in withholding the sacrament from parishioners whom he did not think were ready to receive it. In 1887, the bishop arrived on one of his periodic inspections of the settlement and forced Duncan to leave. Simultaneously, the federal government turned down Duncan's request to make the residents of Metlakatla citizens of the country. However, as soon as the bishop departed, a delegation of Duncan's admirers persuaded him to return; Duncan, however, had already decided to uproot the settlement and relocate 800 of his most ardent followers to Alaska. He named his new village, located on Annette Island near Ketchikan, New Metlakatla.

Alfred Adams had not been among those who relocated. He was a very bright boy, and though he was probably aware of the negative repercussions of Duncan's stringent methodology, he had revelled in the education he received at the Ridley School, so that reading, learning and music became his lifelong passions. Delores, Adams's daughter, remembers that her father's "hands were so soft because he played classical music, and his brother would chop all the wood so his hands wouldn't get rough." Playing the piano, however, was not his only musical talent. Delores remembers that:

> he played the French horn... the trumpet and... the flute. When my
> Dad came from the Ridley Home for Boys, the steamboat went to

Skidegate instead of Masset, and it wouldn't be going to Masset until the spring, so he started walking with all these musical instruments that he had, and Peter Kelly's mother [and]... two of these aunts... walked with him until they couldn't, and they stood on a hill and... saw him walking on the beach and going toward Masset with all his musical instruments.[39]

The 100-kilometre trek was nothing for this resolute young man whose stern demeanour masked such a warm heart. After he had been singled out for special treatment by Bishop Rix, the third bishop of the Diocese of Caledonia, Adams had not only excelled in his studies—according to Delores, "he could read in Hebrew and... Greek,"[40] and Jane, another daughter, recalled that he became a practitioner of yoga[41]—but more importantly he began to absorb the skills necessary to become an effective leader of his people. He began teaching piano to the village youth, managed the community band and choir and performed ministerial work in his capacity as lay minister for the Anglican Church when he wasn't stocking the shelves of the Masset general store, Alfred Adams & Sons, General Merchants, which he and his wife, Selina, had built on land purchased from the Hudson's Bay Company. He also served effectively as village constable, enforcing unpopular laws with an even hand, and ran for office on the village council, even serving as chief councillor for several years.

The reason Adams had come to talk to the fishermen in the camp at Egeria Bay soon became apparent to them. He had an idea that he wanted to share, one that he had the foresight to recognize would work in BC. Some years earlier he had visited Sitka, Alaska, where he had relatives, and while there attended a couple of meetings—one at Hydaburg and one at Klawock—of a unique organization established by Native Americans in 1912 to fight discrimination, gain recognition for their rights and seek compensation for expropriated land. It was called the Alaska Native Brotherhood, and although it was an organization of men, it coexisted alongside a women's equivalent, the Alaska Native Sisterhood.

Somewhat ironically, the organization had been started by a Canadian Tsimshian man, Peter Simpson, who, like Adams, had been a resident of Metlakatla. When Reverend Duncan uprooted the community, Simpson, who was then 13, had moved with him to Alaska. It is likely that his model for the Brotherhood, however, had not come from either Duncan or Metlakatla but from another body established a few years earlier: the Arctic Native Brotherhood. Simpson had become the first chair of the Alaska Native Brotherhood and the only member of the board who was not Tlingit.

It was this organization that Adams was now endeavouring to emulate on the BC coast. But Adams's vision for the Native Brotherhood of British

Columbia was not specifically to tackle discrimination. Instead, it was principally to deal with "grievances that included requests for better schooling, for increased recognition of aboriginal rights in hunting, fishing, trapping and timber harvesting in off-reserve traditional lands, and for a meeting with Ottawa officials."[42] As well, although not overtly stated, Aboriginal Title figured prominently in the minds of Adams and the other Native Brotherhood organizers, who were determined to protect their Aboriginal identity against the ravages of assimilation.

Alfred Adams, the Brotherhood's first president, posing with his wife Selina and children: Ivan, Oliver, Livingston (standing), Loren (sitting), Julia (standing by her dad) and Victor (sitting by his mother). Photo courtesy of Selina Hobelman.

Casting his eyes about the circle of men on the beach at Egeria Bay, Adams implored them to "come together, we must talk as one, we must act as one. We will have an organization by organizing into a body. Then we will be able to talk to the government of the land, for only through an organized, united body will our voice be heard by the world." He finished with "My good friends, it is near morning. Come back tomorrow and we will talk some more for I am sure we have another beach day coming."[43]

Guy Williams, writing in the *Native Voice* thirty years later, described what happened next:

So there were more talks and many tons of sand passed through their fingers. They talked of the glories of the past before the white man came, but all the talks usually ended with their present family needs... The men listened long into the night, no one noticing that the fire had gone completely out and the great rollers were still pounding the beaches heavily from the grey cloud wall at the edge of the world, as their people had once looked upon the horizon, believing that the world was flat.[44]

The quality of Alfred Adams's leadership had never been more apparent than on September 9, 1913, when, as chief councillor for the Haida Nation, he had eloquently addressed the Royal Commission on Indian Affairs for the Province of British Columbia. So poignant were his words that some of them still grace the Proclamation of the modern Haida Constitution.[45] The members of that royal commission, which became known as the Reserve Commission or the McKenna-McBride Commission, had been sent to Haida Gwaii, as part of a federal government directive to "examine the state of reservations"[46] in the province.

However, the path leading up to the federal government's appointment of the five men who sat on that commission had been very long, arduous and conflict-ridden. There had been numerous disputes between the provincial and the federal governments over reserve land in BC, both bodies maintaining that they owned the land. In 1901, Premier James Dunsmuir had been turned down when he petitioned Ottawa to cut down the size of BC's reserves, complaining that some of the more sparsely populated ones were harbouring valuable agricultural land. Dunsmuir was followed as premier by Richard McBride (1903–1915), who had begun his political career as a minister in Dunsmuir's cabinet; for him the land locked up in reserves was an inconvenient barrier to his own policy of giving liberal land grants to railway, mining and timber companies. In addition, the province's rapidly expanding population was also demanding more land, and some of the land they coveted belonged to the reserves. McBride's negotiations with Ottawa on this score went nowhere, and he finally ran up against a brick wall with the Liberal government of Prime Minister Wilfrid Laurier, which on May 17, 1911, passed an order-in-council authorizing the Exchequer Court of Canada to "institute proceedings on behalf of the Indians"[47] against the province. It was Laurier's intention to settle the matter in court.

McBride's response to Laurier's order-in-council was to pass his own law, giving the province the authority to "grant, convey, quit claim, sell or dispose of, on such terms as may be deemed advisable, in the interest of the province, reversionary or otherwise, any Indian Reserve or any portion thereof."[48] This act directly contravened the federal Indian Act in addition to being an overt challenge to the authority of the government in Ottawa. The province also argued that it still held the "reversionary rights" granted to it by an agreement made in 1875, four years after it joined Confederation. That agreement had stated:

> in the event of any material increase or decrease hereafter of the numbers of a nation occupying a reserve, such reserve shall be enlarged or diminished as the case may be, so that it shall bear a fair proportion to the members of the band occupying it... the extra land required shall be allotted from Crown Lands, and any land taken off a reserve shall revert to the province.[49]

The final clause of this agreement effectively prevented the federal government from selling any extraneous reserve land for the band's benefit because, as soon as it ceased to be band property, it would become a provincial asset. On the other hand, at this juncture the province still had not transferred its reserve lands to the federal government as it had agreed to when it joined Confederation in 1871. This transfer would not actually take place until 1938.[50]

Another sticking point on any kind of agreement between federal and provincial governments was the actual size of the reserves granted prior to and by the Indian Reserve Commission, which had been established by the federal government in 1875 to allot and survey reserve lands. Some of the problem had to do with the policy in BC of permitting Indian bands to choose their own reserve boundaries, a policy that had been introduced by Sir James Douglas during the 1850s when he was governor of Vancouver Island. This largesse was rescinded by Joseph Trutch, who in 1864 had become chief commissioner of Lands and Works and began to roll back the size of the allotted reserves. (Trutch was no friend of First Nations people, often referring to them as "savages.")

There was a 180-degree compass change in Aboriginal lands policy after September 21, 1911, the date on which Laurier's government was voted out of office, replaced by Robert Borden's Conservatives. Borden ignored Laurier's order-in-council and settled the impasse by signing the McKenna-McBride Agreement, whose sole purpose was to investigate the land question but avoid any discussion of Aboriginal title. In fact, the "events of 1911 and 1912 give the impression that the McKenna-McBride Agreement was made so that the broad issue of 'Indian title' would not have to be faced."[51]

The two signatories to the agreement were Dr. J. A. J. McKenna, who was a special federal appointee, and BC premier Richard McBride. According to its terms, both governments consented to the establishment of a commission to determine "the final and complete allotment of Indian lands"[52] in the province, the commission having the authority to reduce or enlarge the size of reserves with a band's consent. Although a veto had been built into the Indian Act—the majority consent of adult males in the band was required for any reserve changes—which should have provided First Nations with protection against the erosion of their reserves, this new commission took the approach that they would simply go ahead and recommend cut-offs and let the federal government deal with obtaining consent. In addition, the agreement stated that if any reserve land were to be sold, the province and the federal government would split the proceeds equally, the federal portion being held in reserve for First Nations. The province also gained a partial victory with the "reversionary interest" clause, according to which the federal government agreed that the lands of any band going extinct would revert to the province.

When it was Alfred Adams's turn to address the McKenna-McBride Commission at Masset on September 9, 1913, he already knew what had happened to all the Aboriginal people before him who had attempted to force the federal and provincial governments to hear their grievances and provide justice. He had read the report written by the Interior Tribes of British Columbia after the representatives of this organization, formed at Spences Bridge in 1909 by Interior Salish chiefs, had travelled to Ottawa in 1912 to speak with Dr. McKenna and Prime Minister Robert Borden about the BC government "stealing" their lands. Adams also knew about the Indian Rights Association (formed in Victoria in 1909 by an assembly of mostly North Coast and Coast Salish leaders, although the Nisga'a were known to take a lead in it) and the Nisga'a Land Committee (formed in 1907 by some Nisga'a chiefs) who had asked for their grievances to be heard in the Canadian courts. All of them had been brushed off by one or both governments; McKenna had merely furnished the Interior Salish chiefs with a copy of the McKenna-McBride Agreement, which they had immediately rejected as being biased and unfair.

But Adams took advantage of his opportunity on the commission's podium to educate his guests:

> On these Islands our forefathers lived and died, and here we also expect to make our home until called away to join them in the Great Beyond. Here we are raising our families, and all we have in this world, with the traditions and associations, lands and household goods, are bound up on the islands that once were our own but are now becoming the homes of others. Since the coming of our white friends, we have been wards of the government, and the limits of our land have been drawn, giving to us an interest in six acres apiece of the many thousands over which we formally roamed and held against invaders.
>
> As you are aware, each of our separate tribes had places of their own and were governed by their chiefs. The missionaries came among us, and the government took charge of us. We were asked to centralize, to be Christianized and educated, and we came here to Masset and built our homes, returning now and then to our old homes, where we fished and where the bodies of our forefathers are laid. At the mouth of every river and stream, you will find our old camping grounds. All along the coastline are our former hunting grounds and the places where we fished, hunted and made our boats and canoes. These places are now covered by coal and timber licences and occupied by pre-emptors. Year by year, the limits have been drawn, and we are now restricted to a small piece of land, here and there, the whole Band not having as much land as one prospector can cover with coal licences. Where a foreigner can obtain 160 acres, we are allowed six, and we have always been British subjects since the flag of Britain was raised on our Islands."[53]

Britain, however, was not interested in these distant subjects, preferring not to meddle in Canadian affairs, a fact that King Edward VII had made abundantly clear on August 3, 1906, with his empty "royal promises" following a fifteen-minute meeting at Buckingham Palace with chiefs Joe Capilano (Squamish), Basil David (Shuswap) and Charlie Isipaymilt (Cowichan). The three chiefs had been looking for his support in repealing the potlatch ban, to press their case for hunting rights and to request compensation for their land. Although the king did not keep a diary and no notes were taken during that meeting, Chief Charlie Isipaymilt later recalled the event:

> I went to the King a few years ago to try to get some settlement from the King, and when I got there, the King gave me this photograph. His Majesty promised to do something for us, and said he would send somebody out to look into the matter. The King told me that I need not feel very sorry about these things as, if there was anything he could do, anything for me, he would do it. His Majesty promised to give each male Indian on the reserve 160 acres of land as this land belongs to us Indians.[54]

Three years later, another delegation of BC chiefs met with the king, this time requesting that the Privy Council in London make a judgment on "Indian title." They left similarly disappointed.

Although Adams knew all this, he carried on with his speech to the commission, lamenting that his people had only sixty years of "so-called civilization" and that although they couldn't possibly meet the standards set by twenty centuries of Christian teaching, their progress had been remarkable:

> But the marks of advancement will show most favourably with those of any country where the people were in bondage but a half-a-century ago... Without any treaty, without being conquered, we have quietly submitted to any laws made for our government, and this we intend to be our course. With other Indians who claim to have the same grievances, we asked that our claims be taken before the Privy Council of the Nation, to be finally settled there once and for all time.[55]

Although the commissioners were empowered to recommend small adjustments to the boundaries of reserve land where warranted and where not already pre-empted or under timber lease, their reply to the grievances put forward by Adams and the other councillors that day was all too typical of the standard response from the federal government with respect to "Indian title": "Insofar as the rights which you speak of are concerned, we have nothing to do with the question of Indian title."[56] That Adams and his colleagues had "tactfully avoided the trap of accepting reservations and the agenda of the Commission,"[57] was perhaps in anticipation of such a reply, but it was more than likely a reaction to the fear that any discussion of their rights might place those rights in jeopardy.

On June 5, 1914, after another year had gone by since the McKenna-McBride Commission's hearings in Haida Gwaii with no action from the government, the chiefs of the Interior First Nations met at Spences Bridge where they drafted a memo to the prime minister:

> We have spoken to you many times already in various ways. We have related our grievances to you and asked for redress. You must know our position. We have told you what was in our hearts, what we consider to be our rights as the original occupants, possessors and sovereigns of this country, and we have asked that you consider our case and see that we obtain justice... It now seems to us that this matter of our rights cannot be settled in Canada but must go before the Great Court in England. Therefore, we respectfully urge that you will at an early date have our claims referred to the Judicial Committee of the Privy Council for settlement.[58]

A year later the chiefs of the Interior First Nations met again at Spences Bridge, this time welcoming people from the Kootenay district, and together they endorsed the famous Nisga'a Petition, which asked that lands should be allotted on a per capita basis to all Nisga'a and that they should be compensated for the remainder of their former holdings.[59] This petition had been written with the intent of having the Privy Council in London make a judicial determination on the aboriginal rights of the Nisga'a people and title to their traditional lands. Ottawa's refusal to discuss these fundamental issues had left them with no alternative but to seek redress elsewhere.

The commissioner's report, which was finally published in 1916, was a précis of the twenty-seven volumes of material it had collected over the four years of its inquiry and covered oral testimony that explored land and resource rights grievances. It revealed that 87,291 acres of land had been added to the province's reserves but that 47,058 acres had been removed. Many First Nations now questioned the legitimacy of the commission itself, asking how the government could add to or take away what was already theirs. And they noted that the 47,058 acres removed from reserves, valued at $1,522,704, were considered to be prime land "coveted by whites for a number of years"[60] while the 87,291 acres that had been added, valued at $444,838, were relatively poor land.

The report became a rallying cry to action that was led by a new organization known as the Allied Tribes of British Columbia. Although it was based on the Squamish reserve in North Vancouver, it had arisen from a meeting of a small group of Aboriginal leaders in Victoria in 1911. From there it had quickly expanded into an organization comprising sixteen First Nations from virtually every part of the province. Two well-known and respected leaders, Reverend Peter Kelly and Chief Andrew Paull, were elected to the executive of the new organization. The chiefs came together again in June 1919 at Spences

The leaders in the fight for justice. From left to right: Andy Paull, who called himself "a lawyer without a ticket," Chief William Scow, president of the Brotherhood, and the Reverend Dr. Peter Kelly, chair of the Brotherhood's Legislative Committee. Photo courtesy of the North Vancouver Museum and Archives.

Bridge, where Kelly and Paull were reaffirmed as president and recording secretary respectively and discussions were held on how to block the implementation of the proposed cut-off lands, the greater aim being to "take the land claims through the court system to the Judicial Committee"[61] of the Privy Council. Kelly and Paull were the ideal men to lead the charge and they set out to travel the entire coast, visiting every camp and village to generate interest and attract members.

Peter Kelly was a well-respected, high-born Haida leader who, first in his capacity as a school teacher and then as a Methodist minister, had brought revolutionary change to the First Nations communities where he had served. Despite his noble birth, he was a humble diplomat and stood fast by his beliefs, even at times setting himself against the very church that employed him. Intelligent, outspoken and fiercely loyal to the cause of bettering life for First Nations people, he walked the talk, never forgetting who he was or just how close he was to the ways of his ancestors. His maternal grandmother had been killed in a raid as had the slave who had been conveying her child. When the slave was struck down, her body protected the infant, who would survive to become Peter's mother, Sarah Kelly.[62] Being enslaved had always been a point of shame for the Haida people as for many other First Nations in the province, but Peter Kelly had one foot firmly planted in the Western world as well and was endeavouring to change the mindset that was still burdened by a once-valued class system, a system that was so pervasive it was no further away than his front door. Once, when a Tsimshian man came to the Kellys' front door wanting to speak with him, Peter's wife, Gertrude, opened it to allow him to enter, but the man made no comment, turned and made his way around the house to the back door. There he knocked again and was admitted. When asked why he hadn't come in the front door, he confessed that it would not have been right, given that his grandfather had been one of Gertrude's grandmother's slaves.[63] It was this attitude that Kelly was endeavouring to eradicate, preaching that all men are equal. This was welcome news to many, but he alarmed others by also encouraging assimilation in the belief that "Indians must be prepared to be assimilated into the white community, eventually disappearing as a separate race."[64] As long as First Nations people were dressing and eating like white people, using their technology and their currency, he said, then assimilation was the inevitable consequence.

Kelly's co-leader in the Allied Tribes, Andrew "Andy" Paull (Xwechtáal, the Serpent Slayer), a chief of the Squamish Nation, believed that the First Nations in Canada must remain "as a distinct element of Canadian society."[65] That these two men were able to work together while holding such diametrically opposed views said much about their commitment to the cause and their ability to compromise for the good of all. Paull, sometimes referred to as "Canada's Indian conscience,"[66] was "an extrovert, a slap-on-the-back type, with an elementary school education and a sharp sense of propaganda and publicity."[67] He had gone to school, he claimed, not to become a white man—as a child he had often been taunted by his peers as being too much like a white child[68]—but to use the tools of the white man to fight for his people.[69] At the age of 15, he had been placed with a Vancouver law firm, Hugh St. Quentin Cayley, where he worked for four years, absorbing enough legal knowledge and acumen to defend his people. But he could not be admitted to the bar because rule 39 of the Law Society of BC stated: "No person shall be admitted or enrolled who is not of the white race, of the full age of 16 years, is a British subject, and who would, if of the age of 21 years, be entitled to be placed on the voters' list under the Provincial Elections Act." Besides not being of the "white race," First Nations people had yet to be granted the privilege of voting in BC. Paull, therefore, considered himself to be "a lawyer without a ticket," and according to his friend, Maisie Hurley, "could recite cases chapter and verse."[70] He also had first-hand knowledge of the McKenna-McBride Commission, having left his job as a longshoreman to act as an interpreter for it in Salish-speaking areas.

The Allied Tribes rejected the McKenna-McBride Report, not only protesting the poor quality of the added reserve lands and the unfairness of the cut-off lands but demanding that proceeds from the sale of the valuable cut-off lands should be deposited in an "Indian Trust Fund" for the benefit of the First Nations. As well, they pointed out that the commissioners had given no consideration to inequalities among First Nations, and Kelly and Paull were concerned about mandatory enfranchisement and its implications. And finally they insisted that "Indian title" should be settled first.

First Nations people were not the only ones objecting to the report. James Alexander Teit, a Scottish-born, self-taught ethnographer, who was married to a Nlaka'pamux (Thompson River Salish) woman, stated after the report's release that:

> The Indians see nothing of value to them in the work of the Royal Commission. Their crying needs have not been met. The commissioners did not fix up their hunting rights, fishing rights, water [for irrigation] rights, and land rights, nor did they deal with the matter of reserves in a satisfactory manner. Their dealing with reserves has been a kind of manipulation to suit the whites, and not the Indians.[71]

However, over the protests of the Allied Tribes, the commission's report was ratified by the province of British Columbia through provincial Order-in-Council 911 on July 26, 1923, and enacted into statute law by the federal government on July 19, 1924. Neither of these pieces of legislation would in any way signal the end of the matter for the Allied Tribes, and Kelly and Paull met to figure out how the fledgling but still loosely connected body, which had as yet no legal standing, could become more of a political force. The problem was that the Allied Tribes was still a work-in-progress. The organization had gained temporary new life and renewed purpose in 1922 when they met with Charles Stewart, the federal minister of the Interior, and Duncan Campbell Scott, superintendent of Indian Affairs, in North Vancouver. That meeting, however, had only occurred because a few years earlier the Nisga'a had employed a British law firm to present an appeal directly to the Imperial Privy Council to settle their Aboriginal title case, but the Privy Council had returned the appeal in 1918 with the comment that if the claim "involved the invasion of legal right, it should be litigated in Canadian courts."[72]

William Lyon Mackenzie King, who had been a Liberal MP in opposition at that time, had taken note of the matter and, after he became prime minister in 1921, sent Minister Stewart to Vancouver to meet with the Allied Tribes to discuss land concerns. Virtually all BC First Nations were represented at this gathering, although some Interior nations only appeared as interested parties, not members, because they considered the "expenses and demands of the Allied Tribes excessive."[73] To prepare for the meeting, Peter Kelly and James Teit had co-authored a memorandum to the minister, and this became a significant document for future negotiations if only because representatives of so many BC First Nations endorsed and signed it. Minister Stewart went back to Ottawa to digest the report and returned to BC the following July to announce that the Allied Tribes deserved a judicial decision on the question of Aboriginal title, which the federal government would help them to obtain. Unfortunately, BC Premier John Oliver had not only boycotted the meetings but even refused to send his minister of Lands, Duff Pattullo, or any other representative to them.

Two years later Kelly travelled to Ottawa with a delegation from the Allied Tribes to seek some resolution to their demands, and he returned the following year with an appeal to be heard before the committee set up to investigate their Aboriginal title cases. When their cases were rejected, it was apparent that more formal action was required, and in June 1926 they presented a petition to demand that the federal government launch an inquiry "outlining the Indian land controversy since BC entered confederation."[74] As well, because the federal government had ratified the McKenna-McBride Agreement, the Allied Tribes still believed that it had a right to a hearing before the Judicial Committee of the Privy Council in London and requested the consent and funding to do so, even though by law their case had to be tested in a Canadian court before an appeal could be heard before the Privy Council.

This petition had the desired effect, and during the 1926/1927 session of Parliament the Liberal government formally appointed a Special Joint Committee of the Senate and House of Commons to consider it, notwithstanding opposition from BC Premier John Oliver and many BC MPs. This joint committee was referred to as the "Great Settlement of 1927,"[75] although it would turn out to be just the opposite. Five witnesses appeared before it, Duncan Campbell Scott, Chief Johnny Chilihitza (Okanagan), Chief Basil David (Shuswap), Andy Paull and Peter Kelly. Superintendent Scott, while accepting the principle of Aboriginal Title in British Columbia, predictably stated that the BC First Nations received benefits far in excess of any of the treaty First Nations in Canada and that the provincial government was being reasonable and generous in its dealings with them. It is unlikely that he could have stated otherwise, given his assimilationist objective "to continue until there is not a single Indian in Canada that has not been absorbed into the body politic."[76] Chief Basil David had no complaints whatsoever, only mentioning that his sons had fought in World War I; upon examination, he admitted that they had been accorded the same benefits granted white veterans upon their return. Kelly believed that the two Interior chiefs, who spoke little English and appeared uninvited at the hearing with their own counsel, had been permitted to speak merely to trivialize the demands of the Allied Tribes.

Andy Paull, when interviewed next, offered an emotional appeal based on the many injustices visited on BC First Nations at the hands of authorities, though he finally (perhaps reluctantly) admitted that the federal government was, in fact, the "guardian" of all BC First Nations. To this point, none of the witnesses, save for Paull, had made much of an impression on the committee, so when it was Kelly's turn to speak, he recognized he had nothing to lose by being forthright. He was already well known, even by the committee members, as a powerful and thoughtful orator and leader, and now was his chance to make an even greater impact. He spoke of the fact that the First Nations in BC had the feeling of being confined: "Gradually they have been hemmed in, little by little," he said, "until the things which they had enjoyed in the past have been taken away from them."[77] "And," he stated, "fundamental was the issue of Aboriginal title."

"Supposing the aboriginal title is not recognized?" asked the Honourable Mr. Stevens, a Vancouver Conservative MP. "Suppose recognition is refused, what position do you take then?"

Kelly's response was:

Then the position that we would have to take would be this: that we are simply dependent people. Then we would have to accept from you just as an act of grace whatever you saw fit to give us. Now that is putting it in plain language. The Indians have no voice in the affairs of this country. They have not a solitary way of bringing anything before the parliament of this country, except as we have done last year by petition, and it is a mighty hard thing. If we press for that, we are called agitators, simply agitators, trouble makers, when we try to get what we consider to be our rights. It is a mighty hard thing, and as I have said, it has taken us between forty and fifty years to get to where we are to-day. And perhaps if we are turned down now, if this Committee see[s] fit to turn down what we are pressing for, it might be another century before a new generation will rise up and begin to press this claim. If this question is not settled in a proper way on a sound basis, it will not be settled properly. Now that is the point that we want to stress. I said to the Honourable Mr. Stevens last year, when he was acting Minister of the Interior—I think these are the words I used: "Why not keep unblemished the record of British fair dealing with native races? Why refuse to recognize the claim of certain tribes of Indians in one corner of the British Dominions when it has been accorded to others in another part of the same Dominion?"[78]

He continued, repeating what Alfred Adams had told the McKenna-McBride Commission more than a decade earlier, that the First Nations in BC had only been in contact with Western civilization for a few decades: "How could they be expected to understand or accept these strictures?" he asked. He went on to suggest as an example that if it was reasonable to send experienced white farmers to school to better learn their trade, then why was it not important to educate even less experienced First Nations farmers?

Although his reasoning struck a chord, it was insufficient to sway the committee, and five days later the committee rejected the demands of the Allied Tribes, including their request for funding and sanction to appeal to the Privy Council in London. In essence, the committee found that BC's First Nations had "not established any claim to the lands of British Columbia based on aboriginal or other title."[79] But as Wilson Duff pointed out much later in his book, *The Indian History of British Columbia*, just because they had not *established* a claim didn't mean that they didn't *have* a claim. In an attempt at appeasement, the committee recommended that $100,000 be granted annually to BC's First Nations in lieu of the annuities that were being paid to treaty First Nations to assist with such things as education, health care and agriculture. This money would be known as the "BC Special."[80]

Then, just in case Paull and Kelly were planning to pursue their argument in court, the federal government—perhaps alarmed at the duo's organizational strength and erudite presentations—amended the Indian Act to make it illegal for First Nations people to raise funds or hire legal counsel to pursue Aboriginal title.[81] The intent was to ensure that the claims of the Allied Tribes would never reach the Judicial Committee of the Privy Council. That Paull and Kelly had failed so spectacularly, despite their valiant efforts, was no reflection on their ability, but it was the final blow to the Allied Tribes, and the organization withered away quietly shortly thereafter. It didn't end the fight, however, even in these, the darkest days of the struggle, but merely drove it underground. Kelly continued with his ministry, while Paull became a sports writer for the *Province* newspaper.

Four years later, Alfred Adams, warming himself before the comforting fire on the rain-swept beach at Egeria Bay, had no trouble convincing his Haida brothers of the advantages of forming a new organization, and he then set to work convincing the Tsimshian people on the mainland. He had already spoken to a few Port Simpson fishermen—Ambrose Reid, Rufus Dudoward and hereditary chiefs William Beynon and William Jeffrey—who were all leaders of their communities, but he needed the consent of Chief Ernest Dudoward, the brother of Rufus, to appeal to a wider audience. In response to a letter from

Adams, Chief Dudoward gathered his chiefs together in secret, and over two or three meetings the idea gained assent. It was decided that the general meeting should be open to the public, so they booked the Salvation Army hall in Port Simpson, where most public gatherings were held, and sent letters to northern villages requesting that all delegates be in attendance by mid-December.

On December 13, 1931, when Adams arrived at Port Simpson with the Haida delegates to prepare for the meeting, the delegates from Port Simpson, Hartley Bay, Kitkatla, Port Essington and Metlakatla had already arrived. In attendance were Ambrose Reid, William Benyon, William Bailey, William Jeffrey, Tom Gosnell, Johnson Russ, Samuel Gray, Edward Gamble, Wallace Morgan, Joe Daniels, Guy Williams and hereditary Chief Heber Clifton of Hartley Bay. Despite only seven communities responding, it appeared that the idea's time had come, as evidenced by the enthusiasm of the attendees resplendent in their suits and ties.[82] Before the meeting could get underway, Peter Kelly led the delegates in a rousing chorus of "Onward Christian Soldiers," the battle hymn that opened the meetings of the Alaska Native Brotherhood, after which the Native Brotherhood of BC was being modelled. "What can be more impressive or more to the point," Maisie Hurley wrote in the *Native Voice* many years later, "than hundreds of Native voices singing with determination, 'We are not divided, all one body we, one in hope and doctrine, one in charity.'"[83]

The first day was devoted to the delegates' speeches and included a long address from Alfred Adams advocating unity. On the second day the meeting debated and accepted a resolution mirroring a petition launched by the Port Simpson people that spring that was strikingly similar to the demands of the Allied Tribes five years earlier.[84] By the end of the week the Native Brotherhood of British Columbia was a *fait accompli*. A constitution had been drafted, detailing the organization's purpose and structure (as well as establishing an annual membership fee of fifty cents), but the language used in it specifically avoided the term "aboriginal rights" in order to avoid falling afoul of the 1927 law that made it illegal to raise funds to pursue Aboriginal title. Instead, the official purpose of the organization was to "better the socio-economic position of Indian people."[85]

Organized "for the betterment of our conditions, socially, mentally and physically, to keep in closer communication with one another, to co-operate with each other and with all the authorities, for the further interest of the Natives,"[86] the Brotherhood itself was an amazing accomplishment, given the vast geographical, language, cultural and religious/spiritual differences among the participants. Perhaps, as Adams had suggested, its formation was in recognition of the vital need to speak with one voice.

It was now up to the delegates to inform their own people and to convince them of the advantages of becoming members. Where they were successful, local branches of the Brotherhood were established. Chief Heber Clifton of Hartley Bay and Chief Edward Gamble of Kitkatla were especially vigilant in prospecting for new members, and Chief Clifton made his seine boat available for the task, footing the cost of the sometimes extended voyages. He was also instrumental in launching forays into the Gitskan and Nass territories. There was no question that at this point the Tsimshian people dominated the Brotherhood, even though it was a lone Haida who had envisioned it, but there were soon many others co-operating to make it a success. In contrast, the Metlakatla delegates quickly lost interest, and it has been suggested that they considered themselves better educated and more progressive than their brothers and were therefore disappointed that none of their number were elected into any of the senior positions. As well, there was still some lingering hostility between them and the people of Port Simpson dating back to the sale by the people of Metlakatla of a large tract of land for the establishment of the townsite of Prince Rupert. The Port Simpson people considered this land part of their ancestral territory, but when they requested a share of the proceeds, they were rebuffed, deepening the divide. Later, when Metlakatla relented and offered a share, the Port Simpson people refused to accept it out of pride.

Adams and a few followers, including his nephew, Peter Adams, and Lee Edenshaw, also travelled the coast with Douglas Edenshaw in his fifty-foot seiner, *Edenshaw*, to visit isolated fishing camps and villages in an effort to educate people about the value and need for the Brotherhood. Since the organization also required funds, Adams solicited for these as well, but because he wanted the Brotherhood to be principally a First Nations initiative, he eschewed all government handouts in favour of donations from the people it would directly benefit. He also spent many of his own resources on organization and travel and would often have to apologize to his family and friends for his lack of money. "I may never see the fruits of my labor," he told them, "but it is because you and your children may get some benefit from my work that I must strive to better conditions for our race."[87] His penury is evident in a letter he wrote on September 19, 1933, to W. A. Newcombe, assistant curator of biology at the provincial museum in Victoria: "I will by all means forward you the old relics on coming Saturday as I need money in worse way. My children are very much delayed from going back to southern school owing to lack of funds, your help will make things easier."[88] The $26.50 he received for the few "relics" as well as $42 each for three eight-foot wooden totem poles—with traditional narratives to be furnished—suggests the desperate financial position he was in. His sacrifices and selfless devotion earned him the presidency of the Brotherhood, a position that he would hold until his death in 1945.

By the mid-1930s the Brotherhood had close to 500 members, but was only represented by fourteen branches. In order to spread the word south, in

1938 Adams, Chief Heber Clifton and Douglas Edenshaw made the long foray into Kwakwaka'wakw territory on Edenshaw's seine boat to attract new members. The fishermen there were already aware of Adams, who some years earlier, together with some Masset fishermen, had made several trips to Rivers Inlet to fish. They respected that he was a man of the cloth, but they were still reluctant to join the organization. Two years earlier these southern fishermen, believing they had been duped by unionized white fishermen who were on strike at Rivers Inlet, had turned to George Luther, the mission teacher at Alert Bay, and he had helped them form their own successful union, the Pacific Coast Native Fishing Association (PCNFA). They were understandably reluctant to abandon it in favour of the Brotherhood, an untested northern initiative.

In 1942, however, the Native Brotherhood's value became more apparent to them after the federal government began to tax First Nations fishermen on the premise that their revenue was generated off-reserve, although income generated on reserve remained non-taxable. The outcry was loud enough to catch the attention of Andrew Paull. Convinced that Aboriginal fishermen could win this battle if they spoke with one voice, Paull visited Skeena Crossing during the Brotherhood's AGM there and, after outlining a plan of attack, left with the new title of business agent for the Brotherhood, although the office's duties had yet to be defined. At Alert Bay, where a number of the leaders of the PCNFA lived, he outlined the Brotherhood's case and by the end of his visit had not only received the PCNFA's complete endorsement but succeeded in wrapping up the entire union as a significant member of the Brotherhood.

Buoyed by his success, Paull opened an office in Vancouver and gave himself a modest salary of $75 per month from the dues of the members he signed up. Although he deposited the balance into the Brotherhood's account, the fact that he was taking a salary rankled the northern leaders, who had not taken a cent for their efforts, but their hands were tied: the Brotherhood's coffers were empty while the PCNFA's were full. Given that the Kwakwaka'wakw fishermen were aligned with Paull, if he were to depart, so too might the funds needed to launch an official tax protest in Ottawa. As a result, the issue of the Vancouver office and Paull's modest salary soon evaporated, but his success signalled the beginning of a power shift away from the north,[89] especially after he convinced the Coast Salish nations from the Gulf Islands and the Nuu-chah-nulth from eastern Vancouver Island to join.

Even the Nisga'a people, whose Land Committee had served their needs in the past, were now beginning to show more interest. They had been concerned that the Brotherhood was strictly a Tsimshian organization with whom they were disputing overlapping territory, the land at the mouth of the Portland Canal immediately across the water from the Tsimshian stronghold of Port Simpson. But when the prominent leaders Peter Carter and Johnson Russ explained the advantages of joining the Brotherhood to the Nisga'a people of Greenville, they quite happily joined. Given that the Brotherhood already had such a presence on the coast, it was difficult to ignore the organization after the Nisga'a joined, making it almost fully represented from the province's north to south.

Membership by the Interior nations, however, remained spotty as the people there considered the Brotherhood primarily a fishing organization and Protestant in contrast to their predominantly Catholic faith. They were therefore opposed to the Brotherhood's push for day schools on reserves rather than the existing residential schools, which were principally Catholic in the Interior. It is also possible that Catholic missionaries may have discouraged them from joining. However, the fact that most of the province's First Nations were now represented by the Brotherhood was duly noted by the government in Ottawa.

3—The Native Voice

Seeking justice for First Nations clients in court one at a time had been satisfying for Maisie Hurley, but after her meeting on the street with Alfred Adams in 1944, she began formulating a plan to help on a broader scale. Those plans were interrupted when she was blindsided by a crippling personal tragedy.

Despite her fervent pleadings, two of her sons had gone off to war. Terry, although born American, was serving with the Canadian Army in North Africa. Writing to his mother in the fall of 1943, he couldn't help but reflect on the uncles he never knew whose abbreviated lives had ended in the carnage of the Great War:

> I just have to write to you tonight, dear. All our company are around the fires and are cleaning kit etc. and just on the edge of camp there is a piper practicing on his chanter, and the wild notes of the songs of our Celtic ancestors ring through the night, quickening my blood. I can see Granddad, Ronnie and Alec, and it seems that all the old heroes, Bruin Boru, Douglas, Bruce are saying words of encouragement to us, the new clans. I feel so huge, strong and unafraid that I know I shall never fear anything.[90]

Maisie passed copies of Terry's letter around to her family, even sending one to her cousin, the 10th Duke of Argyll, who had known her two brothers. She wrote that Terry was:

> deeply affected by the anticipation of getting into action, the excitement of getting ready and the feeling of unknown danger. He wanted to tell me that he knew how I felt about our ancestors, the bonny Celtic fighters, and that he too loved the stirring call of the pipes, and he knew that he had Highland blood in his veins... the call of our Fathers to protect the flag of our beloved Empire.[91]

On April 16, 1944, some of that Highland blood stained the soil of Italy when a bursting shell sent shrapnel into Terry's legs. He was rescued under fire by another BC boy, Sgt. Leon Poppell, who then cared for him until medical aid arrived. Despite his injuries, Terry would return injured but whole to Vancouver nearly a year later, but his brother, Michael, was not so fortunate.

Maisie's eldest son had been serving in the US merchant navy as an officer aboard a munitions supplier, the SS *John Burke*. The 130-metre-long liberty ship was part of a 100-ship convoy bringing supplies to a South Pacific

Maisie, dressed in black, walking with her son, Terry, who was injured in the war but returned safely to Vancouver. Photo from the family collection.

invasion force, and they arrived off the island of Mindoro in the Philippines on December 28, 1944. Although the weather was considered too poor to launch aerial support to protect the convoy, six Japanese Aichi D3A dive bombers with kamikaze pilots aboard had lifted off from the island of Cebu earlier that morning. One of these planes survived the gauntlet of heavy anti-aircraft fire from the ships to crash into the *John Burke* amidships. There was a brief flash of fire, followed by billowing smoke issuing from the ship's holds. For several seconds there was some hope that the ship might survive, but then a tall pillar of fire shot into the air, followed by another great draft of white smoke before the ship was engulfed in an immense fireball, which instantly obliterated the ship and its crew of forty merchant mariners and twenty-nine armed guards. A ship just aft of the *Burke* sank and several nearby vessels were damaged.

Maisie's son, Michael, died in the Pacific during the war after a Japanese kamikaze pilot crashed into his ship, the *John Burke*. Following his death, Maisie refused to acknowledge that her friendly local green grocer was Japanese, referring to him instead as Chinese in a bit of self-deception to mask her resentment. Photo from the family collection.

When Maisie received the news, she was as shattered as she had been when her brothers were killed twenty-six years earlier, but she was powerless to do anything but carry on in the fashion that her pedigree demanded. Fortunately, she had the support of Tom Hurley, with whom she was now living at the Silverdene Apartments, 975 Denman Street, in the West End of Vancouver. It would take her years to get over her son's death at the hands of the Japanese, her anger reflected in her bitter retort to a CCF party initiative after the war advocating that Canadians of Japanese descent be permitted to return to the coast: "Wake up, citizens, and fight against this menace to our home and loved ones. Go vote against the [CCF Party Leader M. J.] Coldwells and Mitchells who dare to suggest placing our enemies on equal footing with our soldiers."[92] And uncharacteristically, according to her grandson, Bill Bell, she even refused to acknowledge that her friendly local green grocer was Japanese, referring to him instead as Chinese in a bit of self-deception to mask her resentment. "Thus we never had Japanese oranges around at Christmas,

Maisie, wearing her trademark black beads, teardrop earrings and black cross, was making plans that would consume her for the rest of her life. Photo courtesy of Ralph Bowers and *The Vancouver Sun*.

but rather Mandarin Oranges,"[93] recalled Bell. A granddaughter's only comment was that Maisie "was not without human foibles."

At the age of 57, Maisie had borne more than her fair share of tragedy and disappointment, which perhaps spawned her stern demeanour, complimented by the habit she had cultivated of dressing entirely in black. She wore long black dresses and horn-rimmed glasses and arranged her black hair in a bun held in place by a black comb. From her ears dangled pendulous black teardrop earrings, and about her neck hung coils of heavy black beads, probably jet, a variety of carvable lignite that had been popular in England during the previous century. A four-inch black cross completed her accessories.

The ascetic look generated an imperiousness that would become her trademark, along with the threat of the crooked black cane with its African head handle that was always at hand. "If anyone comes in here—a man or anyone—I can fix him,"[94] she once said of this potential weapon. (The late Judge Alfred Scow recalled that she looked harmless "until she waved her cane."[95]) Clasped in her other hand was a large black handbag that she would occasionally rummage through to find "press clippings, pieces of Indian artwork, and at times for a small bottle of something."[96] Whether she was trying to emulate her beloved Queen Victoria who had dressed in black to mourn the death of her loving consort, or whether she was in perpetual mourning herself is unknown, although one of her granddaughters thought that her appearance was a sort of uniform, and another suggested that she wore black because it could be worn longer before cleaning.

Thomas Berger, who was practising with the law firm of Shulman, Tupper, Southin and Grey in the same building as the Hurleys, and who often sought Tom out for advice on his own cases, remembered her as a "wonderful, gregarious person, but [she] could be intimidating." When he went to the Hurley apartment on Denman Street, he recalled that hair from their three Pekinese dogs covered everything and that "she and Tom would shout at each other... you know, while I was there and Tom and I were having a discussion. Most of the shouting was Maisie shouting at Tom actually, and she would turn to me and say, 'Don't worry, Tommy. This is just our way of making love.'"[97] Ron Rose of the *Vancouver Sun* was also intimidated by her powerful personality. He was a cub reporter when he was first sent to Tom Hurley's office around 1940 to interview him, and it was there that he met Maisie. He recalled that "I hadn't run across anybody with such zeal and it was a little scary."[98]

Maisie's intimidating presence and her admission that she was an "angry woman," served her well in her next venture, the *Native Voice* and the defence of those she called "her people." To accommodate her new publishing undertaking, in 1946 Tom moved his practice from his one-room office on the fourth floor of the Standard Building down the hall to #429, a two-room suite with a secretary's desk in between them. Those who visited the room from which Maisie now ran the *Native Voice* must have thought they had entered a museum because all the walls were graced with First Nations masks, clothing, weapons and other objects. She had been in desperate need of a place to store the considerable array of memorabilia given to her by appreciative clients, so why not an office whose clientele would appreciate it?

When Charles Dudoward from Port Simpson, a hereditary Tsimshian chief, carver and artist, visited Maisie there, he was astounded at her collection. Given his knowledge of totems and other First Nations traditions, he thought that he had pretty well seen everything but was amazed to find an ancient medicine man's regalia, including a stick and headdress, in her collection. This was something his mother had described to him, but that he didn't think he would ever see. It had belonged to a Skeena chief by the name of Gutzen who had lived a hundred years earlier; the stick had "six carved heads, each with a white feather. At the bottom is a snake crawling up the stick. The old medicine man had the power to cause the death of the people whose images were placed on his stick."[99] Maisie's collection continued to grow, and after she launched the *Native Voice* in December 1946, she complained in frustration to Roland Wild, a *Vancouver Sun* reporter who was interviewing her about her life and collection, that she didn't have enough room for her work anymore. Then she announced, "I'm going to shift all this into Tom's office." When asked whether Tom would have to move out, she said: "Never! He'd never leave this office."[100]

It was in this office with its considerable collection of Native objects and art that she began work on the project that would consume her for the rest of her life, a voice for the Aboriginal people of BC to tell of their work and activities, to speak of their grievances, of their wish to educate their children—a voice that would be heard all over North America. And her plans would dovetail neatly with those of one of the most powerful First Nations organizations in the province, the Native Brotherhood of British Columbia. It was a relationship that would become as indispensable as it was inseparable.

Before he died, Alfred Adams made two requests that would have a definitive impact on the battle for justice by the First Nations of BC. He did not live long enough to see the results of his request to Maisie Hurley that she become a voice for his people, having succumbed to his illness in June 1945, the year before the *Native Voice* was launched. His second request was made on his deathbed: he decreed that Chief William Scow (Gla-Whay-Agliss), a hereditary chief of the Kwie-kwa-su-tineuk Nation of the Kwakwaka'wakw, should be his successor as president of the Native Brotherhood of BC. Fortunately, Chief Scow was the right man to take on this important leadership role, and to a certain extent he had been preparing for it all his life. Brought up in a community house on Gilford Island (Gwayasdums), he straddled both the old and new worlds.

The Gilford people, represented by four groups living in fourteen community houses, four families to a house, had traditionally moved between the village on Gilford Island and a camp at Kingcome Inlet where a significant portion of their annual food gathering occurred in the late fall and early spring. Scow had been a participant in this annual harvest until he was removed to residential school, but his father, Johnny, had taken him out of school after he completed Grade 4 in order to prepare him to become a chief and leader of his people. Johnny Scow was not only a successful businessman but politically motivated as well: he had been a delegate at the McKenna-McBride hearings, was involved with the beginning of the Allied Tribes in 1916 and was one of the delegates at the Special Joint Committee of the Senate and House of Commons hearings in 1927. As a result, young William grew up believing that political activism was just a normal part of daily activity.

At Gilford he participated in the rituals and customs of his culture, although he was too young at the time to understand their significance or that his father figured prominently in their preservation. He was also unaware that the great potlatch ceremony that his people had so revered had been outlawed by the federal government on April 19, 1884, by an amendment to the Indian Act of 1880:

Every Indian or other person who engages in or assists in celebrating the Indian festival known as the "Potlatch" or in the Indian dance known as the "Tamanawas" is guilty of a misdemeanor, and shall be liable to imprisonment for a term of not more than six nor less than two months in any gaol or other place of confinement.[101]

Scow's son, Alfred, later reflected on this injustice:

This provision of the Indian Act was in place for close to 75 years and what that did was it prevented the passing down of our oral history. It prevented the passing down of our values. It meant an interruption of the respected forms of government that we used to have, and we did have forms of government be they oral and not in writing before any of the Europeans came to this country. We had a system that worked for us. We respected each other. We had ways of dealing with disputes.[102]

Kingcome Inlet had offered his people a degree of escape from introspection, Scow recalled. As a result, in the 1920s,

they really moved up there—the four tribes—and stayed and made it their permanent village. It was due to the suppression of the old customs, you know, when the government really put their foot down and prohibited them from practising the potlatch... And when the government changed their policies, they approached the heads of the tribes and says, "You don't suppose to live here. Your reserve is in Gilford, or your reserve [is] in Wakelman, or yours is in Hopetown." So they kind of divided the four people that was in the habit of living together... it was one means of depriving them of practising the old customs. Because you can't practise very well within your own family, you have to have an audience. So there's four bands living together, you naturally have three tribes of Indians being your audience any time you conduct this ceremonial potlatch that they have carried on, you know.[103]

The government was hardly subtle in its condemnation of the cultural practices of the First Nations; the potlatch and other ceremonies were considered to be wasteful of both time and resources, and the government wanted to shift the economy from one of redistribution of wealth via the potlatch to one characterized by ownership of private property. An urgent circular sent on December 15, 1921, by Deputy Superintendent-General Duncan Campbell Scott to all the Indian agents in his charge demonstrates how determined he was to disrupt them:

It is observed with alarm that the holding of dances by the Indians on their reserves is on the increase and that these practices tend to disorganize the efforts which the department is putting forth to make them self-supporting. I have therefore to direct you to use your utmost endeavors to dissuade the Indians from their excessive indulgence in the practice of dancing. You should suppress any dances which cause waste of time, interfere with the occupation of the Indians, unsettle them for serious work, injure their health or encourage them in sloth and idleness. You should also dissuade, and, if possible, prevent them from leaving their reserves for the purpose of attending fairs, exhibitions, etc. when their absence would result in their own farming and other interests being neglected. It is realized that reasonable amusement and recreation should be enjoyed by Indians, but they should not be allowed to dissipate their energies and abandon themselves to demoralizing amusements. By the use of tact and firmness you can obtain control and keep it, and this obstacle to continued progress will then disappear.

The rooms, halls and other places in which Indians congregate should be under constant inspection. They should be scrubbed, fumigated, cleansed and disinfected to prevent dissemination of disease. The Indian should be instructed in regard to the matter of proper ventilation and the avoidance of over-crowding rooms where public assemblies are being held, and proper arrangement should be made for the shelter of their horses and ponies. The Agent will avail himself of the services of the medical attendant of his agency in this connection.[104]

As a young man, William Scow, dressed in a ceremonial costume, had been initiated before 2,000 visiting First Nations people in a massive ceremony at Fort Rupert on northern Vancouver Island. He quickly became a polished orator as well as an expert on the potlatch, Hamatsa and other ceremonies, although he would later be strongly opposed to the potlatch, remembering that his father had been left virtually destitute after hosting such an event. Additionally, he may also have taken a lead from the Alaska Native Brotherhood, which had strict rules against potlatching.

For his role as president of the Native Brotherhood of BC, he donned a business suit and looked every inch the executive he was expected to become, but beneath that Western veneer was a sadness that certain elements of the culture he had grown up with had been suppressed right out of existence. "The impact was so great on my own generation," he recalled, "that we decided the thing is not worth it... so we just dropped it."[105] That this was exactly the government's intention was obvious to him and his generation, which had the difficult task of transitioning an ancient culture into a modern world. One way to do that was through education and communication, the vehicle for which was now available to him through the Brotherhood and the *Native Voice*. In the inaugural edition of the paper he implored readers to give it full support:

As President of the Native Brotherhood of British Columbia, I most urgently appeal to all Native people to lend their full support to the *Native Voice.*

For many years we have discussed the ways and means of having a paper for ourselves and unfortunately never did progress beyond the discussion stage. Now we have started. We have established ourselves and will go forward. Through our *Native Voice* we will continue to the best of our ability to bind closer together the many tribes whom we represent into that solid *Native Voice,* a voice that will work for the advancement of our own common native welfare.

The Native Voice will bring about a closer relationship between ourselves and our good white friends who we also appeal to at this time for their support in our struggle for advancement... Through the *Native Voice* we will blend the whole of our problems into a common meeting ground for the discussion of whatever action that is necessary to benefit the well-being of all natives of BC.

We will work together. *The Native Voice* will be the voice of the Native Brotherhood of BC in action which in turn is the voice for *all* the natives in B.C.[106]

The paper was an immediate success, attracting letters of congratulation from BC Premier John Hart; the Indian Commissioner for BC, D. M. Mackay; and the head of the CCF party, Harold Winch; as well as various churches and Indian agents throughout the province. Of significant note was a generous tribute from Major-General B. M. Hoffmeister, extolling the virtues of the First Nations under his command during World War II and what splendid examples of Canadian citizens they were. Apparently he was unaware that First Nations in Canada had yet to be granted that privilege.

The Native Voice very quickly became a valuable link between the widely separated First Nations communities in the province as well as an educational tool for the white population about the trials of belonging to First Nations in Canada. Chief Dr. Robert Joseph recalled "that the *Native Voice* was so instrumental, so needed. We had a real paper... everyone looked forward to it."[107] And the late Alvin Dixon had been surprised when he received a copy of it while he was at residential school because the principal opened everyone's mail, coming and going. "I don't think anybody can underestimate the importance of the paper," he said, "because it provided all the coastal communities [with] all the information they needed to know about what was happening... not just in the commercial fish business, but in aboriginal rights."[108]

A common thread in all the early discussions about the goals of the paper was the need to educate the white population, but it was also decided that the paper would be non-denominational as well as apolitical, permitting it total editorial freedom, although it unabashedly supported anyone in power who was sympathetic to the cause. In an effort to make up for decades of communication blackout, Maisie wanted it to be biweekly, but she very soon discovered that the "trials and troubles of breaking into the ranks of journalism for Native people had not been fully appreciated, nor had we anticipated the responsibilities that would be heaped upon your organization when the start was made."[109] The result was that the paper would remain a monthly publication.

Almost from the beginning, the *Voice*, as is the case for many new publications, suffered from a lack of funds, which the $1.50 yearly subscription rate and the bit of advertising revenue failed to assuage, but Maisie was determined to make it a success and poured her own resources into it, sometimes to the point of her own penury. Her initial plea for membership and funds appeared on the last page of the first edition under the heading: "Are You a True Brother?"[110] She made it abundantly clear that the Brotherhood would only do as well as what people put into it:

> It is wrong to think of this organization as something that gives and gives and gives to you. This organization is fighting for the very existence of the Natives of British Columbia and Canada. We are fighting for existence and a high standard of living, and it is not what you take out of this organization that counts, but what you put into it. It is a war for existence, and like all wars, some will be sacrificed that others may live. The effort you put into building up this organization must be selfless and enduring so that we will win the fight for future generations of Natives...
>
> Maybe the Organization has at times made mistakes, but the good it has done and is doing can never be written in mere words or will the true story ever be fully known except by the few. Its power is growing, and the glorious ideals upon which it was founded by those noble Indian founders who were determined to save their people, the true Natives of Canada, determined that they should not die out but live and come into their own and help to build up and share the magnificent future of the great Dominion of Canada. Their own, Their Native Land.
>
> Brother and Sister, get behind the Native Brotherhood and Sisterhood of British Columbia in their fight for freedom by paying your dues and contributing money.[111]

She signed her piece: Maisie Armytage-Moore, Honorary Life Member. Her reward for the selfless act of advocating for First Nations had been an associate life membership in the Brotherhood conferred upon her in 1944, two years before the paper was launched, and she had the distinct honour of being the first woman to be granted that privilege. Although a Native Sisterhood of British Columbia had been established by this time, and although the two organizations worked in concert to organize such events as AGMs, the Brotherhood remained an association of men, while the Sisterhood, keenly aware of the need for funds, supported the Brothers with fundraising drives and bake sales. Although the Alaska Native Brotherhood permitted Sisterhood delegates to vote at conventions, no such privilege was granted to BC Sisterhood delegates. The Brotherhood, however, viewed Maisie as a sort of den mother, which was not too unusual given the matriarchal hierarchy of BC First Nations, and her seemingly inexhaustible work on their behalf was hugely appreciated by the growing organization.

As well, she was not just an arm's-length participant. In addition to writing for and publishing the paper each month, the doors of her office and her home on Denman Street were constantly being opened to welcome someone in need of a meal, a chat or just a few dollars to tide them over. "Anyone who wants to see her

Maisie's portrait of her friend, August Jack Khatsahlano, of whom she said, "He taught me to think as an Indian." Photo (1986 19 101) courtesy of the North Vancouver Museum and Archives.

just shouts through the window—they are always open—and Maisie comes to the door. 'Darling, I'm glad to see you. Don't mind the clutter.'"[112]

One of her frequent visitors was August Jack Khatsahlano (X̱ats'al-anexw), a hereditary chief of the Squamish people, medicine man and spirit dancer, who, according to Maisie "went into the silence for 10 years to get the 'Power.'"[113] He at first claimed that he was born in 1877 at Snauq (the False Creek Reserve just below the present-day Burrard Street Bridge), from which he and his brother had watched the city of Vancouver burn in June 1886, but he later informed Major James Skitt Matthews, Vancouver City archivist, that people had told him that he was actually born at Chaythoos just inside Prospect Point in Stanley Park. His father, Supple Jack (Khay-tulk) died "when I was just old enough to cut wood—about six years old"[114] after being kicked by a cow. August recalled that as a boy he had listened to the Elders recounting stories of life and war before the arrival of the Europeans.

His grandfather, Khatsahlanogh (he had no European name), was a great chief of the Squamish who had been born at a village a few kilometres up the Squamish River, although he later migrated to the village of Chaythoos.

(The Vancouver neighbourhood of Kitsilano is named for him.) The patronym of his grandfather was conferred upon August Jack in a large ceremony held at Snauq in the summer of 1938, after which, he became known as August Jack Khatsahlano. To return the honour, he and his brother Willie, who had taken on their father's name of Khay-tulk, hosted a potlatch of their own at Snauq, financing it from their earnings at a local sawmill; they reportedly gave away 100 blankets to their guests.

August Jack was a simple, peaceful man whose study of the history of his people and his close ties to his ancestral roots made him a living link from what was then incorrectly referred to as the "Stone Age," although he preferred to call it the "Relief Age,"[115] referencing the cycle of unemployment and relief that even then influenced life. He was not only a legend among his own people but also among Maisie's grandchildren. Young Maureen Murphy, when visiting from Seattle, recalled her visit with him one day at her grandmother's apartment:

> Nana finally came home from her office and she arrived with not only Tommy, her new husband, but with ancient Chief August Jack Khatsahlano of the Squamish. Nana's guest politely refused her invitation to sit on her chesterfield with its broken springs and seated himself on a sturdy chair instead. Tommy, who looked like Winston Churchill to me, slipped off his suit coat and vest, poured himself a tall scotch whiskey, tucked the evening newspaper under his arm and politely excused himself. Like a lord of the manor, he went to his bedroom with Chang, Beijing, and Shanghai happily yapping at his heels.
>
> August Jack was more than just a lord; he was a royal chief. His skin looked like crumpled brown tissue paper. His hands were so thin I could see the bones just below the surface. He appeared to be as fragile and dry as the old cedar baskets I had been playing with earlier, but his voice was strong and eloquent. I curled into the corner of the chesterfield and kept silent while Nana interviewed him for an article she was writing. It was hypnotizing to listen to the ancient chief speak. Even though August Jack spoke English, it was his second language, not his first. There was a lilt to his words, a way of stressing some and softening others that was different. He almost sang English as if every word, even an insignificant one like "it," was more valuable coming out of his mouth than mine. Sentences started out sounding high and ended low, or began low and ended high.
>
> As August Jack talked I felt like I was riding up and down the mountain trails of language. It was a beautiful jaunt and I nearly missed the gist of what he was saying. "I am last of the medicine men who are Squamish dancers," August Jack said. "I was born over there

in Stanley Park." He lifted his arm and pointed north towards the Lions Gate Bridge. "I was born before America's Custer and their Little Bighorn, before the sawmill that grew into this city was built, and not long after the White Men divided my people's land into different countries."

"Canada and the United States?" I asked.

The chief nodded. "They divided the family of rivers and mountains, inlets and lakes from each other. The White Man drew a line on the face of the earth. Don't you think if the Great Spirit wanted such a line he would have created one?"

It was my turn to nod. "In the old days, I bet you could bring your family a gift and not have to ask permission."

"That is true," August Jack said. "But now I have to stop at the invisible line and ask permission to visit my grandmother at Seattle."

"I'm so sorry," I said, feeling guilty for being white. Then it hit me. Grandmother? August Jack must have been almost a hundred years old and he was still going to see his grandmother?

The Squamish chief saw his joke had finally clicked in my brain and he laughed at the befuddled look on my face.[116]

August Jack was a keen prospector and in a letter to a friend Maisie recalled how the two of them had "travelled together with packs on our backs... He taught me to think as an Indian."[117] In 1943, on one of their last treks together, August Jack led her on an arduous fifteen-day adventure up Mount Donaldson at the head of Salmon Inlet on the Sunshine Coast in search of "the mother lode" of the Howe Sound Copper and Silver Company at the 3,100-foot level. It had been staked in the mid-1870s and abandoned ten years later when the company found it impossible to build a road up the precipitous slopes. Maisie and August Jack didn't find it, but Maisie had been in her glory, harkening back to trips with her father in her youth, prospecting and living off the land. This expedition almost did her in as they ran out of food and Maisie sustained a serious leg injury in a rock slide, but it was almost as if she had been on some sort of spirit quest, and she wrote about it upon her return:

August Jack Khatsahlano and Maisie resting after one of their prospecting expeditions. Photo from the family collection.

I have heard people say so many times, "Oh, if I could only get away from it all, just keep on going." I wonder how many have done so? I have, with a heavy pack on my back, fighting my way through underbrush, swamps, fording rivers, climbing up wearily, slowly, aching all over with fatigue, exhausted from the weight of my pack, physically weary, but mentally growing stronger. Carried on by sheer power of my will to escape. When you reach the top thousands of feet up, a great loneliness surrounds you. Silent, deserted by the living, towering mountain ranges reach out as far as the eye can see, vast eternal monuments to the Almighty for centuries past and centuries to come, when you and I are gone and forgotten. It takes the lonely grandeur of these mountain ranges to teach one values, to show the shallowness of worldly gain, the pettiness of human ambition.[118]

August Jack was so enamoured of Maisie that he gave her a *sxwayxwii* mask belonging to his family, a spiritually powerful object that is rarely, if ever, viewed by the public. Used by the Coast Salish in cleansing ceremonies, it "has unique features that include eyes with round bulging plugs, a nose in the shape of a bird's head and horns carved like serpents or birds." "When you give a gift of that significance," offered Damara Jacobs, who is a *sxwayxwii* society member through her family, "it is really monumental. You are tying yourself for life to that person."[119] And perhaps that was August Jack's intention since he once proposed to Maisie, despite already being married. Maisie politely declined his offer while trying not to hurt his feelings, preferring to remain lifelong friends with the beloved and respected Elder. But it was perhaps August Jack's benevolent nature, his wisdom, counsel and friendship that encouraged Maisie to try to right the injustices that she heard about and witnessed on a daily basis. Some of this she and Tom Hurley were able to do in the courtroom, but now that she had the *Voice* as a pulpit, she jumped right into the deep end of First Nations disquiet, namely the Indian Act, in the first issue of the paper. In May 1946, six months before the *Voice* was launched, a Special Joint Committee of the Senate and House of Commons had been struck to "revise the Indian Act and examine the whole life and anything that pertains to the welfare of the Indians of Canada."[120]

The Indian Act had been passed a little over a century after the first legislation governing First Nations in North America came into being. That first document had been a Royal Proclamation signed by King George III in 1763 following the Treaty of Paris, which ended the Seven Years War and ceded much of French colonial territory in North America to Britain. The proclamation of 1763, which laid out the system of governance for the newly acquired French settlements, also had a First Nations component, which provided a framework for their treatment, specifically within Quebec, East Florida and West Florida. It decreed that:

> And whereas it is just and reasonable, and essential to our interest and the security of our colonies, that the several Nations or Tribes of Indians, with whom we are connected, and who live under our protection, should not be molested or disturbed in the possession of such parts of our dominions and territories as, not having been ceded to, or purchased by us, are reserved to them, or any of them, as their hunting grounds...

All of the lands west of the Appalachian Mountains were considered to be "Indian Territory," and British Columbia, which was even more remote at that time, was just marked on the maps as *terra incognita*, although the proclamation anticipated its settlement along with that of other unsettled lands when it made the following provision:

> And We do further declare it to be Our Royal Will and Pleasure, for the present as aforesaid, to reserve under Our Sovereignty, Protection, and Dominion, for the Use of the said Indians, all the Lands and Territories not included within the Limits of Our said Three New Governments, or within the Limits of the Territory granted to the Hudson's Bay Company, as also all the Lands and Territories lying to the Westward of the Sources of the Rivers which fall into the Sea from the West and North West, as aforesaid; and We do hereby strictly forbid, on Pain of Our Displeasure, all Our loving Subjects from making any Purchases or Settlements whatever, or taking Possession of any of the Lands above reserved, without Our especial Leave and Licence for that Purpose first obtained.[121]

This Aboriginal component of the proclamation, which became known as the "Indian Magna Carta" or the "Indian Bill of Rights,"[122] was largely due to the work and influence of Sir William Johnson, superintendent-general of the Indian Department, who recognized that there would be conflict if the First Nations were not dealt with fairly. It recognized the rights of First Nations peoples to their land, and as lawyer Thomas Berger points out, "Equally important and the basis of all the Indian Acts that followed was the principle that the Indians could not be divested of these lands except by a surrender to the Crown. No settler could make a deal with the Indians for their land. A representative of the Crown had to hold a public meeting with the Indians."

By the time the first version of the Indian Act, which was a consolidation of that Royal Proclamation of 1763 and other pre-confederation policy, was drawn up by the federal government in 1876 under the provisions of Section 91 (24) of the Constitution Act of 1867, Britain had been transferring responsibility for the First Nations in Canada to the federal government for over twenty-five years. Further, the government in Canada had been altering the terms of that responsibility by introducing legislation of its own, such as the 1850 Act for the Better Protection of the Lands and Property of Indians in Lower Canada and an Act for the Protection of Indians in Upper Canada from Imposition, and the Property Occupied or Enjoyed by them from Trespass and Injury.[123] These two statutes, legislated by the Province of Canada, which was still then a British colony, served to define what it meant to be an "Indian" in Upper and Lower Canada and what was considered to be "Indian Status"—but these definitions were crafted without input from the very people they would affect.

Then in 1857 the government, growing impatient with the slow progress of Aboriginal assimilation, passed what was known as the Gradual Civilization Act, which introduced the concept of Aboriginal enfranchisement in the belief that First Nations people would welcome the opportunity to lose their "Indian Status" and become full voting citizens. This assimilationist view would swamp the new Indian Act and taint all future legislation. Three years later, the Indian Lands Act was passed, centralizing control of First Nations in Canada under a single individual, the chief superintendent of Indian Affairs, who was given broad discretionary control over all First Nations people living on reserves. The new Indian Act replaced the largesse granted by the king over a century earlier with a paternalistic approach reflected in an annual report (1876) from the Department of the Interior that read in part:

> Our Indian legislation generally rests on the principle that the aborigines are to be kept in a condition of tutelage and treated as wards or children of the State... The true interests of the aborigines and of the State alike require that every effort should be made to aid the Red man in lifting himself out of his condition of tutelage and dependence, and that is clearly our wisdom and our duty, through education and every other means, to prepare him for a higher civilization by encouraging him to assume the privileges and responsibilities of full citizenship."[124]

By 1946 this act had gone through several iterations, the intent always being to gradually chip away at the customs, culture and land of First Nations people until they blended seamlessly into the greater fabric of the nation. But when the government announced its intention to revise the act again and promised to consult with various First Nations across the country, Peter Kelly, who had been elected to the position of chair of the Brotherhood's Legislative Committee due to his burgeoning interest and vast experience, became hopeful that the revised act would become another "Magna Carta for the Indians." However, when time passed and no one from the revision committee called upon the Brotherhood to come to Ottawa to make a report, Kelly travelled there on his own accord to generate some activity. There the committee assured him that the Brotherhood delegates would be able to make a presentation soon as Ottawa was indeed impressed with the organization, given that it was the largest democratic body of First Nations in the country, but they were still bogged down in hearings with government departments and officials. Fortunately, Kelly's trip was not completely wasted because the committee interrupted its schedule of proceedings to make room for his extemporaneous presentation.

But all was not harmonious back home on the BC First Nations front. The Interior chiefs were upset that Ottawa had only recognized the Brotherhood as being worthy of making a presentation,[125] which was likely why Oscar Peters, representing tribes from the Fraser Valley and Interior of the province, had prepared his own submission. The list of changes to the Indian Act that he and his colleagues recommended, which were strikingly similar to the list compiled by the Brotherhood, would have made the revised act a true "Magna Carta for the Indians" had they been implemented. The first item on his list was the establishment of a separate ministry to handle the affairs of First Nations in Canada; at that time they were governed by the Ministry of the Interior, although in 1949 responsibility was transferred to the Minister of Mines and Resources and later handed off to the Minister of Citizenship and Immigration. Second, Peters protested compulsory taxation of BC First Nations individuals, stating that since all First Nations people were wards of the Crown, pursuant to treaties made with other First Nations in Canada, BC First Nations people should be tax exempt. He supported his point by referencing a letter written on March 25, 1861, by BC Governor James Douglas to Henry Pelham Fiennes Pelham-Clinton, 5th Duke of Newcastle, then Secretary of State for the Colonies, wherein Douglas requested £3,000 to purchase First Nations land, warning that failure "to extinguish title and the occupation of such portions of the Colony by white settlers, unless with the full consent of the proprietary tribes, would be perceived as national wrongs, engender feelings of irritation against the settlers, and endanger the peace of the country."[126] Seven months later his request was denied on the basis that, although important, it was a colonial affair and to burden the British public with it would be unfair. With that, the purchase never did transact, despite Douglas having made fourteen similar arrangements, known as the Douglas Treaties, on Vancouver Island between 1850 and 1854. This was ample evidence, Peters stated, to substantiate "the fact that our Aboriginal Rights to this country were never bartered nor purchased."[127]

Peters' report also protested involuntary enfranchisement and requested that "recognition of us Natives as people with equal intelligence and integrity, eligible to exercise equal status of full citizenship privileges, as we are, viz., maintaining all our traditions, aboriginal rights, interests and benefits, a system identical to that granted to the Maori Indians in New Zealand."[128] He was referring to the fact that in New Zealand for the previous eighty years four seats had been set aside in the eighty-seat House of Representatives for Maori MPs who had identical privileges to other members and had been having an equal say in the house. Peters' concept of full citizenship, while simultaneously preserving important elements of Native culture, was, he stated, the only way that the franchise would gain consent among First Nations peoples. His report also protested encroachment on reserve land and the stealing of natural resources by white people, requested that day and residential schools be brought under provincial control, and demanded that the government restore unrestricted fishing rights at traditional sites for domestic purposes. His report concluded with:

> The Doukhobors and Mennonites were granted lands, horses, farm implements and cows, and adequately financed, and they are foreigners without interest in this country. What of us natives who own this country? Are foreigners greater than people who own a country?"[129]

Coincidentally, on January 1, 1947, the same month that Maisie summarized Oscar Peters' report for the *Voice*—including his comment about the Doukhobor immigrants—the federal government declared that "all people residing in Canada regardless of their birthplace, foreign or British, are entitled by law to call themselves Canadian." With complete disbelief, Maisie editorialized her anger: "which makes further comment from the *Native Voice* unnecessary at this time excepting to mention that under Canadian laws INDIANS ARE NOT PEOPLE."[130]

Maisie was inclined to shoot first and ask questions later, indiscriminately blasting away at whomever she felt responsible for a lapse in judgment, a flawed bit of legislation or the slow pace of progress. But it was a character trait born out of frustration. Her reporter friend Paul St. Pierre, reflecting on why she was so fearless, told an interviewer in 1964 that: "She would give everything for a person and damn little for an establishment. To her all things were personal. She is not very much interested in creeds."[131]

Articles published in the *Voice* were soon being picked up by the national dailies, which in the past had never adequately covered the "Indian story." As a result, early in 1947 when the *Voice* published Chief William Scow's telegram to Premier John Hart expressing his displeasure that the BC government was considering enfranchising Chinese and East Indian people while simultaneously ignoring BC's Aboriginal people, the story made the evening news. The premier's glib response that "your representations will be given every consideration,"[132] left a chill not only within the ranks of the Brotherhood but also among the general public, the majority of whom believed that the offer of the vote to Chinese and East Indian people before that of First Nations was manifestly unjust. The mayor of Vancouver, Gerry McGeer, formerly an MLA, MP and senator, wrote:

> I feel and have always felt that our administration of the affairs of Indians forms one of the sad and sorry pages in our Canadian history... Our treatment of Indians in Canada constitutes a brutal and unwarranted repudiation of every sentiment that is contained in the doctrine of the Golden Rule.[133]

The almost two pages of letters to the editor in the eight-page February 1947 issue of the *Voice* supported the fact that it was being read across the province, and the general tenor of the letters was one of excitement that the paper would serve to unite the voices of First Nations people wherever they were. Among those letters was one from Alfred Adams's nephew, Arthur, who was convalescing from tuberculosis away from his home village of Masset, and he wrote to say he viewed the paper as a "letter from home."[134] But Maisie must have been even more pleased that the fledgling publication had already found its mark abroad since it had been one of Alfred Adams's dying wishes that the paper would attract that level of attention. A letter from H. Lyle La Hurreau (Chief Shup-She), in Fort Wayne, Indiana, requested a subscription; he would later become a frequent contributor.

Although the fight for justice was the paper's prime endeavour, the publication was not all gloom, as evidenced by a piece of satire penned by Maisie and Paul St. Pierre and hatched one night in the newsroom of the *Vancouver News-Herald* where he was working at the time. It appeared on the front page of the February edition, but it was cheekily assigned to the pen of Chief William Scow without his knowledge or consent. Scow awoke the next morning to learn that he had just taken over the province from Premier Hart. According to St. Pierre:

> I'm not sure where the original idea came from, but I said, "Why doesn't Bill Scow—who was at that time head of the Native Brotherhood of BC—take over the province and tell the whites they are resuming all rights... that the whites would be taught useful trades and various other promises." We couldn't get hold of Bill that night—phones were even less reliable than they are now—and that's pretty unreliable. We literally could not reach him by phone, so Maisie said, "We'll put his name on it anyway and it'll be all right." So the next day Bill discovered that he had seized the province of British Columbia and declared the coalition government and interim government dissolved.[135]

Scow recalled that he had been working on the docks at Alert Bay loading fish that morning. "I hadn't read the papers or anything that day so when the fellow I worked for walked up and congratulated me, I asked him why. 'Well, I just heard that you are the new premier of BC.' I just laughed and asked him if he wanted a job."[136]

Paul recalled that the story:

> caused a bit of a stir in the province because much of what [Chief Scow] was saying was true, although he himself was extremely irritated when he found out about it—he didn't like his name used on things he knew nothing about—but he never said anything. The province stepped out of its subservient position at that time and said that anything Indian was Ottawa's responsibility. They didn't even want to know about it, you know.[137]

As well as promoting Chief Scow to premier, Maisie and Paul assigned the attorney general's role to Maisie's partner, Tom Hurley, then quoted him as saying:

> This de jure government, solicitous for the welfare of white wards and assuming toward them a paternalistic attitude, will see that native agents are appointed at proper places where white wards may bring all their troubles, great and small, and be assured of sympathetic advice and encouragement.
>
> Whites will be guaranteed freedom of worship, of the press, of speech, and from want. There will be no discrimination; white wards will get the same treatment Indian wards have received.
>
> And for white property taken over, compensation will be paid "at some future date... at the discretion of the native government... with some provisions."[138]

The article also included a list of proscribed activities, including potlatching, being abroad during curfew hours, voting, drinking and betting. Jack Greenwall, executive director of the BC Federation of Labour, who was in on the spoof, protested that seniors and destitute white people were only receiving $4.50 per month in support; in reality, this was exactly what was being paid to senior First Nations persons—only not in cash but in kind—compared to the $30 per month being granted to white senior citizens. The *Vancouver Sun* joined the discussion as well, noting that although the article was a prank, it made many white citizens stop and reflect on the plight of their First Nations neighbours, and on February 3 that newspaper told its readers: "The economic and social conditions of the wards are proof of the failure of the administration of Indian affairs."[139] The *Vancouver News-Herald* noted that: "Now that the franchise is being broadened in the interests of Chinese and Asiatic Indians, there is little enough excuse for failing to make a start with the enfranchisement of native sons."[140] Two days later the *Prince Rupert*

Daily News agreed: "Certainly if the Chinese and the East Indians are to be given the franchise, we would think it to be a fair and just thing that the natives should also have the privilege."[141] Even the IWA spoke up, pointing out that since First Nations people had fought so valiantly in the last war, and as they bore a "full share of the economic responsibility of our country through income tax and indirect taxes, etc. without any representation on any governing body,"[142] they should be offered the franchise as well.

But not everyone in the Aboriginal community agreed. At meetings in Sardis and Harrison Mills in late February 1947, Andrew Paull, now president of the North American Indian Brotherhood, an organization he had founded after his relationship with the Native Brotherhood of BC had soured over an accounting of funds,[143] sharply criticized the Brotherhood's push for enfranchisement; he believed that it was tantamount to trading one's birthright for the doubtful privilege of marking a ballot every four years. He went even further, appearing before the provincial cabinet with a delegation of Interior chiefs to argue, controversially, that First Nations people in the province "want to remain wards of the government."[144] But Guy Williams, Oscar Peters and Maisie, representing the Brotherhood, also attended the Sardis meeting, and it was decided there that the two organizations would unite to press for a system of representation similar to that held by the Maoris in New Zealand.

Three months after Maisie began publishing the *Voice*, the paper's editor, Jack Beynon, retired due to ill health. In time Ruth Smith, a member of the Salish community from Yale, would take over, at first on a *pro tem* basis but eventually becoming the full-time editor. In the interim, however, Maisie picked up where Jack had left off, penning a questioning piece for the March issue about tolerance towards minorities and asking the paper's readers to examine their own actions and motives. She wrote:

> Race hatreds explode suddenly. We read about them daily in the papers the world over. When we read these news items, we probably say, "Too bad. Why can't people do as we do in Canada?" But think—do we? In stories and news items the "bad" characters are nearly always belonging to one of the minority groups—Negroes are labelled lazy, Jews wily, Irish superstitious, Italians criminal, Natives shiftless, etc. There is much we can do in our daily life. Ask yourself, what do you really think? What degree of tolerance do you have?[145]

The March 1947 issue also included a plaintiff piece penned by Big White Owl (also known as Jasper Hill) of Ontario. It was titled "We Are Left Alone to Die," and it questioned government policies that meant:

The Indians of Canada, the first citizens of this fair land, are denied the right to participate in the life of Canada on the same level as that granted to other so-called Canadians of European descent. Why are the Red Indian people held in bondage? Why are they denied every vestige of human rights? ...

I sincerely believe that our real chance for complete emancipation lies in the fact that we must continue to everlastingly expound and rigidly adhere to our faith and ideals. Ideals which have been forged out through countless generations of effort and struggle. We must never completely surrender our grand heritage. We must try to recapture the spirit of our forefathers who were willing to share privileges and rights. Like them we must be brave and courageous and true. We must have faith in ourselves and in our children. We must think and build for the future. And lastly we must remember that we are the NATIVE CANADIANS and that it is our sacred duty to continue to contribute our share for the culture and welfare of the Canada of tomorrow... As a race of people we must continue to live. We must not give up hope and die.[146]

Articles like this stirred public debate, and because of the *Voice*, First Nations readers were now more in step with what was happening across the country as well as south of the border, especially when the paper highlighted the stark differences between the welfare of First Nations peoples in Canada and Native Americans. An article in the March issue of the *Voice* told the story of the Alaska Brotherhood, after which the Native Brotherhood of BC had been modelled, and reported that in Alaska, where fully one-half of the population was Native American, Aleut or Inuit (formerly referred to as Eskimo), Native Americans were considered to be truly equal with their white neighbours. Three had been elected to the territorial legislature—one as a senator and two as representatives—and after the passing of the Anti-Discrimination Act of 1945, which was "really a bill of equal rights for the people of all races and color in Alaska," Native Americans there were enjoying "an equal footing with the white man in all walks of life."[147] Not all states were united in this progressive thinking, however, as Navajos in both New Mexico and Arizona were still being denied the vote. The *Voice* also reminded its readers that the *Free Press Weekly* in Manitoba had pointed out that in Canada the federal government had yet to grant First Nations a separate ministry, let alone hire any Aboriginal people to manage their own affairs, while "more than half the staff of the US Indian Department are Indians."[148]

While the province of British Columbia was still withholding the franchise from its First Nations people, the idea gained a little momentum when Saskatchewan Premier Tommy C. Douglas (who had been awarded the name

Red Eagle) considered offering his province's 11,000 First Nations residents the vote. Previously, the offer had been stalled when legal experts had to consult the British North America Act and its many amendments to determine whether it was within the province's right or whether it was the federal government's responsibility to offer them the franchise. But Douglas, who was planning on passing a Bill of Rights in his province, felt that it would not be fair to introduce such significant legislation when an important element of the population could not participate. On the other hand, Saskatchewan's First Nations were not even sure they wanted the vote; they feared it would mean paying taxes and losing their treaty status despite Douglas's assurance that they would not lose the latter.

In the March issue, Maisie also pointed out that the *Voice* would double the number of pages published in previous issues, and would even have a two-colour cover in future. Unfortunately, this was mostly wishful thinking because the use of colour was spotty at best in the following issues, and although she did strive to double the number of pages, she did not always achieve that goal. As diminutive as it would remain, however, the *Voice* continued to punch much higher than its weight as evidenced when the Indian Association of Alberta sanctioned it as the voice of Alberta's First Nations and advised that the association was copying the Native Brotherhood of BC with respect to aims and aspirations. Similar sentiments were forwarded from First Nations in Saskatchewan who, one year earlier, had established the Union of Saskatchewan Indians; they were now in the process of writing a report to present to the joint committee in Ottawa. Both organizations were excited that the *Voice* had given "courage and strength to the Indians of many other provinces."[149]

Meanwhile, in Ottawa the Special Joint Committee of the Senate and House of Commons had begun distributing the minutes of the evidence presented to it, and in the April 1947 issue the *Voice* reported on them, revealing some shocking admissions of abuse and neglect across the country. Two doctors, one an expert nutritionist, had reported to the committee that the diet of First Nations children at the Norway House residential school in remote northern Manitoba was worse than that of children in the poorest neighbourhood of Toronto. In fact, the children exhibited such serious signs of malnutrition that, had they been part of the doctor's family, he would have demanded their immediate hospitalization. What that doctor did not know was that researchers who had visited Norway House in 1942 had discovered an ideal population and perfect conditions for an abhorrent nutritional experiment. They had abandoned compassion in their zeal to take advantage of these isolated and desperate people who were already suffering from a collapse of the fur industry. Even more alarming was that no one had sought to stop these insidious experiments, which remained hidden until researchers discovered them in the summer of 2013.

Moreover, the joint committee was never told that malnutrition was rampant in the residential schools right across the country. The late Alvin Dixon remembered always being hungry at the Port Alberni, BC, residential school, which in 1947 was another of the schools singled out for special nutritional experiments. He recalled milking cows there, but the milk the children were given to drink was powdered milk from a can. They were literally starving and stole potatoes from a neighbouring farm and ate them raw. It didn't help that Alvin rarely made it back to his village of Bella Bella, but even if he had gone home and told his parents or the Elders about the deprivations at the school, they would have been "very closed mouth about the whole experience... they didn't talk about anything that they thought might offend the Indian agent."[150]

When Dr. Robert Joseph, a hereditary chief of the Gwawaenuk First Nation and a leader of the Reconciliation Canada movement, spoke at his honorary doctorate of laws ceremony in 2003, he recalled being beaten and hungry at residential school:

> When I was six years old, I ended up in an Indian Residential School. I spent ten lost years of my life there. The only language I knew was Kwakwala. Almost from the very first day I entered that school I was beaten for speaking my birthright. I would cry myself to sleep at night, alone and terribly lonely. When I ran out of tears, I would fantasize about being at home with my family and being in my home community. There were many times that I was very hungry and sometimes the worms danced on top of my porridge. There was so much pain, so much harm, so much change in those ten years at this school. There was so much trauma. Sometimes the details are difficult to remember, but you can never really forget.[151]

Evidence presented to the joint committee also identified one community whose members had to walk three miles to get water because the local wells were polluted and another where the schools were so dilapidated that the children had not attended in three years. One man told the investigators that his government relief consisted of $5 per month to feed his family of seven. It was discovered then that the amount of relief provided was based entirely on the discretion of the local Indian agent. Housing was a huge issue as well, and on one reserve the housing was considered to be unsuitable even for cattle. It was obvious from these reports that there was no standard level of care or service and, even worse, that First Nations were often left to the mercy of the Indian agents—some of whom had God complexes—with little to no accountability or oversight.

Chief Dr. Robert Joseph, Ambassador of Reconciliation Canada, giving a presentation. Photo courtesy of Indspire.

The report that the Brotherhood intended to present in Ottawa could hardly address any of these disturbing issues because the struggle for basic rights in BC still had to be won. It was also true that treaty rights were of little concern to BC First Nations since only a few bands were considered to be "Treaty Indians." However, Guy Williams, the Brotherhood's business agent, in a brief to the BC legislature in March, highlighted the deplorable state of Aboriginal education in the province when he advised that:

> It is our contention that the Indian population of this province has received a far lower standard of educational, health and welfare services than other citizens and that much of the deplorable conditions under which Indians are living today can be traced to these low standards. For example, of the 25,000 Indians in BC, 12,000 are less than 17 years of age and of these only 4,100 were enrolled in school during the 1945–46 school year. It is estimated that 10 percent of these 12,000 young people, future citizens of this province, are receiving no education at all. We need at least 20 more day schools to give all our children education, and as it is, 55 of the existing schools are in dire need of extensive repairs and replacement.[152]

Only a few months earlier, these shocking facts would have reached very few, but now that the *Voice* was exposing this sea of neglect to any and all who cared to read about it, the impact was palpable. Sympathetic mail arrived from as far away as Mexico, Alaska, Nova Scotia, New York and North Carolina. But according to Maisie, the paper had "received ten times more publicity" in New York than it had in Vancouver. In fact, the Mohawk people of that state were clamouring for the *Voice* to become their paper, too. In an effort to encourage more First Nations writers to submit their work to the paper, Maisie wrote:

> If the *Native Voice* is to entertain, educate and enlighten our people, then it should encourage any and all Indians to write—if they have any writing abilities—for the *Native Voice* to make known their knowledge and opinions on any subjects of vital interest to readers.
>
> *The Native Voice*, in order to succeed and gain power, must reach and speak for all Indians, whether in all Canada, the United States, Mexico or even South American Indians. If the *Native Voice* is only an Indian journal locally, instead of nationally and internationally, then the paper depends on its support locally only. Now any Indian journal is my paper, whether produced in Canada or the United States, and I wish it to become a big powerful Indian journal for all real, true Natives of America.[153]

In the five months of its existence, the *Voice* had already become an indispensable tool for communicating the struggle for justice, but the notion of true unity that the Brotherhood and the paper had envisioned was still not fully appreciated by all.

4—THE PROVINCIAL VOTE

As the members of the Native Brotherhood delegation—President William Scow, Legislative Chair Reverend Peter Kelly and Business Agent Guy Williams—waited for their turn to make their presentation to the Special Joint Committee of the Senate and House of Commons in the spring of 1947, they reviewed the list of amendments to the Indian Act that they considered absolutely essential. They wanted the right to choose or reject their own band members, a right that was now controlled by the federal government. They felt that taxation without representation was unfair, and they requested a similar style of representation to that enjoyed by the Maoris in New Zealand. The federal franchise was also on their list, but they wanted it without any attendant loss of land and status, and they wanted control over their own reserves to prevent the habitual stealing of resources. Another request was that day and residential schools be removed from denominational control and be managed by the federal government directly. This was not, as one might suspect, due to the abuses that were occurring in these church-run schools since these had yet to be exposed, but because existing schools were in dire need of repair and construction of new schools had not kept pace with population increases.

When at last the joint committee sent a request for the Native Brotherhood to get ready to present its report in Ottawa at the beginning of May 1947, excitement began to mount, but Williams was worried about the outcome of their presentation. Back in 1927 he had been just 20 years old when Chief Johnny Chilihitza (Okanagan), then 80 years of age, had stood before another joint parliamentary committee. Peter Kelly had been there, too, as had Andrew Paull, both of them leaders of the Allied Tribes, an organization that would founder shortly after the disappointing news came that the men had failed to make their case. Old Chief Chilihitza, however, had not been interested in politics, land grants or fishing rights, widows' pensions or education as the others were. He had been more concerned about irrigation and grazing rights and had told the parliamentary committee:

> All the Indians want is to be just Indians and not to be taken as white people and made to live like the white man; they want to be the way their forefathers used to be, just plain Indians. That is what my people want.[154]

Guy Williams wondered why the old man had chosen to undermine the Allied Tribes, an organization that had worked so diligently for more than a decade to gain some measure of equality; it was a question that Kelly and Paull had asked at the time as well. But something good had come from the defeat of the organization, and for the April 1947 issue of the *Native Voice*, Williams wrote:

> The efforts and the cause of a once noble race seemed altogether lost until one day a Haida chief and Tsimshian noblemen gathered together the embers and coals of the fires of the beaten Allied Tribes of BC.
>
> Then was born the Native Brotherhood of BC. Now after 17 years this organization is recognized as the largest and most democratic Native organization in Canada and has continually strived for a change of status and for the betterment of existing conditions among the Natives.[155]

His tone suggested that the Brotherhood had the affairs of the province's First Nations in hand, and the path ahead would be straightforward. But just recently Andrew Paull, who had withdrawn from the Native Brotherhood to form the North American Indian Brotherhood (NAIB), had attended a provincial cabinet meeting with a delegation of twenty chiefs from the Interior to request that BC First Nations continue to be wards of the government. His

argument was that they should not have to give up their land and status just for the privilege of marking a paper with an X every four years. But Paull's rejection of enfranchisement was not only a step backwards for the Brotherhood but directly contradicted its goals as well, and Williams questioned whether the unity once envisioned by the Brotherhood was slowly unravelling. In the fervent hope that history would not repeat itself, he concluded his piece for the *Voice* with: "Now that we are appearing before the parliamentary committee this year, unity is what we need; why should we not take a lesson from the past?"[156]

The Brotherhood Business Agent and Maisie's friend, Guy Williams would go on to become the Brotherhood President and later a Canadian Senator. Photo courtesy of Louiella Bolten.

It is interesting that within a year of Paull's controversial comments in Victoria he would be eased out of the presidency of the NAIB, a position that was quickly assumed by Frank Assu of

Steveston who would serve out the remaining three years of Paull's five-year term. "Whether or not the Indian people of Canada want the vote will be decided by the Indians themselves,"[157] Assu said matter-of-factly after accepting the position.

On May 1 and 2, 1947, William Scow, Reverend Peter Kelly and Guy Williams, who was appearing on behalf of the unaffiliated First Nations people of the province, plus an independent representative, Thomas Gosnell, who had been one of the founders of the Brotherhood, travelled to Ottawa to represent the organization at the joint committee hearings. All were hopeful that the revisions to the Indian Act they were about to suggest would make the new document a true "Magna Carta for the Indians." President William Scow wrote of the optimism that he and his fellow delegates were feeling:

> This is our most critical hour, the hour for which we have waited 80 years. For over three-quarters of a century, ever since the enactment of the Indian Act, our people have suffered discrimination and exploitation. Now at long last our chance has come to present to the people of Canada our hopes and desires in the revision of that Act, so that we may walk as free men in this land of our fathers.[158]

The Brotherhood set the tone for their submission by recalling the words of their late president and founding father, Alfred Adams: "To co-operate with all who have at heart the welfare of the Natives and to co-operate with the government and its officials for the betterment of all conditions surrounding the life of Natives."[159] Their lengthy presentation struck at the heart of the failings of this "anachronistic and moribund piece of legislation"[160] and how it could become more of a progressive document. The old talking points were reintroduced: treaty rights, band membership, income taxes, enfranchisement, residential schools, medical care and agriculture, but the delegates also included a request for an accounting of how the $100,000 that had been granted annually to the BC First Nations since 1927 in lieu of treaty money (the "BC Special") was being spent. Over those twenty years, $2 million had been expensed by the Indian Affairs Department with no accountability, even though this money had been earmarked for education and health on BC reserves. The Brotherhood believed that the funds had been used for "affairs for which the Indian Department already receives a grant."[161]

Guy Williams spoke of education being the key to correcting some of the most deplorable conditions imaginable on reserves, and Chief William Scow told of the unfair influence of Indian agents when it came to supporting young people in the pursuit of higher education:

At our convention in Masset last month, a young man stood up and gave his own life experience. He came from Port Essington. He wanted to have higher education and finally he got into high school. He applied to the Indian agent at Prince Rupert at the time, who told him there was no money for it.[162]

Thomas Gosnell relayed a similar, but more personal story. After his daughter had finished her exams and qualified for high school, he took her to Prince Rupert where he paid the $75 a month fee for room and board, but after a year he went to the Indian agent and told him that the burden had become too heavy and that he would like some assistance from the Indian Affairs department. He was told, "You ought to be ashamed of yourself, coming into this office and asking for assistance when you are in a position to carry your own daughter's higher education." Gosnell finished his story with "There was no assistance."[163]

Chief William Scow spoke of his son, Alfred, who was destined to become the first First Nations judge in Canada but who had been rejected for educational assistance as well because of the Indian agent's belief that the chief was wealthy and could support the cost himself. Finally, in a fit of desperation, Alfred had applied for provincial welfare and that had worked until the Indian agent found out and stopped it, forcing him to withdraw from his studies. And when Chief Scow approached the Indian agent about funding for his daughter's higher education, he was told that "the policy of the Indian Department was that no two members of a family could have higher education."[164]

Despite the good grades obtained by many First Nations children in the public system, the barriers were formidable. In a *Vancouver Sun* article about this time, Ruth Smith, who came from the Salish community in Yale, reported:

One little girl topped her class through school but during her first years she was taunted about being an Indian, so that her mother could only watch and comfort her when she came home time after time to throw herself on the bed shaking with great tearing sobs. What could her mother do? What could she tell her little girl?

Those who want high school education must leave their families and home when they are 11 years old to board in the cities. A little imagination gives an inkling to their loneliness.

Education is the key, so this is the way we obtain it.[165]

At the time the Brotherhood was making its presentation in May 1947, fully 42 per cent of school-age First Nations children in Canada (41 per cent in BC) could not attend school because there was none. This report recommended that funding for reserve schools be doubled from the department's $2 million annual commitment and that 400 new classrooms be built immediately.

Medical care was another contentious issue because the authority of Indian agents was such that they could countermand the orders of a physician, even when a physician had ordered a patient into hospital. Indian agents were also permitted to act as judges in trials of First Nations people within their jurisdictions. In one case, an Indian agent sentenced a Sechelt man to two months in jail for possession of liquor on his reserve. While incarcerated, the man enlisted Tom Hurley to appeal the sentence, and he was released for time served, but the appeal brought to light the potential for partiality in this unusual practice. In his remarks Judge R. A. Sargent, who heard the appeal, said, "Our laws must not only be just, but obviously just," and he suggested that "it was too much to ask of human nature first to hear the evidence, then divert oneself of pre-conceived opinions and sit as an impartial judge."[166]

To a certain extent Reverend Peter Kelly defended the position of the agent with the comment that by law the agent has the right to decide what happens to his charges, but Kelly also stated that agents were not being selected with much thought: "Some of them learn to do the job after they have been in office for some time," and some "have been appointed who [know] nothing about Indians."[167] The committee replied that appointments to these positions were meritorious, but Kelly advised them that when Brigadier O. M. Martin of the Six Nations had applied for an agent's position at Hazelton, he was not even accorded the courtesy of a reply. If anyone was deserving and competent to fill the role, it was the brigadier, as he had served honourably in two world wars; he eventually became a magistrate for the County of York.

Kelly told the committee that although First Nations people were beginning to walk on an equal footing with their fellow citizens in most avenues of life—for example, employment and education—there were still holdouts that refused to respect their rights. Movie theatres in Prince Rupert, for example, still had a segregated section for First Nations—a back corner of one section—despite them charging First Nations people the same price as everyone else. The Aboriginal person "is segregated," Kelly reported.

> The effect, psychologically, I think is damaging. Treatment such as that unconsciously breeds an inferiority complex... An Alaskan Indian came into that theatre with his wife. They were very well dressed. He came in and was going to sit down in the body of the theatre. The usher came in to him and said, "No, you cannot sit here; Indians do not sit here." He wanted to know why. He said, "I appeal to the manager; I am a citizen of Alaska. I have never been treated this way before and I have a right to sit where I please. I have paid the same admission fee as anyone else." The manager was brought. The manager apologized to him and told him to pick his seat.

Our people have not done that. I was going to say they have been browbeaten to a point where they simply accept those things. I mean to say [that] personal dignity, somehow, can be just beaten down until it is broken down.[168]

Alfred Adams's daughter, Jane, wasn't afraid to challenge the system when she went to see a movie in Prince Rupert. She paid the admission and without any forethought or malice chose a seat outside the segregated area in the almost empty theatre. The projectionist refused to start the picture and sent a young man to tell her to move. "The young man and I were very upset and embarrassed,"[169] she recalled, but she refused to move and the picture started anyway.

Kelly finished the Brotherhood's report by telling the committee that it had not always been dark, and that there had been moments of light and understanding, but once "again in connection with the actual revision of the Indian Act, a great deal of sympathy and understanding will be required, for I want to say once more that this will affect the destiny of a race fighting for survival."[170] The committee members thanked the Brotherhood for their intelligent presentation and commented that it was by far the best they had received. But now it was the committee's turn to deliberate and the Brotherhood's to wait and wonder, and it came as no surprise that there were significant delays. The march to freedom was becoming something of a slow shuffle at best.

November 1947 marked the first anniversary of the inauguration of the *Native Voice*, and Maisie wrote:

Naturally we had dreams about the scope of the material we would one day use, the territory we would cover, the quality and number of people we would interest. But the progress made in the last few months has left us giddy... Our subscriptions come in from every part of the continent with very few states south of the border not represented.[171]

She was especially proud that the paper had received a letter from the Canadian Broadcasting Corporation offering "complete sympathy with the [*Voice*'s] effort to combat racial discrimination in all its forms"[172] and requesting an interview with her. Claire Wallace, the first female national radio broadcaster, who had her own CBC show, *They Tell Me*, wanted an interview as well. There was also a letter from Violet McNaughton, women's editor for the Saskatoon-based weekly farming publication *The Western Producer* and one of Maisie's most ardent fans, asking permission to reprint *Voice* articles.

Maisie's earlier request for writers had borne fruit with the conscription of the next generation of First Nations journalists. Peter Kelly's youngest son,

Horace, a World War II veteran who, as a member of the Canadian Scottish, had been among those in the first wave of soldiers to storm the beaches of Normandy, joined the paper as a roving reporter and assistant editor. As he travelled the coast with his parents aboard the missionary ship, MV *Thomas Crosby*, he sold subscriptions to the *Voice*, gathered the news from these isolated camps and villages to bring back to the world and brought the world to them.

Maisie also enlisted Alfred Adams's son, Oliver, who provided a "News from Masset" column, and Frank Arthur Calder, who had the distinction of being the first First Nations individual in the province to attend the University of British Columbia, graduating in 1946 with a degree in theology. Although he was soon hired by the *Vancouver News-Herald* as a reporter on the "Indian desk," he also had plans to take degrees at the University of Washington in anthropology and sociology in order to carve out a career as the journalist who would "put the Natives on the map."[173] In the meantime, he became a frequent contributor to the *Voice*, where his first article, published in the October 1947 issue, began controversially with:

> In the United States, Indians are treated as human beings. Compared to Canada's treatment of her native population, which is little removed from a civilized form of slavery and oppression, theirs is a land of hope and promise.[174]

Then he detailed the history of the US government's early initiative to "de-Indianize" or "Americanize" the Native American population, which really didn't change until about 1920 when their voices began to be heard. With the Indian Reorganization Act of 1934, much of the culture and control over reservation land had been restored to Native American people, and they were being encouraged to adopt some form of self-government.

While Calder was a catch for the nascent paper, given his education and understanding of First Nations issues, Maisie still wanted the *Voice* to have a broader reach. Despite subscriptions coming in from all across Canada and the United States and interest from a few major educational institutions south of the border such as Harvard University and the Smithsonian Institution, only a smattering of articles were being contributed from outside the province. One of those articles, albeit very tiny, was from the famous American humorist and actor, Will Rogers, Jr., who had been born into a prominent Cherokee family. He wrote to say that "[The *Voice*] is by long odds the largest Indian publication I have seen. We have nothing as good in the country."[175]

On this side of the border, one of the most prolific contributors was Big White Owl (Jasper Hill), whom Maisie appointed the paper's "eastern associate editor." He had begun writing for the paper with its fourth edition and was happy to have found a home for his advocacy. He wrote:

I have, during the past years, been striving and struggling against great and sometimes overwhelming odds in the attempt to achieve greater and better human rights for my people. So you see, I do greatly appreciate this opportunity offered to me by the *Native Voice*, and I shall do my very best to be fair and just and truthful in all my writings.[176]

The keeper of the Delaware Nation Moravian Thames Reserve library, Darryl Stonefish, who was related to Hill, recalled that he had either been given or had taken the name Big White Owl after seeing snowy owls on the reserve during an especially cold winter. Hill was born on October 30, 1902, on the Thames Reserve in southwestern Ontario as a member of the Munsee branch of the Lenni Lenape, also known as the Delaware, the name assigned to them by the British. He took his early schooling in the settlement but later transferred to the public school system of Ontario, and on July 12, 1920, proudly became enfranchised and a full Canadian citizen. He spent World War II and the early postwar years in the employ of the Canadian Red Cross.

Big White Owl (Jasper Hill) from the Delaware Nation in his ceremonial costume, of which he said: "I wear all this stuff, not because I don't know where I come from, but I know who I am... Every time I put those things on, I'm honouring that person." Photo courtesy of the Hill family.

Over the years he became a staunch supporter of all First Nations causes, using both his talented voice and his poetic pen, and signing most of his submissions with the definitive declaration: "I Have Spoken." For his public presentations, he dressed in a Plains' First Nations war bonnet and leggings, which a friend from Alberta had given him; Darryl Stonefish said that his reason for wearing this adopted costume was: "I wear all this stuff, not because I don't know where I come from, but I know who I am... Every time I put those things on, I'm honouring that person."[177]

As Big White Owl, Hill was especially vocal about the anticipated revisions to the Indian Act, and he wrote that:

As this group delves further into this matter, they find cause for rejoicing that the Indian is at long last considered as having reached maturity, and that his judgments have merit in the preparation of a "Magna Carta," and hope arises in their breasts that a sufficient number of recommendations submitted by progressive-minded Indian groups throughout the Dominion shall be included in the new Indian Act, that the Indian nations shall be satisfied and the same measure of co-operation shall exist between them and the federal government of Canada that existed formerly, guaranteeing a new era of happiness, prosperity and contentment for a nation that has been too long down-trodden.[178]

However, all of the Brotherhood's efforts appeared to have come to naught when the joint committee issued its recommendations to Parliament in December 1947. It was, perhaps, a lesson in managing expectations, and in the December edition of the *Voice*, Maisie wrote:

> It is generally admitted that the faith and promises made were faithlessly broken with little respect for honour... The report is disappointing in that there is little to suggest elimination of the type of "patronization" which tends to keep our native sons in a state of personal wardhood and apathy. There is no bold proposal to give native Indians the vote, [or the right] to run for office, to buy liquor or to become a full-fledged citizen of his native country. Worse, there is little or no attempt to improve the unsatisfactory educational set-up.[179]

Reverend Kelly was disappointed that the committee had left enfranchisement as a voluntary initiative and still hoped that the act would be amended before it passed into law. Even the Indian agent for Bella Coola, F. Earl Anfield, speaking at the 18th Annual Convention of the Brotherhood on December 11, encouraged the Brotherhood to keep making their wishes known to the joint committee. Did the Brotherhood want denominational schools? Did they want enfranchisement? These were just two of the many questions that still needed answers despite the Brotherhood having made a solid presentation on these very points in Ottawa months earlier.

In May 1948 Ruth Smith, Maisie's editor, wrote in frustration:

> It is now two years since Parliament appointed a joint Commons-Senate committee to "examine and consider the Indian Act... and report on the Indian administration in general." We cannot estimate how many hundreds of thousands, perhaps millions, of words of testimony the committee has heard since it began its sittings. We do know that it has sent its members to various parts of the country to examine conditions on reservations. If nothing else, the case is being exhaustively documented. The committee is still sitting this year. But what is lacking is assurance that reform will follow. Reports of this kind have

a depressingly poor record. Too many—dealing with any number of subjects—are resting forgotten in pigeon holes.[180]

On May 19, 1948, Frank Assu, the new president of the North American Indian Brotherhood, met with the joint committee and Prime Minister Mackenzie King and requested that the First Nations in Canada be able to review the revised Indian Act before it was passed into law. He was assured that the act would be available for review sometime later that year and that it would not become law until the following year. However, one of the main sticking points for both the government and the First Nations in the revised legislation was enfranchisement and all its repercussions. There was no doubt that First Nations viewed the vote as the key to many other privileges, but important though it was, it had to be granted to them unconditionally.

Although a report issued by the joint committee in December 1947 had only recommended extending the vote to First Nations on a voluntary basis, by the following May, due to public pressure from the many First Nations organizations across the country, the committee unanimously recommended that the federal vote for First Nations people in Canada should be offered on the same basis that it was administered to urban voters. Each person would be enumerated and a list prepared for that riding. The bill, however, still had to be debated in the House of Commons. Watching the proceedings from the public gallery on the day the motion was introduced was Peter Kelly, who was now the Reverend Dr. Peter Kelly, having just received his doctorate of divinity.

After presentation of the motion by the Liberal member for Essex West, Donald Brown, who had also served as the chair of the joint committee, the house recessed for dinner. Following the break, Brown resumed his argument for granting the vote, reasoning that First Nations people in Canada pay all the taxes expected of citizens except for taxes on income generated on their reserves. He continued:

> It was unanimously felt by the committee that the giving of the vote to the Indian would create in him a desire to help himself—the theme of the Indian Affairs committee since its inception has been that we were endeavouring to help the Indian help himself—and that it would create in the Indian a sense of obligation to society. It would train him in our democratic practices and make him realize that he has a place in the Canadian economy and in the Canadian society.
>
> On the other hand, the giving of the vote to the Indian would result in a recognition by government agencies and by members of parliament that the Indian was not a chattel but a human being and as such had certain rights in our society and that he should be looked to and his rights be protected. In other words, the thought of the committee has been that the giving of the vote to the Indian will help us

to assimilate the Indian. When I say assimilate, I do not mean that the Indian would lose his rich background of cultural achievements or any of the rights that he enjoys under treaties, or any of his rights, statutory or at common law, but that he would be recognized as being a human being and subject to the attention of those seeking office.[181]

Following Brown, John Gibson, the Independent MP for Comox-Alberni, rose to voice his concern over the various levels of educational development of the 130,000 First Nations people in the country. He told the house:

The more advanced professional people among the Indians live near the United States border, and the Indians who are still in almost an aboriginal state live farther north. I do not think it would be wise to grant to the aboriginal native Indian without an education and without a knowledge of English the same privilege that we grant to his brother who may be a professional man.[182]

Colin Gibson, Liberal MP for Hamilton West, recommended that the amendment be dropped altogether until the elections committee could study its implications, and James Sinclair, Liberal MP for Vancouver North, commented that:

I feel that one of the great incentives in the way of getting the Indians off the reserves, so that they might live as the rest of Canadians do under normal circumstances, would be to say to them, "If you cease being wards of the government, if you move out of the reserve and live as other Canadians live, you will get the vote. That would be a great incentive to the Indians."[183]

This "great incentive" was actually the barrier that had historically kept First Nations from accepting enfranchisement. As well, Sinclair's suggestion was no better than the status quo, which had always offered citizenship to First Nations on a voluntary basis in exchange for them vacating their reserves and perhaps, in corollary, their culture. David Croll, Liberal MP for Spadina, defended the motion with:

I suggest to the committee, agreeing with the mover of the resolution, that the time has come for us, not only to consider the discontinuance of the practice, but actually to put an end to it, of treating the Indians like children. Let us, instead, allow them to live normal adult lives.[184]

At the close of the day's session, MP Brown was forced to withdraw his motion for enfranchisement with the retort that: "We have a sincere responsibility over the lives and habits of 130,000 people, and it is no time for us to be playing politics."[185] It was a dismal end to a promising beginning and left Maisie furious. She expressed her anger in the July issue of the *Voice*:

A motion in favor was made and seconded, discussed further, then voted down; voted down mainly on the grounds that our people are illiterate and disunited... The evidence presented in the last two years revealed heartbreaking conditions in every part of Canada, such a morass of bungling and neglect that to put our people on a par educationally, physically, economically and spiritually with the whites would take many years.[186]

She was now fundamentally questioning whether there was a need for a revised Indian Act at all, and two months later she wrote:

When the present Indian Act was compiled, it literally took away all responsibility for his tribe from the chief, and he was left chief in name only. Now that responsibility should be given back to the chiefs and to councillors—eventually this would obviate the need of an Indian Department.[187]

Maisie's advocacy for her people and attention to the paper were sidetracked on September 9 when her mother, Amy Ellen Chadwick Campbell-Johnston, herself a staunch advocate of First Nations justice, died in Vancouver at the age of 88. Not only had she been a great supporter of First Nations rights, but she had figured prominently in the suffragist movement as well as the struggle for Sikh wives to become residents of Canada. Like her daughter, she had done this out of a sense of *noblesse oblige*, the obligation of the advantaged towards the disadvantaged. Representing the Brotherhood at Amy's funeral service was Ed Nahanee, the Brotherhood's business agent, who acted as one of the pallbearers, proudly conveying her to her final resting place. The curator of the Vancouver Museum, T. P. O. Menzies, sympathized with Maisie's loss when he wrote:

Vancouver has lost a wonderful lady who befriended the Native people of our West Coast Tribes and championed their causes right through the years... Mrs. Campbell-Johnston has now stepped through the curtain (purdah) which we all eventually pass through and I am certain that there will be many friendly hands thrust out to guide her footsteps and welcome her.[188]

A few months later Maisie's attention to the paper was again temporarily suspended when she got caught up in the shenanigans of her boss and partner, Tom Hurley, who was intent upon challenging what he considered to be an unfair section of the Liquor Act. His client, Aladino Fanini of 336 Union Street in Vancouver, had received three citations for bootlegging, and under instructions from Magistrate Oscar Orr the police had padlocked his house. Fanini, expressing concern for the welfare of his precious canaries, had refused to leave and was locked inside without benefit of sustenance.

Hurley responded to his client's imprisonment by announcing, "It's hypocrisy in our democratic way of life to imprison a man without food or water."[189] Six days elapsed before he decided to break into the residence, which would free his client while setting himself up, not only for arrest but for the opportunity to challenge the constitutionality of the Liquor Act, specifically Section 83, subsection 4, which read: "Any person who enters padlocked premises without permission in writing from the inspector or constable shall be liable to arrest without warrant and guilty of an offence against the government liquor act." With screwdriver in hand, Tom attacked the door, but when he had difficulty springing the lock, the incarcerated Fanini yelled through the locked door, "Tom, do you know what you're doing?"

Tom Hurley freeing his client, Aladino Fanini, from his padlocked residence in order to challenge what he considered to be an unfair section of the Liquor Act. Photo from the family collection.

"I'm breaking a lock, not a law," Hurley shouted back before finally gaining entrance.

At that point a number of Vancouver City Police cruisers skidded to the curb, sirens wailing. Inspector Harry Whelan, a detective and two prowler officers piled out of the cars, ready to quell the riot that they had been forewarned was brewing in front of the residence. Pushing through the crowd of thirty or forty interested onlookers, they mounted the steps and backed a none-too-surprised Fanini and a solemn-faced Hurley from the front porch through the front door and into the house. Maisie then breezed in past the inspector, despite his warning, summarily brushing his arm aside with the comment that she "needed instructions from her boss."

After Hurley and the inspector had exchanged a few intense words about the charges against him, the police promptly relocked the residence and departed, leaving all three inside. Before Maisie was trapped, however, she threw her keys to her daughter, Katherine (Kitty) Kennedy, who was also in Hurley's employ by this time. "Here, feed my canaries," she said, grinning mischievously. "And get me some food—I'm starving."

Tom and Maisie were arrested and jailed following Tom's challenge of the Liquor Act. Maisie remarked, "They've got nothing on me." Photo courtesy of the *Vancouver Sun*.

Tom yelled out to the press, "I'm going to starve to death! Next move is up to the police!" after which he and Maisie were removed from the residence, although the briefly liberated Fanini was re-sealed inside. When the detective sergeant moved to arrest Hurley, Maisie protested volubly. "Take that woman along too," he said.[190] So Maisie and Tom were taken to the city police cells, and "the police matron burst into tears when she was told to lock Maisie up. 'Tom Hurley,' she scolded, 'you should be ashamed of yourself for getting Mrs. Moore into trouble.'"[191] After a three-hour detention the two were released on a $100 surety each.

Hal Malone of the *Vancouver Sun* reported that in the corridor outside the courtroom the next morning, Maisie, bundled in her fur coat, fedora cocked rakishly, laughingly quipped:

"They've got nothing on me." Then she added, "Mr. Hurley is going to make this a test case... He has been worried about the danger to our Canadian freedom ever since Fanini was locked up. Yesterday he decided to do something about it."[192]

Tom's plan had been to invite the attorney generals of all ten provinces to the hearing, in accordance with his advice that the British North America Act required them to hear his constitutional argument, but this was met with "I don't think that will be necessary," from Magistrate McInnes who was hearing the case.[193] Calling the charges against Maisie, "an absurdity,"[194] he dismissed the "entering charge" against both of the accused but not before the prosecution had lured Fanini from his residence with a subpoena to testify against his lawyer. The police promptly re-padlocked the door behind him, leaving his canaries to fend for themselves.

To the readers of the *Voice*, Maisie explained:

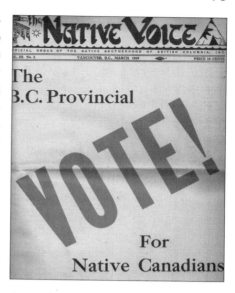

> I feel that there should be some explanation with regard to my arrest by the Vancouver police in the now famous padlock case.
>
> I am secretary and legal clerk to Mr. T. F. Hurley, barrister and solicitor. In the course of our duty connected with his practice, Mr. Hurley and myself were arrested and detained for several hours before being released on bail. After being tried by His Honor W. B. McInnis, Esq., magistrate, and acquitted, his honor said, "The arrest of Mrs. Moore was ridiculous."
>
> This padlock case was a test case which has been given nation-wide publicity, hence my explanation. I am now suing the Vancouver police for wrongful arrest.
>
> It is to my Indian friends that I am giving this explanation because their friendship and trust in me... means more to me than any mere words could express. I am not guilty.
>
> P.S. Any money received for damages will be donated to a school to educate Vancouver police to discriminate between an elderly grandmother of eleven grandchildren and other criminals.[195]

One of the most important covers of the *Native Voice*'s young life. "I never thought I would live to see this day," said a relieved Mr. Isaac Skulsh, the oldest man in his village. Photo from the *Native Voice*.

With this adventure concluded, Maisie plunged back into her work, appealing for First Nations people to stand up and be counted, to take charge of their own affairs and to contribute articles to the *Voice,* no matter what their level of education or eloquence. Some positive news was on the horizon, she wrote, given a recent Department of Indian Affairs announcement that assistant Indian agents, all of whom would be First Nations individuals, would be hired forthwith to teach band members fishing and agricultural skills as well as almost every facet of daily living and working. The recommended skill set required an elementary school education plus practical knowledge. There was no question, however, that these positions were sub-management at best and the people employed in them would be at the beck and call of the Indian agent.

Meanwhile, the *Voice* continued to attract new talent, including Doug Wilkinson, a UBC agriculture student. His maternal grandmother was the sister of the famous Sioux chief, Sitting Bull, whose visions of victory just prior to the Battle of Little Big Horn inspired the defeat of the 7th Cavalry Regiment led by Lieutenant Colonel George Armstrong Custer by such notables as chiefs Crazy Horse and Gall. "With such a romantic and blood-stirring background," Maisie wrote, "the *Native Voice* feels that he will be a most valuable addition to the staff."[196]

The paper was also expanding south, thanks to negotiations led by Chief Shup-She of the Eagle Clan of the Potawatomi Nation, who had become a regular contributor to the paper. He reported that the *Voice* would soon become the official organ of the League of Nations Pan-American Indians. With councils in the United States, Mexico, Panama, Yucatan, Chile and more, the paper had stretched its reach and its influence exponentially. Maisie welcomed the exposure and anticipated more news from south of the border, the first of which was a report that Native Americans in New Mexico had just secured the vote.

And then quite suddenly the First Nations of British Columbia were given the provincial vote. Caught off guard by the unexpected announcement, the staff of the *Voice* just had time to design one of the most important covers of the paper's young life. The front page of the March 1949 edition, splashed with red, screamed: "The BC Provincial VOTE For Native Canadians."[197] Maisie wrote:

> It is my privilege to have many Indian friends, and knowing them I feel sure that they will be cautious and give the vote careful study before doing so. Each Indian will, when he accepts the vote, feel a deep responsibility and take it as a sacred trust, studying what is best for his fellow Indians.
>
> This gaining of the vote has been so unexpected and sudden it leaves many bewildered and in many cases suspicious, fearing for the safety of their rights.
>
> There is need for careful instruction and enlightenment as to the benefits of their new citizenship. We are all standing by them, respecting, loving and ready to help to the end.[198]

There were many letters of congratulations, a few of them cautious but most hopeful. The Reverend Dr. Peter R. Kelly visited the attorney general and the premier and reported afterwards that: "They gave the Indians of BC the first real chance they ever had. Mr. Attorney General assures me he wishes to help and explained that the vote in no way jeopardizes Indian rights." Kelly, who had sat in the House of Commons gallery to hear the debate over the Indian Act, continued, "I sometimes have felt very discouraged since my last trip to Ottawa, but now I am full of hope." William Scow, president of the Native Brotherhood, stated that "it was a great step forward," and Guy Williams offered that "Indians will have a very powerful weapon in their hands to back up demands for the rights of citizenship."[199]

Even the Honourable Gordon Wismer, attorney general, wrote to the *Voice* to express what many had been thinking for years:

> I feel that in granting them the franchise, this Government has recognized a principle which should have been invoked long ago. These new voters are the only true Canadians; the rest of us came to this country from other lands, and it is only fit that they should have a voice in the affairs of their own country.
>
> I might point out that the amendment to the "Elections Act" does not grant to the Indian any more than the franchise itself, but this is a priceless possession to all free men in a free country and thus for the first time the Indians in British Columbia will have an opportunity of voicing their claims to all of the other privileges which are accorded Canadian citizens. It also PRESERVES ANY RIGHT HE HAD IN THE PAST, but it gives him only the additional right to vote in the election OR BE A CANDIDATE IN THE ELECTION.[200]

The *Voice*'s editorial that month called for a "new thinking trend" to figure out how reserve life could be blended into the new reality post-vote. It was an acknowledged happy story, one that ended with a simple "Thank you, British Columbia, for the first step in equality. We are grateful. It is through such acts of faith-keeping that resentment crumbles, clearing the way for better understanding."[201]

The granting of the provincial franchise, however, had not been entirely unexpected. Although the Brotherhood had not initiated any of the most recent discussions, after the furor a year earlier over the government's intention to offer the vote to people of East Indian, Chinese and Japanese descent, members of the legislature had begun asking why the resident First Nations population had not been included in the bill. This had motivated the government to reach out to the Brotherhood to initiate discussions about how an offer of the vote would be perceived within the First Nations population.

The Brotherhood had taken decisive action, abandoning "their ambivalence on enfranchisement and the avowed preference for the only vaguely understood Maori Plan,"[202] in favour of the government granting them the vote. Their cause had not been helped by Andrew Paull and his Interior Chiefs organization advising the government that First Nations in British Columbia wanted to remain wards of the state to protect their rights, advice that had left the government perplexed over the conflicting opinions. It had taken some quick action by the Brotherhood to set the matter straight. Now it was time to celebrate, and perhaps some small measure of satisfaction was gained by the fact that Aboriginal British Columbians were not last on the list; the Doukhobors would not be granted the privilege of voting for another four years.

The Reverend Dr. Peter Kelly told the *Voice*:

> My family and I will now vote for the first time... For the first time the door is opened to us and if all villages march shoulder to shoulder as the upper Skeena villages are doing, we will go through that door in final triumph... BC is the first and only province in Canada whose lower and high schools are now open to native boys and girls on a basis of complete equality. We still have old age pensions and other benefits to win, but the government in Victoria has put a strong lever in our hands and we are going to throw all our weight against it to move Ottawa to action.[203]

Maisie's pleasure in this triumph, however, was short-lived. It had come to her attention that three BC Aboriginal men had been charged with murder, and two of them had been denied their own choice of counsel. Because they were wards of the state, the government had left this important decision in the hands of the Indian agents, who were more inclined to reward party and government faithful than the wishes of their clients—and who at that time faced the death penalty for murder.

The third accused, Mike Duncan Antoine, a resident of the Squilax reserve near Tappen, had been charged and found guilty of the murder of Daniel Elkins of Williams Lake. He had been sentenced to hang and had been languishing in prison for eighteen months, six of them under threat of the gallows, when Tom Hurley appealed his conviction in Victoria and won the right to a retrial. During the new trial at the Kamloops Assizes in April 1949, Hurley sat and listened as twenty-three prosecution witnesses shuffled in and out of the witness box. He called no witnesses himself, instead availing himself of his considerable talent at cross-examination. One of the key witnesses stated unequivocally that he had seen Antoine commit the crime. "Are you sure it was Mike Antoine?" Hurley asked, then waited for an answer for four nearly silent minutes, broken only by the very audible ticking of the court clock. Then he suddenly thundered, "I have waited in vain for four minutes for an answer to my question. That means that you are not sure." The witness broke down and said, "Yes, I am not sure."[204] Twenty minutes later the jury declared Antoine not guilty.

"I will never forget Mrs. Maisie Armytage-Moore and Mr. Hurley," Antoine said happily as he gazed fondly upon his family and then up at the sun. "I can't write. Please put in the *Native Voice* that I thank Mr. Wismer. He saved my life."[205] BC's attorney general, Gordon Wismer, had paid for Antoine's defence when the federal government had refused. That Antoine was released in time to exercise his franchise was judicious as well.

With the June 15, 1949, provincial election looming, the *Voice* was filled with the proselytizing of Premier Byron Johnson's coalition government, shilling for votes from the province's newest citizens. Countering them was an ad from Frank Calder, the CCF candidate for Atlin, emphatically declaring that "I am proud to be an Indian and proud of my race." He reminded First Nations people that it had been Johnson's coalition government that had earlier turned down a proposed amendment to the Elections Act that would have given them the vote. He continued:

> Why am I a CCF candidate? The reasons are very simple and understandable. Not only was the CCF the first party to fight for Native Indian representation in parliament, it was the first to fight in both provincial and federal houses for equal rights and privileges for the Native Indians.[206]

First Nations British Columbians had suddenly become an important political demographic, and while the rest of the population might wonder whether they were ready for the responsibility, had they seen the activity at Kispiox in the northern part of the province, they would have been disabused of that notion. "I never thought I would live to see this day," said a relieved Mr. Isaac Skulsh, the oldest man in the village, who was so giddy when he registered to vote that his son, Walter Skulsh, the head of the local chapter of the Brotherhood, declared that "My father is walking in a dream today."[207] All of the Kispiox village Elders registered for the vote, and the Brotherhood was kept busy arranging evening courses on citizenship, which included a mock election complete with polling booths. It was as impressive a demonstration of democracy as had been witnessed in many years, and it was further supported when the Brotherhood completed the registration of all eligible Aboriginal voters in the province within the first few weeks after the provincial franchise was granted.

"It was a big job to trace them in all the remote inlets and rivers and bays of the coast," said Chief William Scow, but he acknowledged that they were all appreciative of the franchise. "I feel and know," he said, "that the granting of this franchise to our people is the beginning of giving them many privileges which they have not had in the past."[208]

5—NORTHERN ADVENTURE

The lure of the north was as irresistible to Maisie as it had been for her father, Ronald Campbell Campbell-Johnston, who had spent much of his working life prospecting and assaying potential mining properties in the northern part of the province, often accompanied by Maisie's mother, Amy. Entranced by her parents' reports of their adventures, Maisie had long been determined to see it all for herself. She was already familiar with many of the northern chiefs and their villages through her work, and they, of course, were very familiar with the *Native Voice* and Maisie's involvement with the Brotherhood. So, soon after the announcement of enfranchisement for BC First Nations was made in March 1949, Maisie set off for northern BC. Her tour would also be an opportunity to explain to her First Nations friends how the provincial vote worked and to encourage their informed but cautious participation as she was worried that they were going to be taken advantage of by opportunist politicians who would promise anything to win them over.

Her first stop was Fort St. James on Stuart Lake where she was received by Chief Felix Antoine, who introduced her to many other chiefs and asked her to speak to his people. They called a meeting where Maisie explained the voting process, emphasizing the importance of unity, which would provide the vote with meaning and strength. She lauded the Brotherhood and its president, Chief William Scow, telling them how the Brotherhood "helped to open the door and make this great step forward possible."[209] However, the vote being a somewhat foreign concept to many in her audience, who still very much depended upon the land for survival, the direction of the meeting soon moved on to a discussion of fur prices and protection of their traplines that were being destroyed by logging.

While in Fort St. James, Maisie also met an old friend, David Benoit, a war veteran known to his army buddies as "Bambie" and who referred to Maisie as "Mother." A trapper, logger, miner and cowboy like his father, he had enlisted in 1942 with the Army Corps of the Seaforth Highlanders and served out the war in Europe. Upon his return he had joined the Vancouver Police Force, becoming, according to Maisie, the first First Nations policeman in Canada. The fact that she had taken a hand in his employment further endeared her to him, but he soon left the force, because he hated arresting people, and returned to Fort St. James. Less than a year later he had written to say he had re-enlisted in the army and was on his way to Korea.

Frustrated with the injustice of it, she wrote about him in the November 1950 issue of the *Voice*:

> The North is cruel to those who have no money and who are wards of the government... The price of fur was low and trapping was cold and wet—he landed in the hospital—bad chest...[210]

She then addressed the rest of her article on Bambie Benoit to Citizenship and Immigration Minister Walter Harris:

> Mr. Harris, I can't seem to make you understand. You told me you were a "practical politician"—I believe you now... Sitting here thinking and, yes, weeping a bit, thinking of my own boy who can't go with him this time, I felt a fierce burning sense of injustice. Why, why should dear, kind, gentle Bambie fight for us if he is not good enough to share our freedoms and benefits?[211]

It had been Maisie's intention to travel to Hazelton and the surrounding villages after visiting Fort St. James because she had many friends there in both the Brotherhood and Sisterhood, but en route her party passed through the tiny settlement of Burns Lake where she was shocked to discover First Nations living in substandard housing and coping with almost non-existent incomes. "The place is depressing," she wrote in the June 1949 issue of the *Voice*, "and in bad condition, the houses are poor and in some places on Babine Road they are absolutely hovels." She poked her head into one such shack to find an injured trainman, his wife and five children. He couldn't work and the monthly family income had been reduced to $20, barely adequate to feed his family for half that time. In another she found an old woman bedridden and in great pain. "Her son and his wife and three children and a brother all lived in this tiny shack,"[212] she wrote. The settlement was between the territories of two Indian agents but far enough removed from either to make visiting it inconvenient for them.

At Hazelton, Maisie was welcomed by a contingent of the Sisterhood, and she was amazed at how progressive the community was in comparison to Burns Lake. Under the guidance of the Indian agent, Mr. Boyse, plans were afoot to construct an integrated school for both white and First Nations children. At Kispiox (Kisbyox), Maisie met a few men who had worked for her father as packers, and she was toured around the area by Constance Cox, whose father, Thomas Hankin, had worked for the Hudson's Bay Company prior to building his own store, around which the settlement of Hazelton had developed. Although Constance's mother had Tlingit ancestry, Constance was considered to be the first white child born at Hazelton. Constance's mother had spoken seven First Nations languages and passed this proficiency on to her daughter, who often acted as a court interpreter. Later Maisie would recall that Connie, as she called her, "had spent her youth among the natives of Northern British Columbia. They treat her as one of themselves." While at Kispiox, she and Constance were invited to the local hall where Maisie gave another talk on the vote with Constance interpreting. She told them of "the need for unity and how this vote, if properly handled, would enable them to protect their rights."[213]

Later, reflecting on her visit there, she wrote:

> I left the village with many kindly wishes for our success and with a feeling of how wonderful these Christian people are—their kindliness, their faith in spite of hardship and sorrow, truly a noble race. What a mess the whites have made of this world of ours and how shabby and snobbish we act! Thank God we still have these Christian people to show us the way. "Kisbyox" means "the place of hiding."[214]

Continuing on her journey, still in the company of Constance, she visited Skeena Crossing or "Kitwizgulth, meaning the people of the pass in the mountain,"[215] where she received perhaps the most important tribute of her life. She was met there by Chief Martha Molthan, the head chief of the village, who told her people:

> Young men and women, I am nearly 100 years old. I have been your leader and chief. Be wise—listen to the voice of your elders. CCF is something very new. We have not heard of it before, so again I say be careful. Whichever way you go, bring God with you, you will need His help. Listen to the voice of this white lady who has come so far to help. I will soon leave you all to go to my rest. I will not benefit by this great honour that has been given us—so I say again, young men and women, give thanks to the Great White Chief who has opened the door and has asked us to come in.[216]

Chief Jeffrey Johnston brought tears to Maisie's eyes when he recounted:

> the sorrow and tragedy of his people since the white man came, saying that it was as if all their life a hand had been placed over their mouth— they could not speak, only hear and see, and they were beaten down lower than the animals, but now that hand was removed and the heaviness was lifted away, giving them this great new hope and freedom.[217]

Following Chief Johnston's talk, Chief Arthur McDames "rose from his seat with great dignity and stated that he wished to show his gratitude and that of his people to Mrs. Moore, who had come such a long way to show them what was right."[218] He then honoured Maisie by conferring upon her the senior name of his house. It was, she wrote:

> the Order of Gooksun, meaning "the gambler or the man who took a chance," in the tribe of the Finback Whale, the crest of the Eagle.

This tribe originated from the beginning of the world, the oldest tribe of ancient origin, clan of the Lathsalia—[a] relationship stronger than blood relationship. My name is "Chief Simlouax" meaning "Chief Queen of the Moon"... I feel very humble, very frightened, that I may not be worthy of such a great honor and I humbly pray that I may never fail these great Canadian people.[219]

During the ceremony Maisie was presented with a beautifully carved spoon engraved with the crest of the chief's house, and she probably mused upon the similarity between the clans of these noble people and the regal septs of her ancient Highland ancestors.

The next day Maisie and Constance travelled to Kitwanga, a name that means "the Place of the Rabbits," where she was again honoured and presented with an exquisitely carved chief's staff. From there they drove along the rough, perilous road to Kitwancool, "the Narrow Valley," where Maisie viewed "beautifully carved, ancient totems, bleached by sun and rains, [that] stood tall sentinels to honor a great, fighting, noble race."[220] Returning to Kitwanga for the evening, they prepared to travel to Hazelton the following morning to meet with the premier and his party who were stumping the province for votes.

Maisie departed for home on May 10, but on her way south she stopped to visit the Stoney Creek Reserve near Vanderhoof. There, she was welcomed by Chief Jimmie Antoine and Dick Patrick, another World War II veteran and decorated hero. In a story published in the *Omineca Express* in 2001, Patrick's younger sister, Arlene, is quoted as saying: "Maisie was really close to my brother... She did a lot for him,"[221] even considering him her adopted son. Dick Patrick's Military Medal for bravery had been pinned to his chest on October 23, 1945, by His Majesty King George VI at Buckingham Palace, and now even the premier wanted to meet him and have him recount the story of how he had earned the medal. Patrick, however, had another story to tell. After the war he found that nothing had changed in his home town: regardless of his achievements and honour, he was still "just an Indian."[222] Despite some discrimination in the ranks, in Europe Dick Patrick and other First Nations servicemen from Canada had been treated largely as equals. They could enter restaurants with no restrictions and enjoy the same privileges as other soldiers. However, the comrades-in-arms code had ceased the day they were discharged, and that day Patrick began to fight another war, the war against discrimination.

Dominic Richard (Dick) Patrick was born on the Stoney Creek Reserve (Saik'uz First Nation) on February 27, 1920, to Isaac and Lizette Patrick, and as the oldest of their ten children was the first to attend the infamous Lejac Indian Residential School at Fraser Lake where physical, sexual and

Dick Patrick, a decorated war hero, was determined not to be treated as a "second hand citizen" in his own community. Portrait of Dick Patrick by Tracy Cogan.

psychological abuse were rampant. He quit school at the age of 15, having completed Grade 6. His sister Arlene remembers him as a "jolly, happy guy... a tall, laughing cowboy"[223] who enjoyed the rodeo, hunting, fishing and some reading. He loved sports, playing baseball as first basemen in the drowsy days of summer and hockey in wing position in the chill of winter.

He was 22 and had been married to Vitaline for three years when he volunteered for military service in April 1942. At the time of his enlistment, he weighed 153 pounds over his rangy 5-foot 8-inch frame, honed lean by his work around the farm, in the bush and with the Dinsmore Gold Mine at Manson Creek, where he had mucked and timbered. Following basic training in Vernon, he was assigned to E Company of the Seaforth Highlanders, 5th Anti-Tank Regiment, RCA, as a gunner and driver. Although his lack of higher education would prevent his advancement, his personnel report noted that "his M-score of 143 indicates a better than average learning ability."[224] E Company was "taken on strength" for overseas duty on October 31, 1942, his unit landing in the UK several weeks later, but the attractions and temptations were too great, and he was counted AWL and charged with drunkenness and insubordination. Drink had been an admitted problem for him while growing up, and it was perhaps the fact that possession and consumption of alcohol was illegal for First Nations people in BC that made it so attractive in Europe, where it was not only legal but abundantly available. On July 28, 1944, his company embarked for France, and Patrick was quickly in the thick of the fighting. The citation for his medal tells the next part of his story:

> [His company] secured and for two days held a small bridgehead on the east side of the canal at Moerbrugge during which time a bridge was built. The bridgehead was limited in depth to about 300 yards due to heavy mortar and machine gun fire. Gunner Patrick was a member of a 17-pounder M-10 gun crew which with two tanks of the 29

Canadian Armoured Reconnaissance Regiment crossed the bridge at 0700 hours, 10 September 1944... After the M-10 had shot up several suspected enemy positions, the actual location of enemy positions became hard to establish accurately due to poor visibility and fog. Gunner Patrick asked permission to go ahead on foot and carry out a reconnaissance to locate enemy positions. Despite the enemy fire, he succeeded in getting into the middle of an enemy machine gun position and there opened fire with his light machine gun. His daring attack completely surprised the enemy, who totalled three officers and 52 other ranks, into surrender and cleared out a strong point which had pinned the infantry down for approximately two days. The extension of the bridgehead was due in large part to the daring of this gunner.[225]

Lieutenant-Colonel D. S. Harkness, the commanding officer of the 5 Canadian Anti-Tank Regiment, recommended Patrick for the Military Medal, which was awarded "for individual or associated acts of bravery on the recommendation of a Commander-in-Chief in the field."[226] The recommendation was forwarded up the line until it was reviewed and approved by the great man himself, Field Marshall Bernard L. Montgomery, Commander-in-Chief, 21 Army Group. At the reception following the medal ceremony at Buckingham Palace, at which King George "commended Patrick for his valour on the battlefield, and his people for their outstanding service in the war," Patrick told the King that:

> when my people went into Vanderhoof, they were not allowed to go into restaurants, use public toilets, and had to come in the back door of a grocery store to buy groceries. We spoke for a long time about the injustice to my people. He told me he would endeavor to help my people.[227]

Among the letters of congratulation that poured in was one from the agent general for British Columbia in London, W. A. McAdam, who, under the direction of BC MLA John Hart, was offering Patrick 1,000 cigarettes and wanted to know where to send them. As well, the soon-to-be governor general of Canada, Vincent Massey, sent his congratulations and expressed the belief that "Canadians everywhere will, I know, be happy that such fine service that you have given has been thusly recognized."[228]

Patrick was discharged from duty on March 14, 1946, after serving nine months on domestic soil and thirty-eight months overseas. Having received a sympathetic hearing from the king, he was now more than ever convinced that he must do something to right the wrongs to his people. However, on returning to his reserve, he stayed home for some time, a delay that gave him time to steel himself for the inevitable consequences of what he was preparing to do. He was fed up with the double standard that saw young First Nations men and women freely risk their lives for their country but be unable to enjoy a restaurant meal, a night's rest in a hotel or any other services in their own community. He was now going to offer himself up for the cause by becoming the Rosa Parks of BC's First Nations.

Patrick's first stop in Vanderhoof, approximately fourteen kilometres from his reserve, was the Silver Grill Café on Burrard Street, a restaurant that refused to serve First Nations people. "One community member spoke of her experience working there and trying to understand why she was not allowed to serve her friends who were First Nations. She did not last long in the job."[229] Patrick went in, sat down and waited to be served. Finally the owner of the establishment called the provincial police, who asked him to leave. He refused. He was therefore arrested, charged with disturbing the peace and sentenced to six months in Oakalla Prison in Burnaby.

Oakalla at that time "was notorious for its inmate brutality" and deplorable living conditions. As well, it was overcrowded and the "destruction of prison property was equalled only by the destruction of human lives."[230] It was into this hopeless environment of hard-time criminals that Dick Patrick was dumped, but he was now angry and defiant. He told his sister Arlene that he would not be treated as a second-class citizen, and she remembered that he "just wanted everyone to be treated on an equal basis... He was stubborn... I think sometimes he was very discouraged... He really felt we had such a long way to go."[231]

Patrick placed a call from Oakalla to Maisie that galvanized her into immediate action; she was always most effective when her dander was up and when she had a "cause célèbre," and Dick Patrick neatly fit that bill. She was so incensed at his incarceration for merely wanting a meal in a restaurant that she called Attorney General Gordon Wismer, who immediately ordered the highly decorated war hero's release. Patrick, however, was not finished with his demonstration. After Maisie had paid his $163.80 fine and furnished him with bus fare, he was soon on his way home, but as soon as he got off the bus in Vanderhoof, he marched right back into the Silver Grill and ordered another meal. Again he refused to leave, and again he was arrested for disturbing the peace and sentenced to six months in Oakalla. In fact, Patrick was returned to Oakalla nine more times that year. Each time he called Maisie who in turn called the attorney general. In an interview with Kitty Sparrow in 1980 Patrick said:

> She got me out of Oakalla eleven times in one year; in one year I spent eleven months in prison. I would just get off the bus and walk into a restaurant and they would arrest me and send me back to Oakalla... I was bound and determined to show them they could not treat my people like animals.[232]

Despite his continuing protests, Patrick was never served a meal, although his sacrifice did not go unnoticed.

Maisie's last overnight stop on her northern tour in May 1949 was in Prince George. The next day she went on to Williams Lake where Tom was defending a First Nations man on trial for murder. She was still angry about the refusal of service to First Nations by many northern businesses and made a note to add to her next column in the *Voice* that she "would like to make a test case of refusing Indians in hotels and restaurants... I was horrified at the unchristian discrimination shown towards Indians in some places"[233]

June 15, 1949, the day of the provincial vote, dawned warm but wet as Chief Isaac Jacobs of the Squamish Nation, dressed in his full ceremonial regalia including headdress, arrived at the polling station in North Vancouver to drop his ballot into the box, making him, according to the *Voice*, the "First Indian to vote for the candidate of his selection."[234] The following month Maisie eulogized the long struggle for the vote in her editorial:

> The Natives of British Columbia have made a long step forward. They have secured the provincial vote. They have given up no right. They do not think that the vote is an end in itself, but they know it is a means to an end. The natives need no longer approach government as beggars. They now go with the same spirit as was shown by their forbearers demanding rights and not asking for favors. No longer need they be satisfied with the crumbs that fall from the rich man's table.
>
> They will sit at the table, and the time may not be far distant when one of the natives shall sit at the head of the table. No high-spirited proud people can manifest and maintain the spirit and the soul of their forefathers on alms.[235]

Although not quite sitting at the head of the provincial table, Frank Calder made it to the head of his constituency table when he squeaked by to win the election by six votes after the absentee ballots were counted. By July 8 he was affirmed as the CCF MLA for Atlin District. Harold Winch, the CCF leader, stated:

> I am proud to welcome Frank Calder to the ranks of the CCF members in the BC Legislature... Representation of native Indians on Canadian legislative bodies is long overdue, and it is particularly gratifying to me that the first native Indian to gain a seat in the BC Legislature should do so under the CCF banner, because the CCF has consistently and continually fought for the franchise for our native population throughout the years.[236]

When the 34-year-old Calder rose for his inaugural speech in the legislature to a "thunderous desk-thumping welcome,"[237] it was to thank the honourable members for supporting his people but also to say he recognized that he was not First Nations in the legislature but merely a citizen of BC. Maisie, in summarizing his speech for *Voice* readers, wrote that he had then told his listeners that even though he was now an MLA:

> he, as an MLA, was an Indian outside the house… without such privileges as old age pensions, social welfare rights, liquor rights and other things that go with citizens.
>
> He called the position of Indians "second-hand" citizens, [and] said they have to pay sales tax without getting the social security benefits from it.
>
> Indians were told they got a Magna Carta in the vote, but they are still hemmed in with a "mess of laws, but I'm not blasting anyone for injustices to Indians in the past. I'm talking constructively," he said.[238]

Now that the provincial franchise was won, Maisie and the *Voice* moved the focus back to the federal scene. The fact that the federal government had yet to deliver a revised Indian Act was now front and centre right across the country and somewhat of an embarrassment. *The Globe and Mail* asked:

> What has become of all the efforts to modernize the obsolete Indian Act? In June 1948 a Parliamentary Committee, after two years of inquiry, made its second report which would have done this. The report proposed a separate Indian Department, voting rights, better educational measures, encouragement of self-government on reservations, permission to buy liquor legally and other measures. But there the matter appears to have ended, and Indians are constitutionally no better off than before.
>
> There is something basically wrong with a system which taxes without granting voting rights. Many of the restrictions on Indians are childish and hair-splitting. For instance, so far as the Dominion franchise

Dr. Frank Arthur Calder, the first First Nations MLA (CCF Atlin) in the province, said during his campaign: "I am proud to be an Indian and proud of my race." Photo courtesy of the Nisga'a Lisims Government.

is concerned, they can secure voting rights—which include running for elective office—only by giving up the tribal rights attaching to reservations, which include certain public grants. The bestowal of provincial voting rights is under the control of the province where they reside.

The sooner our government goes ahead to provide them with full citizenship rights, the sooner it will do justice to an apparently forgotten element of our population.[239]

A few months later the *Toronto Daily Star* mirrored these exact sentiments when it reported: "The Indian is the only man without a vote in the country of his origin. Rather than the Indians being backward, our treatment of the Indians marks us as backward."[240]

Maisie hammered this point home at a Burnaby Lions Club meeting where she was invited as the guest speaker. She declared:

The Indian Act is a "disgrace" as there should be only one law for Canadians and not two sets of laws. Indians should be able to receive the same social services as all Canadians. The Indians are hungry for education and should be helped to go to school so they will be able to become doctors, nurses and teachers, then go back to the reservation to help their people.[241]

Brotherhood president William Scow expressed the same sentiment at a conference on Native Indian Affairs held at Acadia Camp, University of British Columbia, in April 1948 when he lectured that:

We are gathered here for one purpose—to solve the problems of the Indian. We do not need to look for the solution to the problem. I am happy to say this before an intelligent well-learned people that the only solution is education. Everything will come with it.[242]

While Native education was definitely one of the Brotherhood's main objectives, the organization had another important role as well, that of lobbyist for its salmon-fishing brothers, who made up the majority of its membership. When the Japanese fishermen upon whom the packers and canners had once relied for their proficiency and hard work—and with whom First Nations fishermen were in direct competition—were taken from the West Coast following Japan's bombing of Pearl Harbor, the supply vacuum that developed had been quickly filled by other fishermen, First Nations included. Now First Nations fishermen were no longer subject to the type of economic discrimination that had typified the pre-war years, being paid on par with the members of the United Fishermen and Allied Workers Union (UFAWU), which had been established in 1945 as an amalgamation of several shore and off-shore unions.

Together, the Native Brotherhood and the UFAWU wielded considerable power and influence, although the Brotherhood on its own had little bargaining power compared to that of the much larger UFAWU. They exercised their joint power in September 1949 when they advised their seine and gillnet members fishing the Johnstone Strait area to tie up their boats until an agreement had been reached with the canners and packers over chum prices. Within a week the issue was settled, and Homer Stevens, secretary of the UFAWU, together with Ed Nahanee, Brotherhood business agent, issued a joint statement advising their members that fishing could recommence on October 4.

The *Voice* detailed the events leading up to this combined action, including a long article challenging the Department of Fisheries over its decision to close certain areas of the West Coast to seine fishing, and the jail-time consequences for three First Nations fishermen who were caught fishing in a closed area out of a desperate need to feed their families. MP John Gibson (Independent for Comox-Alberni), who had known the three men since childhood, told the *Voice* that "their ancestral fishing grounds were closed by the white man's decree because the white man overfished these grounds."[243] He hoped that the federal Fisheries minister would speak with Attorney General Gordon Wismer to right this wrong.

It was into this environment of closures and rancour that Harold Sinclair, vice-president of the Brotherhood for the Northern Interior District, accused the canners and packers of having approached interned Japanese-Canadian fishermen about returning to the West Coast. Although there was an immediate outcry from both the union and the Brotherhood—Maisie remained largely silent at this point—they were careful to say that their objections had nothing to do with race but everything to do with an already crowded industry. The 250 to 300 fishermen allegedly invited back to the West Coast was a paltry number, given that before the confiscation of boats and internment of Japanese Canadians there had been 1,265 licenced fishermen of Japanese descent on the coast with a total of 1,137 vessels,[244] but according to the union this recruitment was a ploy by the canners and packers to destabilize the industry and drive prices paid to the fishermen down. Even MLA Frank Calder in his inaugural speech in the legislature had stated, according to the *Voice*, that he "scorned all racial discrimination but expressed concern that fishing companies are 'recruiting' Japanese back into the fishing industry and threatening the livelihood of the older Indians in the industry."[245]

The idea that the canners had invited the Japanese fishermen back as some sort of retribution for the chum strike occurred to both the Brotherhood and the union, although the canners denied this while at the same time accusing First Nations fishermen of selling their fish to "blind buyers" as well as drinking on the job. The Skeena chiefs, chaired by Harold Sinclair, met on

January 19, 1950, in Hazelton to counter these accusations and stated that the canners themselves sent out "blind buyers" to purchase fish at prices above the going rate, some of them even topping up their offer with a case of beer for every ten sockeye. Those attending the meeting were so annoyed at the possibility of the Japanese fishermen returning to the Skeena River fishery that they drafted a petition to the government demanding that they be kept away, claiming that First Nations had treaties issued by both the provincial and federal governments entrenching their "inherited livelihood claim." Not everyone was onside with the chiefs, however. In the letters section of the *Voice*, a First Nations woman named Hattie admonished Sinclair over his attempts to keep the Japanese fishermen from returning, pointing out that the same racist tactics had been used against First Nations at one time.

The controversy appeared to be a mystery to C. E. Salter of the Canadian Fishing Company, who discounted Sinclair's accusations as being a complete fabrication. He advised that the First Nations fishermen employed by his company were treated as well as any other fishermen and that he had never sent out "blind fish buyers." His statements were corroborated by his First Nations employees, and Henry A. Bell of Alert Bay cautioned against criticizing the fishing companies too harshly when he told the *Voice* in March 1950:

> I, myself, have worked for the Bell-Irving Company [owners from 1891 to 1969 of the North Pacific Cannery on the Skeena River] all my life, and I want to point out that the fishing companies have done a great deal for our people and in part are responsible for the position that we hold in the fishing industry today.[246]

Stories like this, objectively reported over several issues, caught and held readers' attention, making the paper one of the few reliable sources of industry information for isolated First Nations on the coast. Maisie was very encouraged that it was having this impact, further evidenced by a small article in a semi-monthly newsletter published by Columbia University, which called the *Voice*:

> one of the most unusual newspapers in the world... Canada's only paper published exclusively on behalf of the Indians. Established about three years ago, it now has a circulation of well over 3,000 and goes to nearly every state in this country as well as circulating in Canada, Alaska and England.[247]

Beyond the Sky (Pete Hest), an adopted member of the Onondaga Nation, lauded Maisie for her work and told her that each edition of the *Voice* was read so often it turned yellow and looked much like a piece of birch bark. Chief Thunder (J. White Sr.) of Hartford, Connecticut, wrote to say, "I am sure it is helping to make things better and giving the people a chance to show many wrongs—it brings them out in the open. I believe that in this way, good people bring about better conditions."[248] Chief Paul Cooke, secretary of the Alaska Native Brotherhood, thought highly enough of the paper that he jumped at the chance to become the paper's Alaskan associate editor. At the ANB's 37th annual convention he announced with great pride that Maisie had chosen him for the job and that "for the first time in years the towns of southeastern Alaska will be represented in a newspaper."[249]

The paper was attracting attention beyond First Nations circles as well. In November 1949 a letter arrived from Rich Hobson, whose first book, *Grass Beyond the Mountains*, was currently being serialized in *Maclean's* magazine. It was the story of his and his partner's (Panhandle "Pan" Phillips) experiences with their Frontier Cattle Company on the upper Blackwater River, north of Anahim Lake. (After it was published in book format in 1951, it sold more than 100,000 copies.) In his letter to Maisie, he called the paper "your splendid and courageous Indian monthly" and went on to state that his best friends were the First Nations he worked with on a daily basis. He wished her "very best regards and good luck to you, Mrs. Moore, in your very constructive work."[250]

By the time Christmas 1949 rolled around Maisie had reclaimed the editor's chair of the *Voice*. Ruth Smith had resigned from the job in April, and her replacement, Lorne Nahanee, had only lasted six months. Whomever she hired as editor must have struggled against her sometimes overbearing presence; she gripped the paper's reins tightly, her distinctive style characterizing most of the editorials and much of the copy. Her granddaughter Maureen remembers that whenever she was visiting, Maisie would give her money to get her out of her hair while she put the finishing touches to one of her corrosive missives for the paper. "My grandchildren," Maisie once said, "can live on fish and chips, ice cream and pop."[251]

Her editorial for December 1949, entitled "Rights of the Native Folk— What in [the] World Are They?" detailed two specific conditions listed in the United Nations' Universal Declaration of Human Rights, which had only recently been drafted. "Surely this did not exclude Native Canadians?" she continued. "Let us on the anniversary of the birth of Christ resolve that the Native Canadian shall not be excluded from the beneficent maxims and provisions of that declaratory Charter."[252]

For the federal government, perhaps the first step in honouring the United Nations Charter was for that august body to finally deliver on its promise to revise the moribund Indian Act that had first been mentioned in the inaugural edition of the *Native Voice* back in December 1946. Brotherhood President William Scow's beaming face on the cover of the January 1950 edition reflected his joy upon reading in a letter addressed to him from MP John Gibson (Independent for Comox-Alberni) that Liberal Prime Minister Louis St. Laurent had assured him the revised Indian Act would be introduced in the House of Commons during the next session. And in her article in that issue Maisie wrote, "What specific changes will be contained in the revised Act are not known, but the Native Indians of Canada are looking for a status equal to that of any other citizens."[253]

In Maisie's mind, equal status included identical liquor rights, her reasoning being that First Nations people were being incarcerated regularly for no reason other than they had consumed a beverage that white people took for granted. And the First Nations people, believing that the law meted out higher penalties for possession than it did for intoxication, had figured out that it was better to be caught drunk than holding a bottle.[254] Imprisonment, according to Maisie, was just one part of a recidivistic cycle that saw First Nations unfairly targeted. There was no shortage of examples.

Normally, inmates from BC jails were released where they had done their time, and because they had no money to make their way home, First Nations individuals often ended up in Vancouver's skid row district, only to repeat the process. This was potentially the case for Joe Inyallie, a Fort McLeod resident who was released from Oakalla in the fall of 1949 after serving a month-long sentence for liquor possession. He had only $1.75 in his pocket, insufficient to cover the cost of his bus fare home. While the province had no problem paying for his trip from Fort McLeod south to Prince George for sentencing and then farther south to Oakalla for incarceration, they professed not to have the funds to send him home again, although return fare was provided for those released from the federally run BC Penitentiary in New Westminster. In a follow-up editorial—probably written by Maisie—the *Voice* quoted her on the subject:

> "It's a crying shame," says Mrs. Moore, "that Indians should be subject to the temptation of alien city streets, timid and fearful of being stranded so far from home"... Most of these men, she says, are good law-abiding citizens, guilty only of minor infractions.[255]

Maisie and the jail chaplain, Father A. F. Carlyle, teamed up to pay for Inyallie's bus fare home, although the responsible Inyallie later repaid them for their kindness.

The situation was unchanged two years later when Alfred Scow, who was by then pursuing a law degree at UBC, wrote that First Nations should be able to decide for themselves whether they wanted to consume liquor. He pointed to his community of Alert Bay where, he noted, several "very normal Indians have been victims of exorbitant fines simply because they have been in possession of intoxicating liquor... The penalty for possession of liquor ranges from $25 to $100. In some instances, a few have been shot at on suspicion of possessing intoxicating beverages."[256]

In fact, Section 128 of the Indian Act that the federal government hadn't yet got around to amending contained the incriminating clause that:

Every Indian or non-treaty Indian who makes or manufactures any intoxicant, or who has in his possession, or concealed, or who sells, exchanges with, barters, supplies or gives to any other Indian or non-treaty Indian, any intoxicant, shall, on summary conviction before any judge, police magistrate, stipendiary magistrate or two justices of the peace, or Indian agent, be liable to imprisonment for a term not exceeding six months and not less than one month, with or without hard labour, or to a penalty not exceeding $100 and not less than $25, or to both penalty and imprisonment, in the discretion of the convicting judge, magistrate, or justices of the peace or Indian agent.[257]

Alfred Scow argued that the First Nations people in BC had just been made equal citizens with respect to the vote, but they were still feeling inferior due to this draconian section of the Indian Act and urged that it be abolished. Section 128, he stated, was forcing some individuals to obtain liquor through bootleggers, despite these products being of inferior quality. And they were being excluded from functions where alcohol was served, which placed severe social restraints on their activities and relationships. So, if the federal government was still adhering to its plan to assimilate First Nations into the broader fabric of Canadian society, this restriction was surely working against that objective.

The full absurdity of this particular section of the Indian Act was highlighted in a story covered in the June 1949 issue of the *Voice*. A Chinese man had appeared before Magistrate McInnes in Vancouver on a charge of possession of liquor in his own four-room apartment where a First Nations acquaintance was temporarily residing. His friend, a woman, had visited Seattle and on her return had nowhere to stay in the city, so he invited her to stay overnight at his place. She invited a few of her friends over for the evening, and they were followed to the residence by an RCMP constable and a city detective. Although the women were not drinking, a couple of unopened bottles of beer were discovered in the apartment as well as the dregs of a bottle of whiskey. The owner of the apartment, despite advising the officers that the liquor was there to entertain his male friends, was arrested under this retributive section of the Indian Act.

When the case got to court, Magistrate McInnes was incredulous and asked Mr. Masterson, the prosecutor, whether this meant that "I can't have liquor for my own use if I employ an Indian servant?" Masterson had replied, smiling, "I'm afraid it does, Your Worship." McInnes had rebelled. "I think that's straining the Act too much. Case dismissed."[258]

The Reverend Dr. Peter Kelly didn't drink and didn't approve of drinking, but he told the *Native Voice*, "Let us face the facts. The Indian must have full responsibility as far as liquor is concerned or he will never be able to control it."[259] He recalled the words of another magistrate, Roderick Haig-Brown of Campbell River, who had recently written that:

Many Indians appear in my court every year. They are rarely charged with anything more serious than having bought or drunk liquor. But an Indian case is never trivial. Indians come to court on these charges with a sense of injustice and discrimination. They are right. The laws that keep liquor from Indians were passed long ago to protect them from the dirty trading practices of the white men. Out of this has grown a myth, perpetuated by the ignorant and prejudiced, that Indians "go crazy" when they drink. I once heard a retired Mounted Policeman put that in its proper light. "Sure" he said, "a drunken Indian is tough to handle. Goes right back to the savage. He is liable to be just about as mean and ornery and dirty as a drunken white man."

It is not simply a question of liquor, but of freedom and human dignity that belongs with freedom. I am ashamed every time it is the duty of my court to punish Indians for something that is a crime only for them.

I am still more ashamed when I act on the law that forces me to ask an Indian where he got his liquor. The answer is nearly always the same: "A white man I have never seen before gave it to me; it was dark; I don't know what he looked like." I can believe the story and let the man go; or call him a liar and send him to jail. If there is anything in all this that adds to the honour of the court, the safety of the state or the dignity of the individual, I haven't yet been able to discover it.[260]

Of course, alcohol was just one issue among many grabbing the attention of the *Voice*'s publisher. Another and perhaps more glaring problem was that First Nations people in Canada still did not qualify for the old age pension. This was highlighted in an editorial composed and submitted to Maisie by a 13-year-old of European descent, John Hargrove, who wrote that:

The native Indians of British Columbia, who once owned this province, have lately been given the right to vote in it. But in case we feel like patting ourselves on the back about that, here is something to think about.

A white man who is more than seventy years old can get a pension of fifty dollars a month. An Indian living on reserve can get only eight dollars a month in old age.

Why? Is a white man's stomach six times as big as an Indian's?[261]

An eastern magistrate, E. R. Tucker, who was a staunch friend of the First Nations people in his jurisdiction, added his voice to this discussion when he offered that:

> It is hard to understand why old age pensions were not granted to the Indians at the same time they were given to other people. While a white man may often carry on after he is 70, could you follow a trap line in the cold north and pull a toboggan at 70 as the Indian is supposed to do?[262]

At the 19th annual convention of the Brotherhood in April 1950, Reverend Dr. Peter Kelly, still chairman of the Legislative Committee, also pressed for equality with respect to old age pensions when he stated that First Nations were paying the social security tax without receiving any of the benefits the tax funded. But old grievances of a domestic nature also surfaced during this convention when the Native Sisterhood of BC staged a mini-revolt led by Sisterhood President Kitty Green and Secretary Brenda Campbell, who advised that their members wanted the right to vote in Brotherhood affairs as the Alaska Native Sisterhood had done since its inception. They had been trying to obtain this privilege for several years, but the matter had been repeatedly deferred or ignored. In the April issue of the *Voice*, Maisie reported that the Sisterhood, which was the organizing body for all the Brotherhood's banquets and events, would stop all such activity until "the fight against this unjust discrimination by the male Natives of British Columbia" had been settled. The Brotherhood's response was to defer the decision once again to the incoming slate of officers, and this elicited the following response from Maisie: "Brothers, quit passing the buck and remember that the female of the species is more deadly than the male."[263] Perhaps Maisie was mirroring the sentiments of her mother who had been such a staunch supporter of the suffragist movement.

6—THE INDIAN ACT

In April 1950, while Maisie bided her time waiting for the revised Indian Act to be submitted to the floor of the House of Commons, she received a startling communiqué from her cousin, Ian Douglas Campbell, the 11th Duke of Argyll, who had only a few months earlier taken possession of Inveraray Castle in Scotland from his late cousin, Niall Campbell, the 10th Duke and the Campbell family historian. The duke's letter advised that he was now engaged in a search for a Spanish treasure ship that had sunk at Tobermory Bay on the Isle of Mull in 1588. "Modern methods of detection should prove fruitful," he wrote. "You won't be forgotten." Maisie replied: "I have 13 grandchildren,"[264] an ample indication of where her share of the booty would go.

How this treasure ship could have ended up in Tobermory Bay, however, is as murky as the seafloor, but history has it the vessel was part of the Spanish Armada and had sailed, "beaten with shote and wether,"[265] into the protective waters of the bay to beg protection from the Scots. And given the provenance of the few artifacts that have been salvaged over the years, it definitely appears to have been Spanish in origin.

It was likely a large, three- or four-masted Mediterranean carrack, which had probably departed for the campaign against England with a complement of about 340 soldiers and seamen. Severely damaged while fleeing Sir Francis Drake's navy, it was then blown off course during the fierce storm off the Irish coast on September 20, 1588, that claimed so many of the retreating Spanish vessels. It was reported at Islay off the west coast of Scotland on September 23; a week or so later it was harboured on the Isle of Mull making repairs and taking on provisions. Its safety there was assured by the chief of Clan MacLean in exchange for the use of some of the Spanish soldiers and their guns to lay "siege to Mingary Castle,"[266] a siege that was ultimately unsuccessful. Legend has it that the ship burned two days later and most of the men were lost, although it is more likely that it was actually blown up, the result of a deliberate act of sabotage by a local merchant who was actually working for the British. However, a much simpler theory rests with sailors' risky habit of spreading wet gunpowder over the deck to dry.

King Charles I began a salvage attempt after ascending to the throne in 1612, but abandoned the effort in 1641 and granted the salvage rights for "all Armada ships by the mercy of God sunk to the sea ground on the coast of Mull near Tobermory, with ornaments, munitions, goods and gear"[267]

to Archibald Campbell, the 8th Earl of Argyll, for his services to the crown. The contract was in perpetuity on the condition that 1 per cent of whatever treasure was recovered would be forfeited to the royal coffers, although Charles I and his son, Charles II, both later tried to have it rescinded. Their attempts failed, leaving the dukes of Argyll with uncontested ownership of the wreck.[268] The family later employed a rudimentary diving bell, their reward being the recovery of several cannon but no treasure. Since then, generations of Campbells have dedicated countless hours and resources chasing this somewhat illusory pot of gold. Keeping the story alive are the stirring rumours of the vast treasure trove that was aboard the ship, tales that the merchants of the quiet little seaside village of Tobermory are happy to perpetuate for the benefit of tourists.

Maisie's cousin, Ian Douglas Campbell, the 11th Duke of Argyll, who, preparing to search for an alleged Spanish treasure ship sunk in Tobermory Bay, Scotland, in 1588 near the family castle, informed Maisie that, "you won't be forgotten." Photo from the family collection.

Whatever Maisie thought of her chances of receiving a share of the treasure from her cousin is unknown, but she enjoyed telling the story. When her titled relatives also tried to induce her to move to Scotland, however, she refused, telling a *Vancouver News-Herald* reporter that "When I was a child, they tried to make a lady of me, but I didn't like it. I like cowboys and Indians."[269] In fact, Maisie's life would not have changed one iota had she been the recipient of a fortune—which she wasn't—and her focus quickly returned to one of the main themes of her advocacy, the Indian Act, and how to free First Nations from its oppressive constraints.

The proposed amendments to the Indian Act in the form of Bill 267 were finally introduced in the House of Commons by Citizenship Minister Walter Harris in late May, which meant MPs had just two weeks before the house was due to rise for the summer recess to debate a bill that had been under consultation, discussion and debate among the members of the Special Joint Committee of the Senate and House of Commons for four years. All that time Canada's First Nations had been labouring under the impression that the "new deal" embodied in the amended act would place them on an equal footing with their neighbours of European descent. But when Minister Harris began his presentation, it was obvious that this would be no "Magna Carta for the Indians." Most of the changes were merely administrative, some of them already implemented prior to the bill's introduction. For example, band council consent would now be required for the use of any band capital funds by the Indian agent, which was a small step in the right direction, but other changes made it abundantly clear that First Nations in Canada were still very much considered wards of the government.

The Alberni Branch of the Brotherhood pointed out that clauses 5 to 16 of the proposed revisions, which redefined what it was to be a First Nations person in Canada, were totally arbitrary. One clause called for the re-registration of reserve members and the loss of status for anyone with one-quarter First Nations blood or less. This new description would exclude "a considerable number of persons who have [been] considered as Indians and who were considered by the band to be Indians."[270] Clause 12 of the bill even regulated the status of children not yet born because if the mothers and grandmothers of these children did not have First Nations status, the children would have to leave the reserve by the time they were 21. And the alleged illegitimate children of males would not only be excluded from band membership but would be denied status as well. Far from being an act to bring First Nations gently into the twentieth century on terms equal to that of their European neighbours, the revised definition of what it was to be a First Nations person in Canada now appeared to be at the core of a planned government strategy to depopulate reserves and force assimilation. The revised act offered few, if any, of the promised freedoms.

It was also an affront that federal enfranchisement was still denied despite enfranchisement being unconditionally offered to the country's 8,000 Inuit; the government's rationale was that Inuit (and Métis) people were not governed by the Indian Act so they had to pay taxes, while First Nations people were tax-exempt. At the same time, however, a new provision in the act called for the compulsory enfranchisement of First Nations women marrying white men. As well, education was to remain denominational. Disappointed, Reverend Dr. Peter Kelly stated: "Churches of all denominations did an invaluable job in pioneering education for the Indians... [but] the stage has been reached where that education should be part of the non-denominational school system."[271] Minister Harris, meanwhile, promised that copies of the bill would be forwarded to each Indian agent for review by their respective band councils before it was passed into law.

The *Voice*'s editorial that month, written by Elmore Philpott of the *Vancouver Sun*, left no doubt what the people in the BC thought of the new bill. It was headlined "Bill 267...Dead Rat" in large bold type, and continued:

BILL 267 TO AMEND THE INDIAN ACT is one of the most disappointing ever introduced into the Canadian Parliament. It is, in fact, worse than disappointing. It is a disgrace to Canada.

We all know the old saying about the mountain which labored [and] brought forth a mouse.

On this matter the present Parliament has done worse than that. The mountain has labored, indeed, but brought forth a rat—and a dead rat, at that.

Philpott ranted that the promise of change throughout the exhaustive four-year process, which for the first time had included consultation with the very people it would affect, had been an illusion.

Bill 267 does not deal with any of the major injustices and neglects to our natives. It totally disregards Canada's solemn obligations under the UN Charter of Human Rights. It ignores the many fine recommendations made by the parliamentary committee which studied the revision of the Indian Act. About the only change of any importance that Bill 267 provides is that Indians should be allowed to imbibe alcoholic drinks (off the reservations) without getting pinched.

That would be downright funny—if it were not so pathetic.

Then in the same breath that Philpott thanked BC's coalition government for their courage in offering First Nations the provincial franchise, he condemned the federal Parliament for its lack of faith in the country's First Nations people. And then, he said, that such an important act should be:

considered by an exhausted Parliament in which the MPs literally have their suitcases packed for the trip home... is a farce. But it is less farcical than the proposal to ask the Indians of Canada to say "yes or no" to Bill 267—all within the space of two weeks! There are many isolated Indians who will never hear about Bill 267 till long after the stipulated period. [272]

Fortunately, the bill caused such a media storm throughout BC that the federal government had no choice but to withdraw it from the floor. Hunter Lewis of the Civil Liberties Union (CLU) had led the campaign by writing to interested MPs, encouraging them to stall the bill until the next legislative session, when it could be properly examined and debated.

We were greatly disappointed by the inadequacy of the Indian Act now before the House as Bill 267. We were also shocked by the proposal to rush it through the House during the hurried remnant of this Session, when it could not possibly receive the serious debate it deserves, and which is contrary to the promises that both Indians and organizations interested in their welfare should have an opportunity to study it fully.

Although we have not been so optimistic as to expect that an ideal bill would be presented, we certainly did not foresee the introduction of anything quite so negligible as Bill 267... It is a far cry from being the "Magna Charta of the Indians," which the Joint Committee said that it would produce. And it is an instance of trying to propitiate the Indians by listening to their grievances rather than remedying them.

Bill 267 is a travesty of the Special Joint committee's slogan "Help the Indian to help himself," for it leaves him in precisely the depressed state to which our laws have brought him, and it is equally a travesty of Canadian professionals in the United Nations.[273]

The *Vancouver News-Herald* was equally critical of the bill when it editorialized that:

What was to have been the "Magna Carta" of the Indians turns out to be little more than a revamping of administration regulations. The committee's long hours of work have been a waste of time.

The Canadian Indians are a backward and depressed race with shattered morale and lost confidence. They are educationally incompetent and dependent.

The Indians are not to blame for this condition. The white man is to blame. He has maintained the reserve system and neglected to emancipate his native brother.

The new act fails to tackle the franchise question. It provides no measures to liquidate the reserve system. It fails to provide a state of affairs by which Indians, if they wish, can have the same rights as other citizens.[274]

Maisie expressed her sincere thanks to the *Vancouver Sun*, the *Province* and the *News-Herald* for their excellent editorials supporting First Nations and their condemnation of Bill 267. "The fine editorials helped delay the passing," she wrote in the July issue of the *Voice*, although a telegram sent to Citizenship and Immigration Minister Harris from BC Attorney General Gordon Wismer, urging him to postpone the bill, most certainly helped as well. Vancouver Mayor Charles Thompson and Vancouver Parks Board Chairman Rowe Holland had followed suit with telegrams of their own, but C. A. Hayden, the publisher of *Country Life*, a magazine representing the primary producers of BC, credited Maisie and the *Voice* for much of the success:

There is no doubt but that the *Native Voice* played an important part in inducing the federal government to withdraw that proposed legislation, which among other things, set up a sort of barter system for the votes of Indians on reservations—a condition that was out of line with the spirit of Canadian citizenship and Canadian democracy.[275]

Minister Harris reacted to the vitriol flowing east from BC by making a special visit to Vancouver at the end of June to try to overturn objections to the bill. Perhaps, though, he was also taking advantage of the opportunity to garner support for a run at the prime minister's office as he was considered the most likely successor to Prime Minister Louis St. Laurent. When Harris met with Maisie, freelance reporter Erwin Kreutzweiser was there to record her interaction with the quiet and amiable minister. He wrote:

> It was a treat to listen to the impassioned exhortations of Mrs. Maisie Armytage-Moore, publisher of the *Native Voice*, who loves the Indians and calls them "my people."
>
> There was emotion in her voice and tears in her eyes as she begged Mr. Harris to "throw the Indian Act away" [and] "wipe out a black-mark of injustice."
>
> "As minister of citizenship," she said, "you can have a holy mission and your name can go down in history."
>
> "I am a practical politician," said Mr. Harris. "How can I do as you say?"
>
> "By taking a stand as a man of vision and honour," came back the reply.[276]

Chief William Scow, president of the Brotherhood, also took advantage of the minister's visit to the city, penning a critique of Bill 267 and passing it on to the minister. This document, which first politely welcomed Harris to the city and thanked him for his offer to meet with the Brotherhood, continued:

> We were given the assurance out of all the presentations throughout Canada that a new day was being made for the people. With all this publicity, the people were happy for what the Minister and members of Parliament called an Indian Magna Carta for our people.
>
> It took the Committee upwards of four years of careful study, BUT TODAY they have failed to give us a Magna Carta. Therefore, Mr. Harris, it is now up to us to do what we must for the people.

After stating that in this province First Nations did not consider themselves wards of the government and that they worked in the fishing and logging industries with complete equality, he asked the minister to "do away with the Indian Act for the people of the province." He continued:

We accepted with a hope that the federal government would also make the final miracle by giving us the federal vote and making us first class citizens of this land of ours.

I AM AFRAID WE DO NOT WANT TO BE SECOND CLASS CITIZENS; we feel it is contrary to the Declaration of Human Rights which reads: WHEREAS recognition of the inherent dignity and of the equal and inalienable rights of all members of the human family is the foundation of FREE-DOM, JUSTICE and PEACE in the world.[277]

Chief Scow's statement wasn't the only condemnation from the Brotherhood, whose Skeena chapter meeting was even more strident in its categorical rejection of the bill. MLA Frank Calder criticized the continuation of denominational schools and wanted the term "quarter breed" defined. The *Voice* reported that it was "notable at the meeting... that elders were more concerned with the effect the new legislation would have on children than on themselves."[278] Thomas Shewish of the Alberni branch of the Brotherhood questioned the government's legal definition of marriage and argued that First Nations had not observed such formalities before Europeans made it mandatory. The illegitimate children the bill referred to were not illegitimate as far as First Nations people were concerned but were the result of First Nations unions according to their customs. "Certainly this provision will cause a great deal of hardship among the Indians and Indian children of the West Coast,"[279] he said. Chief Peter Dionne of the Six Nations Confederacy condemned the bill as well when he stated:

Of course, I understand that it is against the Department of Indian Affairs doctrine to consult an Indian to find out what is best for him. But remember this, we don't vote to appoint any member of that Department or any member of your government, and yet when there is a war, we are called for military service.[280]

Chief Edward Elliott of the Cowichan band also spoke out against the bill, the content of his plea having been heard by the committee countless times, although to no avail. Maisie reported that: "he said [his band] want full enfranchisement and they want no lands to be sold except by approval of the band. They prefer Indian children to be educated in public schools, but if there must be residential schools they should be non-sectarian."[281] The Cowichan people also wanted social security that would be equal to that of the white man's, perhaps not having heard that on June 21 the federal government had finally increased the Old Age Pension for First Nations people 70 years and older from $8 per month to $25, only $5 less than that granted elderly white citizens. This increase would, however, be subject to an income means test, with $420 being the maximum annual earnings permitted by a single applicant and $900 for a married couple before a clawback would occur.

The Reverend Dr. Peter Kelly, who had been in the House of Commons public gallery when Minister Harris had made the pension announcement, told the *Voice*, "This is one of the great days in the history of the Indians of Canada. I think the $25 for an old-aged Indian on the reservation will mean as much as the $30 federal pension for an old age pensioner elsewhere."[282] But while Kelly was elated over the pension news, he was disheartened that all the years of planning and anticipation of a new Indian Act had been for nothing. He probably felt much the same level of despair he had felt in 1927 when the Allied Tribes had failed to make their case to the last joint committee of parliament.

MP John Diefenbaker, Progressive Conservative MP for Lake Centre, who was to become one of Maisie's correspondents in the years ahead, was equally disgusted with the lacklustre revisions to the Indian Act, and later that year when he spoke to fifty chiefs at a conference of the Union of Saskatchewan Indians, he described it as:

> not a charter of Indian rights as was intended but one to continue the powers of the Indian Department... Some of the clauses have been redrafted, others renumbered, but through it still runs the threat of subservience. It leaves the Indian in a position of worship and the department with near-to-tyrannical powers.

As a legal advisor to the chiefs, it was his opinion that they should press for a royal commission to investigate the injustices and that First Nations should have the right to vote without losing treaty rights as well as to be able to seek justice under the law without the consent of a government minister. Furthermore, he believed that the trial of First Nations people on reservations by Indian agents or local justices of the peace was a travesty and a "denial of freedom."[283]

Less than a month later at a banquet in Saskatoon, Minister Harris defended his bill as a "most liberal document" and emphasized that Canada's First Nations people would lose none of their rights and would even gain some additional ones. He categorically denied Diefenbaker's charge that the bill would leave the minister with "arbitrary powers" or that a "thread of subservience" ran through it.[284] He even defended the clause he had inserted in the bill that made it mandatory for First Nations people to obtain permission from the Indian agent prior to selling cattle, hay or any other product. This level of paternalism had been identified as a problem as early as the 1840s in legislation governing the First Nations in the Province of Canada, and here it was again a century later.

❊

As disappointing as Bill 267 was to her, in the summer of 1950 Maisie suddenly had more practical matters to attend to, having received a call from Dick Patrick, who was once again languishing in a dingy Oakalla cell. This time, however, it was not for any public mischief or demonstration of civil rights, but merely for endeavouring to feed his family. He, his blind father, ill mother, wife and three-year-old daughter had all been on the point of starvation when he went into the bush and shot a cow moose. When the game warden collared him for this transgression, Patrick had been in the process of ploughing his fields for spring planting, and despite admitting his error, he was charged and sentenced. Although his friends, including Constance Cox, had tried to find help to finish his ploughing and planting, no one stepped forward due to the isolated nature of his farm, and by the time Patrick was scheduled for release, his neighbours would already be harvesting their crops. "You don't reap where you cannot sow,"[285] Maisie said as she paid his $163.80 fine from the $200 that had been given to her by a lawyer friend—likely Tom Hurley—for that purpose.

Ever since moose first migrated into the Lakes District in the early part of the twentieth century, hunting cow moose after haying season had been a tradition among First Nations people living there. This was when they would harvest their winter supply of meat and dry it according to their custom. Adona Antoine, writing to the *Voice*, explained:

> This year, however, the game warden has stopped a number of boys out on the hunting grounds and taken some dried meat from them so as to put them in trouble for cow moose. Every Indian from hundreds of years back know and harbour these cow moose. The only reason an Indian will kill a cow moose is when he has nothing else to eat.[286]

This was not the first instance of First Nations people becoming entangled in the country's game laws nor would it be the last, but at least it would begin the discussion of what inherent rights they had when it came to traditional food-gathering practices and privileges. And although there was no broad brush that could make the determination of innocence or guilt, since each case had to be adjudicated according to its own set of circumstances in a court of law, the general subject intrigued Maisie enough that her interest went far deeper than just rescuing Patrick. Knowing that Hugh Dempsey, a journalist with the *Edmonton Bulletin,* was wrestling with this same subject, she fired off a summary of case law on the subject that he might reference for his work. What interested Dempsey at that time were the number of First Nations people in Alberta who had been charged by game officials for hunting out of season, only to have the charges dismissed in court because of their treaty rights. In Saskatchewan the most famous case of this kind had occurred back in 1939, when John Diefenbaker had defended a First Nations man, John Smith, Jr., in the provincial Court of Appeal for carrying a firearm in the Fort La Corne Game Preserve. In reality, his client was only doing what he believed his band's treaty permitted him to do, which was to hunt "on unoccupied crown land." Although Diefenbaker lost the case, he vowed that, when and if he ever became prime minister, he would respect treaty rights. This would also be the subject that would later launch—at Maisie's insistence—one of Tom Hurley's protégés, Thomas Berger, into the field of Aboriginal law, thus beginning a new era of insight and justice for Aboriginal people in Canada.

Of course, because there were few treaties to honour in BC, the legal landscape in this province was vastly different than in other parts of Canada with respect to game and, perhaps more importantly, land. Andrew Paull, now the president of the Grand Council of the North American Brotherhood, approached the legislature on January 9, 1951, with this in mind, demanding that the provincial government pay for approximately 348,000 acres of land taken from the First Nations in the province, a debt he estimated to be worth millions of dollars. He backed this up with a copy of the Royal Proclamation of 1763 from King George III, wherein it was decreed that the crown must pay for any land acquired from the First Nations, and an 1858 proclamation from Queen Victoria that reinforced it. According to the February issue of the *Voice*, Paull stated:

> The province has only bought a few parcels of land from the Indians... This includes land at Sooke, Saanich, Nanaimo, Puntledge and Rupert... We were never conquered and the government has never met the Indians in council for a discussion of native title to the lands of BC. When Canada was under British rule, the Indians got a fairer deal because Englishmen were more conscious of their duty. Since Confederation the Indian rights have been pushed aside by both the federal and provincial governments.[287]

The day after Paull made his presentation in Victoria, the *Vancouver News-Herald* printed a response by historian Bruce McKelvie, who had produced documents from the provincial archives proving that Chief Factor James Douglas had assembled First Nations representatives at what is now Beacon Hill Park in order to conduct negotiations for the purchase of the land. "Every foot of ground from beyond Sooke to Saanich Inlet and including Sooke, Metchosin, Colquitz, Esquimalt, Saanich Peninsula and Victoria and Oak Bay was deeded to Douglas with the exception of reserves and enclosed fields," McKelvie stated, and he claimed that the First Nations consigned their land to the white man by signing the following statement:

> The condition of, or understanding of this sale is this—that our village sites and enclosed fields are to be kept for our own use, for the

use of our children, and for those who may follow after us; and the land shall be properly surveyed hereafter. It is understood, however, that the land itself with these small exceptions, becomes the entire property of the white people forever.[288]

Maisie immediately prepared to do battle with McKelvie and "plunged into her personal record file and came up with a copy of a statement made by Governor James Douglas on February 5, 1859." Her rebuttal was reported in the *News-Herald* the next day:

In that speech [by Douglas], she claims the governor said the Indians "could convey no part of their reserves by lease or sale." Mrs. Moore also claimed Sir Wilfrid Laurier, when prime minister of Canada, pledged that the matter of Indian lands would be settled by the highest court.

"Let's keep them to the record and settle this matter in Supreme Court," she said. "Make the provincial government bring out everything and lay it on the table for all to see. Let's do away with all this smokescreen talk." As a clincher, Mrs. Moore claimed that it would have been "illegal" for the Indians to sign anything "even if someone tricked some of them into it."[289]

McKelvie's response was that "Mrs. Moore and the Indians may be half-right." He said the records in the provincial archives merely showed that "the land on the southern end of Vancouver Island was purchased from the Indians," and that he had "made no reference to the mainland situation." The "prominent *Daily Province* newspaperman, who has written several books on the early days of the Indians in BC" announced that "no definite agreements were signed in colonial days with the tribes on the mainland."[290]

Guy Williams also declared McKelvie's comments invalid, and the February issue of the *Voice* carried his rebuttal:

"We remember hearing the rich Nanaimo coalfields were sold for a bottle of rum," he said. "We were under the impression that we native Canadians were then considered primitive savages. How then could we sign deeds? How could we understand the intricate mazes of the law?"

Williams claimed that when the Indians signed the "traps drawn up by the Hudson's Bay Company" that the marks made by them "were guided by the white man..." The Indians who have fought in two world wars "will not be pushed around," said Mr. Williams.[291]

The *Province* newspaper had the last word in this round by reminding its readers that:

No government and no court can, of course, make [the Indians] the fantastic award they are suggesting. Nor do they really expect such an award. This is far from saying, however, that the Indians have no case. They have a case against the white man, but it is not so much a case for compensation for lands occupied as it is for more considerate, more humane, more intelligent treatment than they have received... The thing to do is make the Indian a Canadian citizen equal in privileges and responsibilities to any other Canadian citizen... But when we make him a full citizen, there is no reason why we should require him to sacrifice his aboriginal rights.[292]

In February 1951, Citizenship Minister Harris introduced his revised Indian Act, now called Bill 79, to the House of Commons. It was apparent that he believed the amendments would be enough to gain approval from the First Nations since it gave them the right to handle more of their own affairs. Newly included in the amended bill was the authority to dispose of grain and livestock without interference from the Indian agent, and the right to unrestricted consumption of alcoholic beverages, provided provincial authorities were in agreement. "The Canadian Indian," Harris said, "has proven himself a capable, shrewd chap, and I think he has the ability, in most instances, to take care of his own affairs."[293]

Brotherhood President William Scow expressed optimism that Bill 79 would be enacted successfully. He gave high marks to Minister Harris who had invited First Nations leaders back to Ottawa to discuss and amend Bill 267 "over three days and three evening sessions" prior to reintroducing it. He said:

For the first time in history the Indian leaders of all Canada have been invited to sit down and assist in the making of their own laws. We went through Bill 267, article by article and section by section, and referred back continually... I do not believe there is any such thing as a perfect law, but I feel in my heart we have made some progress."[294]

The Reverend Dr. Peter Kelly, who had travelled with Scow to those three days and nights of meetings, was less enthusiastic about the new bill. He told the Ottawa press that he had hoped the federal government would give the franchise to Indians without asking them to sign a waiver foregoing income tax exemptions on their earnings on reserves. "We feel that citizenship rights should be given to all Indians with no strings attached," he said, before adding, "I don't think that this new bill is the Magna Carta... but it has been brought somewhat closer to that goal,"[295] he said.

Meanwhile the topic of land rights had so incensed Maisie and Guy Williams that they had begun organizing their own political party to challenge the Provincial and Federal government. On January 16, Maisie wrote about it to her friend Hugh Dempsey:

> "Guy Williams and I are organizing the Indian Non-Partisan Political Party (INPPP) to try and protect [First Nations people]—run our own members and sort of put a brake on some of [the government's] rank stuff. After working for years and spending real dough (which I now haven't got)."

But there was bad news in her letter to Dempsey as well. Maisie and the Brotherhood's president, William Scow, were at loggerheads, and although their public faces indicated nothing but calm, Maisie wrote of their uneasy alliance that:

> these politicians took Scow, whom it took years to build up, turned his head and he is no more use to the Indians—simply spoiled a good man—so now there may be a blow-up, and politics are behind it. I am taking a firm stand and Scow, who is trying to run a one-man job, may ask me to get out and stop the *Native Voice* being the Voice of the Brotherhood. I rather hope he does as Guy and I will be free to show up a lot of stuff. Our organization is steadily being defrosted by Scow who is a Yes-man to the politicians. Keep this under your hat as I don't want it to get out yet. However, we are not looking for a fight unless he starts it openly. *Don't* let this out.[296]

According to an article in the *Voice* in February, the new party Maisie and Guy Williams were organizing would "support the candidates—Indian or white—we feel are qualified." Their ultimate aim was to furnish elected officials to take care of Indian Affairs and to "protect our unsurrendered land and the future of our children." Guy Williams was quoted as saying, "We have always backed the present government and hope to do so in the future. There will be no clashes as long as the Indian is treated justly."[297]

The inaugural meeting of the INPPP was held on February 8 at Maisie and Tom's apartment. In attendance were representatives from high-ranking southern coastal families as well as those from Haida Gwaii, Alert Bay, Bella Bella and Fort Rupert. Letters of support were received from the Skeena River and even from David Benoit who forwarded his encouragement from the battlefields of Korea. He wrote:

> I was really surprised to hear of the forming of the new party, I mean the INPPP, which will strengthen our political tomahawk. We just got to fight for our right, the same as we do on the front lines...
> As ever your adopted son, Dave[298]

Williams told the meeting that women members would hold equal sway with men in the new party, which was in line with the customs that had prevailed before the white man came, and that the deputy leader of the INPPP would be a woman. Unanimously, the founding members of the party demanded that the provincial government bring pressure to bear on the federal government to "recall the amendment made to the Election Act whereby Indians were forced to sign a waiver signing away their rights before they could receive full citizenship."[299] Williams warned that failure to do this would likely be felt by the government in the next provincial election.

On April 3, 1951, Bill 79 received approval in principle in the House of Commons and was referred to a special house committee for detailed consideration. This committee would call witnesses—both government officials and First Nations leaders—to make recommendations to amend the document, which included a few administrative changes and revised and modernized some of the detailed provisions of the old act. Opposition Leader George Drew (Progressive Conservative for Carleton) lauded the government for the new bill but cautioned that "we have no right to be satisfied with this legislation" until First Nations have been provided with full citizenship rights. CCF leader M. J. Coldwell reminded the house that in many parts of Canada native Indians living on reserves were "in a state of economic and social depression."[300]

However, the committee voted down First Nations enfranchisement eleven members to five, unmoved by an emotional appeal from MP E. Davie Fulton (Progressive Conservative for Kamloops) that "the Indians were here first; they should be given this privilege."[301] And Minister Harris, despite his previous assurances that the bill would give Canada's First Nations "near total freedom,"[302] now insisted that offering the franchise without a waiver would be giving them "more than the white man has."[303]

Andrew Paull, now Grand Chief of the 70,000-strong North American Indian Brotherhood, condemned the bill as being "dictatorial and bureaucratic" and said it would "obliterate the identity of Indians in Canada." He stated that the government had yet to compensate the First Nations of Canada for their lands, and because of that, they should be treated fairly and should not be subject to the government's dictatorial powers. He pointed out that under the terms of the revised bill Minister Harris still retained the discretionary power of enfranchisement for First Nations people living on reserves (sections 108 to 112 of the revised Indian Act) as well as the power to tax them, even though they still had no representation in Parliament. Crowning these powers was the absolutely undemocratic edict that there could be no appeal of the minister's decisions. Paull suggested that "no white man would tolerate such action. It would cause a revolution."[304]

Chief William Scow's leadership of the Brotherhood was reaffirmed for a seventh term at the 19th annual convention of the Native Brotherhood of BC in May 1951, and during his opening remarks he recalled the 1943 convention, where he had developed a close relationship with the late president, Alfred Adams, and vice-president Heber Clifton, men who had been his father's friends. He then spoke of the trust and responsibility that Adams had placed in his hands on his deathbed, a trust that was manifest in his actions. He reminded the meeting that when Bill 267 had been read into the House of Commons, he had left no stone unturned in his effort to delay its passage, and he said he believed the Brotherhood's opposition had a significant impact on that bill's eventual withdrawal.

The Reverend Dr. Peter Kelly, who was re-elected to his position of chair of the Brotherhood's Legislative Committee, gave a stirring account of the history of the struggle for justice. He recalled how, twenty-four years earlier, the Special Joint Committee of the Senate and House of Commons had stated that the Allied Tribes had failed to make their case, and he was still bitter towards Dr. Duncan Campbell Scott, superintendent of Indian Affairs who, when he had the opportunity to make a real difference to BC's First Nations, had merely allocated $100,000 a year to them for education and health, money that had never been proven to have been used for that purpose. When it came time for the convention to debate Bill 79, the *Native Voice* reported that, although Kelly said he appreciated the government's invitation to various First Nations leaders to help craft the revised bill, there were still some troubling shortcomings. For example, he said, Section 86, the waiver section of the bill stated that:

> whereby to gain the right to vote, the Indian had to give up his inheritance in order to exercise that right, he had a feeling of unfairness and discrimination. He vigorously opposed it, saying I do not know who will sign the waiver—I don't think it worth it. I value the ballot. It is worth more than you people realize. The provincial government did a magnificent thing when they gave you the right to vote. But the Dominion says we will give you the vote, but we want you to surrender your rights before you will be permitted to exercise your vote. It is too big a price.[305]

The meeting also heard from Superintendent Anfield, who spoke of the progress being made in curing tuberculosis, which at one time had been thought impossible. Earlier that year the *Vancouver News-Herald* had made the tuberculosis problem among First Nations people alarmingly clear, reporting that TB deaths for all of Canada were 37.1 per 100,000 people for 1948 and 30.5 for 1949, but for First Nations, it had been a whopping 549.8

per 100,000 for 1947 and 480.1 for 1948. "Our lack of concern [for] the Indian is one of our national shames," the article had continued. "We herded him on to reservations, there to die out."[306] Kelly stated that "it was like a message from Heaven to hear that TB can be controlled and cured."[307]

In May 1951 Father Carlyle returned to England after decades of administering to First Nations and indigent people in the Lower Mainland, and Maisie wrote:

> My friend and confidant of many years has gone. When sorrow and trouble were too heavy to carry alone, he shared it and somehow lifted the heavy load from one's heart, giving consolation and new strength to carry on with a word of comfort and God's blessing.
>
> Many times in my work when I was confronted with hungry stranded men, homeless and in trouble, both white and Indian, I would phone him for help and shelter. Often I would say he is not Catholic, he is a Protestant, Father, and he would say: "What difference does that make? He is in trouble; send him down."
>
> On many trips to Oakalla Prison Farm where I really got to know him, he was deeply loved by those unfortunates. He gave them courage and spiritual help, even money to hire a lawyer to fight their cases, and when they got out without friends or help, he gave them shelter and help and guidance.
>
> On many occasions he walked the last steps to the gallows with men I knew, giving them courage to pass over the border through the last gate into Eternity. Afterwards, when exhausted, sorrow-stricken, he would tell how the man had gone bravely to face his Master and make peace with his God. It was always a terrible ordeal for Father Carlyle, for he grew to love the men who turned to him for spiritual comfort in their last hours. Father never flinched but gave help and comfort until the soul had passed on into Eternity, poor, bewildered, troubled men.[308]

It was about this time that Maisie was facing a serious threat to her own health, and although it was uncharacteristic of her to relinquish editorial control of the *Voice* to anyone, she passed the job to Big White Owl (Jasper Hill) because she had no option. He had not attended the Brotherhood convention, but he mirrored the sentiments of its various presenters when he slipped into the editor's role for the May issue of the *Voice* with an editorial headlined: "Bill 79 is a Farce" and continued: "The new act is merely a very clever manipulation of words, planned and designed to confuse and pull the wool over the eyes of the groggy, half-conscious, always sleepy Canadian public."[309] And that issue of the *Voice* also reprinted an article from *The Globe and Mail* that thoroughly condemned the new act:

> If the public of Canada were half as interested as it should be in minority justice, this poor measure would never have got through Commons at all. It is surely revealing that the only constructive program put before the Commons came from British Columbia, the only province which has exercised its right to give Indians the provincial franchise.
>
> The Senate still has a chance to block this Indian Act and force a new charter of Indian rights into being. Failing this, some future Parliament with more conscience than the one we now have must do the job. Indian reform has travelled a long and obstacle-cluttered trail. The latest dab at it doesn't even settle the dust.[310]

Although a permanent employee of the Canadian Red Cross, living off reserve and enfranchised, Hill was still very much in tune with his culture as well as being a fierce advocate for First Nations justice. He was also very appreciative of the opportunity Maisie had given him to write for the paper, and he replied to tell her how much he admired her for:

> the wonderful work that you are doing for the Red Indian cause or to be more correct the North American Indian cause... Therefore, you can rest assured that I shall always do all that is within my humble ability to assist you because I honestly believe that the Indians of Canada (and those of USA also) really need a medium such as the Native Voice... Truly, it is the only Indian paper I know at the present time which offers the native Red Indian an opportunity to present his views and beliefs, his traditions and legends, his culture, past and present, before the roundtable of the truth-hungry public... Dear Mrs. Moore, long may you live and continue to guide the destiny of the Native Voice.[311]

A dangerous goiter had been threatening Maisie's breathing for some time and surgery was required, and in August when she had finally recovered, she wrote:

> Sometimes I think it does one good to be dangerously ill—you find out how many friends you have. I am just recovering from years of illness—two dear fine doctors gave me a new lease on life, dozens of real true friends offered their help, visited me and smothered me with flowers. I have never been so important before in my life except perhaps the day I was born.
>
> It is a rich feeling to know that you are loved by dozens of fine, wonderful people. It gives you a new outlook on life. I felt that if I

took time off to be operated on, the Native Voice and everything would stop and go to pieces, but no, dear Phyllis Grisdale and George North kept everything going and lifted my burden and everyone else helped—just told me to rest and forget everything.

Dear beloved friends all, how can I tell you how much it means to me and how rich you and the many letters of cheer make me feel? My associate editor, Jasper Hill, carrying on and giving me strength, knowing he was pulling for me. Thank you, my beloved friends—it is nice to start again. Knowing you are with me with all your kindness and good thoughts, how can I fail you?[312]

It was this attitude and selfless devotion to "her people" that earned Maisie another accolade: on Dominion Day 1951 the Squamish people honoured her by making her a member of their nation and conferring upon her the name of Maithla (the Dancer). It was the name that had also been given to her mother, Amy Ellen Chadwick Campbell-Johnston, a name that had now been in Maisie's family for two generations. This fact was not lost on her friend, Squamish Chief August Jack Khatsahlano, who spoke fondly of her and her parents and their respect for his people.

August Jack was not the only one enamored of Maisie and the paper at this time. As a 10-year-old boy, the noted deep-ocean explorer, scientist and inventor Phil Nuytten, who traces his lineage to the Métis people of Manitoba, learned that Maisie lived a stone's throw from his house in Vancouver's West End. He was ecstatic and decided he must meet her, not suspecting that he had probably served her and Tom Hurley at his family's restaurant, the Chilco Grill at the corner of Chilco and Robson streets. Nuytten had already developed such a keen interest in First Nations art and culture that he was taking painting and carving lessons from the renowned Kwakwaka'wakw carver, Ellen Neel, granddaughter of Charlie James, one of the most significant carvers on the West Coast. When there was no carving to be done at Neel's studio—Nuytten would often help with carving and painting small commercial totem poles for the tourist market—he would curl into a corner of her basement with a cup of tea and read back issues of the Native Voice. Once he took one to read at school when a classmate—Maisie's granddaughter, Moira Kennedy—saw him. Nuytten recalled:

She came over and said, "Oh, I see you're reading the Native Voice" or words to that effect, so I immediately boasted about knowing Ellen Neel and carving with her, and she said—so I wouldn't outdo her with my boast—"Well, my grandmother writes that." And I thought she meant an article in it and I said, "Which one?" And she said, "All of them. That's hers. The Native Voice is hers."

When Nuytten asked if she came often to Vancouver, he was shocked to learn that he passed her apartment every day on his way to and from school. Moira offered to introduce him to her grandmother, and when they met, Nuytten told her how much he enjoyed the paper.

And I said, "I don't want to bother you, but I'd love to come by some-times when you're actually doing it… and watch you do it…" Tom Hurley made all kinds of side comments—he was really funny. Once in a while I'd look in the window and they'd be sitting around having tea, you know, or talking and whatnot—there were white and native people.[313]

The tea parties that Maisie and her friends hosted were a regular part of the social scene in Vancouver at the time, but Maisie was not just having tea. She used these parties to exert her influence on behalf of her First Nations friends. Kwakwaka'wakw Chief Bill Wilson (Hemads-Kla-Lee-Lee-Kla), who was the second First Nations lawyer to graduate from UBC's school of law, re-membered coming to Vancouver with his mother, Ethel Johnson (Puugladee), and attending parties at the home of Maisie's friend Irene Rogers, widow of Benjamin T. Rogers, the president of the BC Sugar Company. Wilson recalled

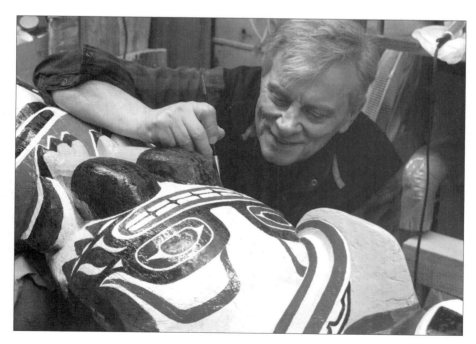

Enamored with Maisie and her newspaper as a young boy, Phil Nuytten, revelled in the stories he read in the *Native Voice*. Here he is restoring a pole carved by the iconic west coast carver, Ellen Neel. Photo credit to Virginia Cowell.

roaming through the accessible portions of the Rogers family's former mansion on Davie Street. This impressive house, which had been called *Gabriola* in its heyday, had been converted into the Angus Apartments (Irene's maiden name) after the death of her husband in 1918, and Irene inhabited one of them. "There was a whole circle of these women," Wilson recalled, "most of them sort of Vancouver's socialites [one was Mildred Valley Thornton, the noted artist] and Maisie, of course, was 'in like Flynn' with them." What Wilson did not know was that Irene Rogers was not only a patron of the arts, but she often provided funds to assist Maisie to pay the fines of her friends who were sent to Oakalla. It was a symbiotic relationship in which advocate was matched to benefactor.[314] Wilson remembered Maisie as "a tall woman in a black dress that was scary... I thought she was mean... I'm sure she wasn't mean but that was my impression."

Joan Hall, from Bella Bella, whose stepmother was Kitty Carpenter, the president of the Sisterhood, recalled that when she and her husband, Jim, first moved to Vancouver, "we met Maisie... she was very active with Native groups... she was an organizer... she wheeled and dealed for us, for the group and she had good connections." Joan, however, remembered that her husband referred to her "as that pushy woman."[315]

On September 4, 1951, Bill 79 became law, and Maisie, back in fighting form after her surgery, editorialized that this bill was still far from perfect. And then she took John Blackmore, Liberal MP for Essex West and the latest chairman of the parliamentary committee, to task for suggesting that "Indians had ample opportunity to make their views on the legislation known." Finally she directed her scathing anger at Minister Harris:

> Mr. Harris' intentions are presumably honourable, but his successor might not be so well intended, and there are several dangerous and deadly sections in this new Act which should be revised.
>
> Consider Section 112 whereby the minister can, after a hearing, enfranchise a band of Indians without their consent. Until these sections are revised, Bill 79 remains, so far as we are concerned, a dangerous and imperfect Act. Why pass an Act unless it is perfect and just?
>
> We cannot, under any circumstances, look on this imperfect bill as anything but a calamity and disaster ending the long and weary fight of those noble old Native chiefs who sacrificed so much in their fight to win justice and freedom for the future young Native Canadians.[316]

Harris's rebuttal that "the aim of the new act is to bring the Indians, by progressive steps, into a position of social, political and economic equality with other Canadians"[317] didn't appease Maisie at all, given the long and arduous path she and the Brotherhood had taken over the years to educate him and influence his policies. But perhaps she might have challenged the revisions with more vigour had she been back into the full swing of her advocacy. A sympathetic friend, *Vancouver Sun* reporter Tom Jarvis, wrote soon after she recovered from her surgery that:

> Mrs. Maisie Armytage-Moore cannot, with more than 50 percent accuracy, be described as a strong, silent woman. When injustice, real or imagined, touches a BC Indian, she is very strong indeed.
>
> Mr. Hurley being engaged these days as crown prosecutor at the Assizes, Mrs. Moore represented an Indian charged with being drunk. His bail, rather curiously, was $50, which is unusually high.
>
> Mrs. Moore: "Your Worship, may I ask a question? (Lovely wedge to work into a speech!) This man is a hard-working fisherman, so hard-working he fell asleep in the taxi. He couldn't be awakened when it came time to pay. So the taxi man had him arrested and someone here set bail at $50 to make sure he'd get the fare money. It's unjust..."
>
> Magistrate McInnes suavely cut short this modern Portia: "He will pay $5 costs or three days. That is the end of the matter."
>
> Ah, yes—but by the tilt of Mrs. Moore's chin as she left court and some remarks [she made] later, I fancy we may read in "The Native Voice" (which she edits) something about the police station being used for a collection agency. Mrs. Moore was much annoyed.[318]

7—Marriage and the Heart

In 1911, following Maisie's split from her husband, John Reginald Rowallane Armytage-Moore, he had returned to England. His subsequent wanderings took him to Australia and then to New Zealand where in 1916 he joined the New Zealand Expeditionary Force and was sent to Samoa. From there he returned to Australia where he enlisted with the 12th Field Artillery Brigade, Reinforcement 35, and embarked for the war in Europe. He arrived too late to join the conflict and was discharged from duty in London a year later. By 1929 he was living in Earls Court and operating a school of dancing. When he died at the age of 75 on June 2, 1951, at St. Georges Hospital, Hyde Park Corner, he was still married to Maisie.

As Maisie and Tom's Catholic faith forbade divorce, they had been left with no choice but to wait for Armytage-Moore's demise before marrying—although as strict as they were about observing this canon, they had been ignoring another that prohibited sexual congress before marriage. However, with his death they were now sanctioned to join in holy matrimony, and in due course Tom proposed to Maisie. The wedding date was set for Boxing Day 1951.

Maisie's reporter friend, Tom Jarvis, spilled the beans in his *Vancouver Sun* column on September 24, 1951, and it was subsequently reprinted in the *Voice*:

> Well, just for a change, this is a wedding bells column, which is a good answer to those who say it's sometimes too sordid with nothing but crime and punishment. I suppose, though, even this time it's concerned with a life sentence...
>
> Now it's out. I can just hear the excited buzz of conversation and the congratulations that crowd in upon Tom as he continues his work as Crown Prosecutor at the Assizes. And Mrs. Moore's telephone, rarely free anyway, will be going for a week. Her Indian friends will flood her with messages.
>
> So now we'll save up for confetti and rice. Methinks I'll be hearing T. F. H. no longer singing softly in his idle moments, "Maisie, Maisie, give me your answer, do!" He has his answer. Courtship days are over and now the stern reality begins.[319]

Maisie broke the news privately to some of her confidants. In a letter to Hugh Dempsey, she wrote:

Did or did I not tell you of my taking the fatal step—marrying—in say, December? to the "BOSS"? You will see same in the *Native Voice*. I am trying to get married somewhere quietly, but it looks hopeless. Everyone has decided to make it a cross between a wake and an Indian Potlatch—Gentlemen will please check their spurs and guns outside etc., etc...[320]

Mrs. Adona Antoine from Fort St. James was one of the many who wrote to Maisie to congratulate her on her upcoming nuptials:

Just a few lines to let you know that we all wish you happiness in your new life.

Somehow, we won't get used to it overnight. We never realized how much you meant to us; now we know that we love you very much. We thank you especially and all those who helped to bring us a better living.[321]

Messages of support poured in from the US, too, and Chief Thunder (Jim White) of Hartford, Connecticut, combined his good wishes with praise for the *Voice*:

The Native Voice is part of me, it keeps alive the Truth, and I love the Truth also a chance to hear from my Brothers and Sisters in the USA and Canada. I pray that the Native Voice grows and I believe it will, because with worthy people like Chief J. Antoine, Jasper Hill, Chief Paul Cooke, William Scow, Rev. P. R. Kelly, Reginald Cook, Dan Assu, Oscar Peters, William Pascal and you, Maisie Armytage-Moore, it will grow. May the Great Spirit be with all of you and may you enjoy good health.[322]

But Maisie had more than marriage on her mind that fall, and in October she announced that she was adding another associate editor to the paper, a Cherokee woman from Oklahoma named Mrs. Jimalee Chitwood Burton, although her father had given her the name Ho-chee-nee, which means "the leader." She was a force unto herself, and in addition to being a talented singer, songwriter, poet, broadcaster and author, she was also a noted artist. "The Indians of BC are fortunate in having a champion in you," she wrote Maisie in response to the invitation to join the paper. "Soon I hope the Voice will stir deep inside them, and awaken them to their great possibilities. We are the Americans."[323]

In October when Princess Elizabeth and her husband, Prince Philip, arrived in Vancouver, Maisie was once again distracted from her wedding plans because the officials organizing their visit to the city had excluded First Nations people from the celebratory welcome at the CPR station. "We consider it outrageous the way that Vancouver ignored the Natives when royalty paid us a visit," she wrote in the *Voice*. Then, always adept at roasting persons in positions of authority whom she considered fools, she called those guilty of this particular crime of omission "drab, uninteresting, unimaginative little civic officials: could any prospect be worse than that some of them may be with us in the Great Beyond?" And she added, "In the same breath, we wish to commend Victoria for inviting the Natives to put on their lovely dances and for including them in the plans of welcome."[324]

She was also pleased that when MLA Frank Calder met Prince Philip at the provincial legislature in Victoria a day later, the Prince had singled him out for a conversation.

"Where are you from?" Philip asked.

"Atlin," answered the young MLA.

Then the Duke [*sic*] wanted to know where that was. When Mr. Calder told him it was just below the Yukon border, he quoted the Duke as saying, "It must be cold up there."

"It is slightly," the MLA replied.[325]

In early December Tom, who had to adjust his busy schedule to accommodate his upcoming marriage, appeared before a panel of judges to request that the four cases he was working on be transferred to the next Appellate Court in Victoria. According to one newspaper report, the exchange between Tom and Mr. Justice Sidney Smith, the head of the panel, went something like the following:

"I myself am about to undergo a life sentence, and before I lose my liberty I have several matters to arrange," Mr. Hurley told their Lordships.

"You have our sympathies," said Mr. Justice Sidney Smith.

"I take it that you mean I have a long life sentence," replied Mr. Hurley.[326]

The wedding took place at 11:00 a.m. on December 26 at the Guardian Angels Church not far from Tom and Maisie's apartment. The Rev. F. A. Clinton officiated. The day was chilly and wet when Maisie, dressed in a black tailleur with a white corsage, accompanied by her daughter Kathleen (Kitty) Kennedy as matron of honour, also dressed in black but with red accessories, strode purposefully down the aisle to meet her betrothed at the altar. Later, according to the *Vancouver Sun*, as the couple made their way to the chancel to sign the register, Tom whispered to his best man, Angelo Branca,

KC, that "This is what's known as a *matrimonial blitz.*" "It was the first time," said another friend, Assistant City Prosecutor William Masterson, "that Tom Hurley didn't ask for an adjournment of his case."[327]

"The aristocracy of BC's Indians attended the wedding reception for their 'White Mother,'"[328] at the home of Mildred Valley Thornton, noted artist and occasional *Voice* correspondent. Included in the crowd of well-wishers were August Jack Khatsahlano, Chief of the Kitsilano Nation; Chief Andy Frank of Comox; Chief Isaac Jacob of Squamish; Guy Williams from Kitimat and Dominic Charlie from Capilano. Each of them, in turn, approached the couple to offer advice as well as to bless them according to the marriage rites of their individual cultures.

August Jack Khatsahlano blessing Tom and Maisie on their wedding day while Moira Kennedy and her sister Louisa look on. Photo from the family collection.

The couple departed for their honeymoon soon after, taking their granddaughter, Moira Kennedy, with them to California. Three days into their honeymoon Tom presented Maisie with the promise of a wedding gift that is probably, if not unparalleled, then at least rare in the annals of recorded human history: the mummified heart of one of her ancestors, James Graham, the First Marquis of Montrose. It would soon be en route from London, although they would be long returned to Vancouver before it actually arrived.

Montrose had been a Covenanter, one of the Scots who signed the National Covenant of 1638 to confirm their opposition to Charles I's interference in the affairs of the Presbyterian Church of Scotland. The Stuart kings believed in the divine right of kings and thus their role as spiritual head of the Church of Scotland. However, when the Covenanters' leadership was assumed by Montrose's cousin, Archibald Campbell, the First Marquis of Argyll, Montrose switched sides to champion King Charles. He distinguished himself at the head of the king's forces during what is known as the Bishops' Wars and in the Civil War that followed, and for his services Charles appointed Montrose lord lieutenant of Scotland in 1644 and a year later commissioned him captain general. But two years later Montrose and his forces were defeated;

The tomb of James Graham, the First Marquis of Montrose, at St. Giles Cathedral, also known as the High Kirk of Edinburgh. On the eve of his execution, he wrote a poem that would affect Maisie 300 years later. Photo courtesy of St. Giles Cathedral staff.

he escaped to Norway but returned at the head of a small force in March 1650, eager to avenge the execution of his king at the hands of the Roundheads. On April 27 he was defeated at the Battle of Carbisdale in Ross-shire, and a month later Parliament condemned him to death. As he sat in his jail cell on the eve of his execution, Montrose wrote a poem, one that would affect Maisie Hurley 300 years later:

> Let them bestow on every airth a limb.
> Then open all my veins, that I may swim
> To thee, my Maker, in that crimson lake:
> Then place my par-boil'd head upon a stake.
> Scatter my ashes, strew them in the air:
> Lord! Since thou knowest where all these atoms are,
> I'm hopeful Thoul't recover once my dust.
> And confident Thoul't raise me with the just.

Montrose was hanged on May 21, his head cut off and placed on a "prick" on the Old Tolbooth outside St. Giles Cathedral while his limbs were divided up between the cities of Glasgow, Perth, Stirling and Aberdeen; his torso was interred in the gallows grounds of Burgh Muir. A short time later, however, his niece, Lady Napier, sent men by night to remove his heart, which she placed in a steel box made from his sword and then encased in a gold filigree box presented to the family by the Doge of Venice. Montrose's head remained on the Old Tolbooth prick until 1661 by which time the monarchy had been restored and a general amnesty declared. Now his torso was disinterred, his arms and legs returned, and all were allegedly reunited with his head for a splendid funeral at St. Giles on May 11, 1661.

But was the heart that Tom gave Maisie as a wedding gift the heart that once beat in the chest of James Graham, First Marquis of Montrose? The man who sold it to Tom insisted it was. He was Captain Henry Stuart Wheatley-Crowe, the president and founder of the Royal Stuart Society, but he had not bothered to pass along the findings of two "experts" who had declared that the specimen he was selling was not a human heart at all. In addition, family and historians disagreed on whether the heart had been taken from its gold filigree box at the time of the funeral and buried with his body. Maisie seemed blissfully unaware or willingly blind to the fact that the heart

Three days into their honeymoon, Tom presented Maisie with the promise of a gift, if not unparalleled, then at least rare in the annals of recorded human history: the mummified heart of one of her ancestors, James Graham, the First Marquis of Montrose. Photo from the family collection.

might not be that of her long departed relative, although her suspicions might have been aroused by the fact that the heart arrived wrapped in cotton wool inside a cardboard box, but minus the silver urn into which one of Lady Napier's descendants was said to have transferred it in the late eighteenth century. But Maisie announced, "If it's a fake, it's a beautiful fake,"[329] and then told reporters that she was planning to have the heart cremated and carry out Montrose's final wish to "scatter [his] ashes, strew them in the air."

Later she abandoned plans to cremate it and said she was leaving instructions for it to be sent to St. Giles Cathedral to join the rest of Montrose's remains after her death. Meanwhile, although Maisie had admitted to her friend Patrick Nagle of the *Vancouver Sun* that "I think it's a young bullock's heart. It's too big to be human,"[330] the heart, besides being a morbid curiosity, had developed more value to her as a prop than as an actual relic. It facilitated conversations about her regal Highland ancestors, a subject her children, grandchildren and associates say she never grew tired of telling and retelling. In the end she repatriated the relic to her closest relative in England, Christopher Campbell-Johnston, who wrote in 1989 (many years after Maisie's death) that he had it mounted on a German silver crown that he placed in a black box especially designed for it.[331]

August Jack Khatsahlano, whenever he visited Maisie's apartment, was shocked by both the heart and an Ecuadorian Jivaro shrunken-head medicine stick that was suspended over the couch. Maisie's granddaughter, Maureen Murphy, recalled discussing the latter with her grandmother one night when she was visiting from Seattle:

> Nana made up my bed on the lumpy chesterfield. "Nana, why don't you buy a new one?" I asked, as I tried to find a space between the cushions for my bottom to comfortably rest.
>
> "Because my mother bought it during the Boer War and my father fell asleep on it while reading his books, and because my brothers, your grand uncles who died in the Great War, also slept on it. I could never throw it away... You probably smell the dust it absorbed when it was in the Punjab or some mildew from Hong Kong. This lovely piece," she said while patting the frayed upholstery, "has been toted from one British colony to another. Now go to sleep." She bent to kiss me.
>
> I wasn't ready to shut my eyes... Abruptly I sat up and pointed to a strange leather-bound, bumpy stick dangling high above my improvised bed. "What's this?" I asked, stretching to grab it and study it closer.
>
> "DON'T TOUCH IT!" Nana bellowed. She yelled so loud I was nearly knocked over by the force of her voice. She grabbed my wrist and drew me back under the blankets. "That is a Jivaro medicine stick and those are shrunken heads. They call it the Devil's Wand. Something terrible might happen to you or you might be cursed for life if you touch it. Only special people who are protected by the right kind of spells can safely put a finger on it."
>
> "Can you touch it?" I asked.
>
> "Yes, I have been through a special ceremony."
>
> "Why do you keep it if it belongs to the Devil?"
>
> "August Jack asks the same question." Nana paused. "He wants to paddle me out into the middle of Burrard Inlet and have me drop it overboard. He says it is bad medicine. I'm thinking of doing it. August Jack is a wise shaman. Now go to sleep. You've had a long day, I think."[332]

In December 1951, shortly before Maisie and Tom's wedding, there had been interesting news from Victoria: the provincial government announced that BC's First Nations people could now drink in BC beer parlours. Previously, only Aboriginal people who had foresworn their privileges as wards of the government had been permitted unfettered access to alcohol, while those who remained wards were restricted to bootleggers if they wanted a drink. Maisie's editorial that month did not celebrate this "good news" from Victoria. Instead, she condemned it as being nothing more than a "tiny step."

> We may drink with impunity in the confines of a parlor where beer is sold at a price much higher than obtains in government liquor stores, but we cannot purchase alcoholic beverages from those stores.
>
> We may consume beer from a bottle in a parlor, but if we wish to take a bottle to our homes, we are forbidden.
>
> We may drink, but if we are considered intoxicated, we are liable for arrest on a much more rigid and unfair basis than the white man.[333]

The "tiny step" taken by the government in Victoria was the result of the clause in Bill 79, passed into law on September 4, 1951, that allowed the provinces to loosen alcohol restrictions for First Nations people. Tavern privileges, however, would be all that they could enjoy, with bootleggers being the real winners. They could continue their lucrative trade unabated as the still restrictive covenants of Bill 79 did not allow First Nations to buy alcoholic beverages anywhere but in beer parlours.

The "progressive steps" argument advanced by Minister Harris when Bill 79 was passed was still a number of strides behind the "total freedom" he had originally promised, and the harsh treatment meted out to First Nations people for liquor offences thoroughly offended Maisie's sense of fairness and justice. It was further evidence, she said, of the rampant paternalism that still plagued the government's treatment of First Nations people. Alexander Lester, a journalist with the *American Indian*, reflected this point when he quoted a First Nations Elder, who wisely observed that: "If the white man treated us as men, we would have been men. He treated us like children, so he finds children."[334]

Liquor rights were also on James Maranda's mind when he, a World War II veteran from Squamish, was refused membership in the North Vancouver Army, Navy and Air Force Veterans' Club because he was a First Nations man and the club was not considered a "public place." Club officials stated they were merely following the law since their club was not open to the general public, thus making First Nations veterans ineligible to consume liquor in it. Colonel Donald McGugan, BC's liquor commissioner, agreed with them, referring to the Liquor Act, which defined a public place as "any building, place or passenger conveyance to which the public resort or to which the public are permitted to have access."[335] The attorney general's office also confirmed that such clubs were not considered public places and were therefore off limits to First Nations veterans wanting to consume alcohol there. At this point Attorney General Gordon Wismer himself weighed in with the comment that this interpretation was "absurd."[336]

At a Liberal Party rally at Smithers in May 1952, Chief Harold Sinclair of the Kitwanga reserve delivered a passionate speech against discrimination while at the same time thanking the attorney general for the advancements that he had procured for them:

> First on behalf of the natives of the province I wish to thank the honourable attorney general who has handed us out of an age of darkness and treated us as equal human beings. We are the Canadians of BC and of Canada. We were the first upon the land and along the shores of the Skeena. I am not ashamed to say we were the first here. We have aboriginal rights and we want the rights of citizens also.[337]

After so eloquent a speech, he retired from the meeting, having slept only one hour on the train while travelling to the event, but he went directly to the local jail because no hotel in Smithers would permit him to stay there. The attorney general later found him and arranged for him to stay at a private residence.

As reports began to surface a month after liquor permission was granted, it appeared that consent had been justified. First Nations people were taking their responsibilities seriously, evidenced by comments from B. J. "Benny" Abbott of the Maple Leaf Hotel in Williams Lake as well as from the management of the Ranch Hotel who offered that:

> With regard to the Indian question and the recent change in the laws giving them privileges under the Liquor Laws to enable them to patronize beer parlors the same as other races: during the past month, the operators and employees of the Ranch Hotel have found them to be good customers and citizens and during the month have found the premises just as orderly as they have been in the past. We extend a cordial welcome to all Indian peoples to come and enjoy their glass of cheer in our parlors at all times.[338]

There were still some detractors, however. The proprietor of a hotel in Smithers stood up at a local political meeting and condemned First Nations patrons for their rowdy behaviour, imploring the government to rescind their drinking privileges until they cleaned up their act. Other businesses had similar complaints. But a look at court judgments in Smithers for the previous month revealed that thirty-four First Nations people had been found guilty of liquor offences compared with thirty-one whites, and for the present month, charges had been laid against six First Nations compared to fifteen white people. The attorney general's response was that: "I say as at-torney general of this province that the Indians have behaved in beer parlors much better than some whites, and I promise that as soon as it can be done they will be given all other privileges of the white people."[339] Native Broth-erhood Vice-President Thomas Squinas wrote to the *Voice* to say that: "I am very gratified at this good behaviour as I am sure that this continued good behaviour will prove to everyone that our Native Indians are worthy of all the rights and privileges accorded a full citizen of Canada."[340]

Once Maisie's convalescence from her goiter surgery, the marriage celebra-tions and the controversy over the Montrose heart were over, she began to reconnect with her advocacy projects and the *Native Voice*. Her editorials and submissions had been spotty during this period, and she had often used stories from the national dailies as the paper's voice whenever those stories were both informative and parallel to her own thinking. But she knew that, given the encouragement she was receiving from her subscribers as well as from her associate editors, she must return to writing more of the paper's editorials. In June 1952 Chief Paul Cooke, her Alaskan associate editor, wrote to Maisie to say that he "was happy to see once again an editorial that was signed Maisie Armytage-Moore—that to me is a sign that the editor-in-chief is in good health."[341]

Maisie's editorial that month had been a reminder to First Nations to cast their vote in the provincial election. "We are confident," she wrote, "that of all those eligible to vote on June 12, the Native Indians will most clearly demonstrate that they as a group do not take voting lightly but will in their numbers turn out and help decide the composition of the next provincial gov-ernment."[342] Back in January Guy Williams, president of the new British Co-lumbia Indian Independence Party, although not ready to launch his party, had begun to formulate plans to upset the shaky Liberal/Conservative Coa-lition that had held power in BC since 1941. Even though the coalition held thirty-nine of the forty-eight seats in the legislature, he figured that the First Nations vote alone could significantly influence nine of those seats, and he pointed out to First Nations readers of the *Voice* "how important their vote [could] be."[343] What neither Maisie nor Williams anticipated was the com-plete rout of the coalition on June 12, and the narrow victory of the new Social Credit Party under W. A. C. Bennett over the CCF. It meant that in future negotiations over First Nations rights they would be dealing with an entirely new and unknown entity.

Although the turnout for the provincial vote had demonstrated that the First Nations were taking their new responsibilities seriously, the federal franchise, which represented true Canadian citizenship as well as freedom from wardship, continued to elude them. Despite sophisticated and well-reasoned presentations from First Nations leaders across the country, Bill 79 had fallen victim to the caution of House of Commons members who didn't think that First Nations people were ready for the vote. More than likely, however, MPs had not been sure themselves what an unencumbered federal vote for the First Nations would look like. How would the Elections Act be amended to accommodate it and how could the vote be offered to First Nations people while also protecting their rights? It was such a complex issue that they had backed off to give the problem "further study."

Given this stalemate in Ottawa, it came as a surprise to Maisie and her colleagues that their neighbours to the south were planning to grant Native Americans the very prize that had eluded them. When General Eisenhower, running for president in the fall of 1952, pledged to grant Native Americans full citizenship, the chairman of the Republican National Committee, Arthur E. Summerfield, issued the following statement:

> It is the sincere wish of General Dwight Eisenhower, Republican candidate for President of the United States, that the American Indian be provided every right and privilege of citizenship. For years, the American Indian has been subjected to abuse, hardship [and] discrimination and has been victimized by unfair policies and legislation. The Republican Party, under the leadership of General Eisenhower, will do everything within its power to right these wrongs. It will be our purpose to carry out in full the promises to our Indian friends as our platform has outlined. It is high time the American Indian is consulted in the matter of selection of the Indian Commissioner.[344]

Maisie fired off a telegram to the general:

> We, the publisher and staff of the Native Voice, British Columbia Indian paper, pray for your victory because of your promise of full citizenship to Native Indians.
>
> Your victory strengthens our fight for full citizenship for Native Canadian Indians with protection of their aboriginal rights. God bless you.
>
> (Signed) Publisher of Native Voice.[345]

Eisenhower's response, made through his assistant, Sherman Adams, succinctly thanked Maisie for her "thoughtfulness in communicating with him."[346] Eisenhower proved true to his word when he signed Bill H. R. 1063 in October 1953, ending firearms and liquor restrictions for Native Americans. Although several states protested that it would contravene existing laws and treaties, Eisenhower responded that "I have signed it because its basic purpose represents still another step in granting complete political equality to all Indians in our nations."[347]

Meanwhile, Maisie had wasted no time renewing the discussion in Canada. In bold capitals she appealed to her friends in the November 1952 issue of the *Voice*:

CALLING ALL INDIANS OF CANADA: NOW IS THE HOUR TO HIT WHILE THE IRON IS HOT AND UNITE TO FIGHT FOR FULL CITIZENSHIP WITH PROTECTION OF OUR AB-ORIGINAL RIGHTS.

Friends of the Indians, Awake! Friends of the Indians, Unite and Lend us your vote. What about the Indian? Isn't it more important that he should live, too, and decently, that all discrimination should stop, that we should have a say in the making of the laws we live and are punished under?

Indians are the real and only Canadians. This is OUR COUNTRY. The fish, the furs and land all belong to us.

You claim no taxation without representation? Still we are taxed and punished and live under the laws that you made and in which we have no say. Are there two kinds of laws, one for so-called whites and one for the so-called colored people?

Now is the time for action. If you are sincere, LEND US YOUR VOTE. There are approximately 30,000 Natives in British Columbia alone. Less than half of them have a provincial vote. NONE have a federal vote. We want that federal vote WITHOUT BARTER and at the same time protect our aboriginal rights and lands. So, if you white friends are sincere, lend us your VOTE.

Look at it this way:

Say you give us five votes for each Indian. That will give us 150,000 votes more than we would have if we ourselves voted. Come to our help or "forever more hold thy peace." Now is the time and the hour to start supporting us in our fight for equality. Let us hear from you. Write Ottawa. Let's start fighting, planning.

We feel the pangs of hunger just as you do. We feel pain just as you do. We suffer blood, sweat and tears, just as you do. We get tired. We get sick. We get hungry. We sorrow over the loss of our loved ones and see them ill and dying, just as you do. Our sons go to war and fight for Canada, and many have died. Yet unless these sons renounce their rights, leave their homes and loved ones, they cannot enjoy the privilege of full citizenship.[348]

Maisie had the bit between her teeth again and wouldn't let go until she had achieved one of the most important hurdles of her life's agenda: the federal franchise. It would not be an easy fight.

8—BUSINESS AS USUAL

The Native Voice was not only a forum for fierce political debate and a pipeline for communicating personal information such as marriages, births, deaths and other significant events pertinent to its readers. Maisie also published stories, starting with her parents' adventures, and in the February 1953 edition Constance Cox revisited Maisie's mother's 1912 journey to the Groundhog country of Northern BC. Known there as the "Lady With the Strong Words," Amy Ellen Campbell-Johnston had not only survived perilous journeys that would have killed lesser mortals, but she had thrived on and written down the First Nations stories and described the cultures with which she came into contact. But more importantly, the *Voice* had become a register of First Nations history, beginning with Big White Owl's stirring account of the Delaware people. This was followed in September 1951 with the first instalment of Newell E. Collins' long saga of the great Shawnee Chief, Tecumseh, a story that did not end until after Collins' death, with the final instalment appearing in the December 1959 edition.

In introducing Collins and his subject to readers of the *Voice*, Big White Owl wrote that he was an "author, lecturer, archaeologist, friend to Indians, distinguished gentleman."[349] He had grown up in the town of Redford, Michigan, which eventually became a suburb of Detroit. Collins' father had befriended local Native Americans there, and the respected Native American leader Shop-ne-gan had often been a dinner guest at the Collins' home. As a result, young Newell became enamored with everything Native American and spent the rest of his life studying and writing about the great leader, Tecumseh.

And this is where the interests of Big White Owl and Collins had intersected. Tecumseh had been killed in the Battle of Moraviantown on October 5, 1813, and had been secretly buried nearby; Big White Owl was born nearby at the Moravian of the Thames Reserve and throughout his life had advocated tirelessly for a memorial to recognize the great Shawnee Chief's contribution towards the founding of the nation. Tecumseh "was a man of high ideals and courage and no Canadian more deserves a life-sized statue in bronze,"[350] Big White Owl wrote.

Acquiring the story of Tecumseh for publication in the *Voice* was something of a coup, as was the story of Crazy Horse, the Oglala Lakota Chief who was one of the architects of Lieutenant Colonel George Armstrong Custer's defeat at the Battle of Little Bighorn. It was the first time the story, as related by Chief Crazy Horse to his sister, Pretty Straight Legs, had been revealed to anyone outside his immediate descendants, and in May 1955 Maisie wrote about the paper's good fortune in obtaining it from Cha-la-nung, grandnephew of Chief Crazy Horse and grandson of Pretty Straight Legs:

> It is with considerable pride that the *Native Voice* wishes to announce commencing in July the publication of a story which we are certain will achieve a high distinction in the field of American literature as it relates to the Native people. It is the story of Chief Crazy Horse, noted Indian military strategist who planned the Custer massacre.

Prior to receipt of the story, Maisie had carried on a correspondence with a Cheyenne Elder named Ee-a-sa-ta (Short Big Talk), who had held the great Dakota chief while he lay dying. Crazy Horse had suffered a bayonet wound inflicted by a military guard after he allegedly resisted imprisonment at Camp Robinson in present-day Nebraska on September 5, 1877.

"Good friend Maisie," Ee-a-sa-ta wrote, "I am good happy with you, much you give me in your paper. I am old and dry like leaves on snow. Soon I die. I am what white man says with years of full one hundred... Crazyhorse when he die in arms of me [say] 'My blood is gone, my people are dead with war of white man.' ... I say with him the same words, 'The good of our blood they do not know, and tears there were many in us.' Then he sleep with this bad dream."[351]

Cha-la-nung, content that he had the blessing of Chief Crazy Horse's old friend to release the story, wrote to Maisie to say that:

> If readers of the Native Voice and you, Mrs. Hurley, would like to read this story, I will give you permission to print it. It is long and will cover many months to tell. But, it is the truth of my people. In it are the words as they were spoken by my people. This is a story the white man does not know... I do not know how to express my gratitude to you for doing so much for the Indian. You have a great spirit in you that will never die. I do not know how old you are, but I feel you will live for many years that you can continue to do your wonderful work."[352]

However, Cha-la-nung made it abundantly clear in a subsequent letter to Maisie that the *Voice* would be the only place that the story of Crazy Horse would be published:

> The story of Crazy Horse was not intended for all the public to read. It was given to you for my people, the Indians. It was meant to help them, to give them the eyes with which they could see their fathers as they actually were, and not the savages and pagans the history

books say... Understand, dear friend, why this story cannot be re-printed, why it is never to be used for personal gain, not ours, not anyone's.[353]

And Maisie honoured Cha-la-nung's request that the story would only be printed in the *Native Voice*.

British Columbia, of course, had its own set of fearless leaders, and the *Voice* reported on their exploits regularly. One of them was MLA Frank Calder who had chosen to take the battle to the political arena. He was an innovative thinker who was not only representing his Atlin constituents but taking on responsibility for the province's First Nations population as a whole. On February 16, 1953, he bravely scolded the MLAs assembled in the BC Legislature, telling them that the provincial Indian Affairs Committee wasn't working and that Indian Affairs should be transferred from federal to provincial jurisdiction: "Indian problems should be brought to the floor of the House and discussed along with those of the white man" so that the Aboriginal population would not have to depend so much on a committee "which is outside this House." He protested that the committee was not reporting all its investigations in its official reports[354] before cheekily advising the speaker that even the legislature itself stood on First Nations ground, land for which no First Nation had ever received a cent. He also stated that there was no mention in the Indian Act of beer being the only beverage First Nations people were permitted to consume, and that the wording of the act actually read "consumption in a public place," which allowed leeway for Indians to consume other liquors.[355] "He said he was sure Victoria could do a better job than Ottawa in dealing with BC Indians"[356] and offered the suggestion that if First Nations people were permitted to drink on reserves, a solution to the policing problem would be to encourage them to join the RCMP so that they might police their own people. He also recommended a form of self-government and said that a portion of the province's sales tax revenues could be diverted to administer it.

Reports on First Nations individuals such as Calder kept *Voice* subscribers excited and engaged, because they were eager to see actual progress being made for the First Nations. But Maisie wanted more from the paper, which was now in its seventh year, and she encouraged letters and articles from south of the border as well, since the political scene there was also heating up. Native American problems mirrored First Nations problems here—the twin issues of discrimination and assimilation being common to both—and solutions for one might apply to the other. And American subscribers were almost more effusive in their support of the paper than their Canadian brothers and sisters were.

So, perhaps it came as no surprise to Maisie when a correspondent wrote from Trail, BC, in February 1953 to complain that there was too much American content in the paper. In fact, that month there had been only five articles from and dealing with the US out of a total of twenty-five. Another subscriber observed there should not be any division between the countries at all, given that First Nations people once roamed the continent unimpeded by borders, which were only implemented by the white man. A month later two more correspondents waded into the controversy—both from the US. One said they were tired of hearing the same old argument, while the other, after describing the *Native Voice* as unique, "being a paper for and about Indians," then continued:

> And all Indians are American Indians, whether they live in Canada, the US, Mexico or South America. Everyone born or naturalized in this western hemisphere is an American, regardless of what country he lives in. And as far as there being Canadian or US Indians, there is the Jay Treaty to stipulate that there is no such thing as a border between Canada and the US as far as Indians are concerned.

This correspondent also mentioned that the argument wasn't one-sided as he had heard Iroquois people from New York State refer to First Nations people visiting from Canada as "Canadians" in a tone suggesting they were "foreigners," despite them sharing a common lineage. He concluded his letter with:

> So I beg of you keep your editorial policy on the same level, printing all Indian news as you get it, regardless of the source, so long as it is interesting reading and true... Your paper is read from beginning to end, every word by more people than you realize as each copy passes through several hands around here. God bless you and your fine work! Robert Gabor "Sagotaoala."[357]

The *Voice* also continued to faithfully report Native Brotherhood news, with convention news receiving special attention. At the twenty-first annual convention held in Hazelton in May 1953 the dominant issue was taxation. Reverend Dr. Peter Kelly, still the legislative chair, advised that the Brotherhood was prepared to take the argument all the way to the Supreme Court if necessary. He informed the assembly that the First Nations in BC were paying millions of dollars in income tax without any representation, and he referred them to the agreement made in 1871 at the time of the union between the province and Canada wherein:

> Article 13 of the terms of Union stated BC would set aside lands for the benefit of the Indians and would follow a policy as liberal as the policy of the colonial government. From time immemorial, Indians were free from taxation, and that right has never been abrogated. The

Indian is still not a citizen in this land. Further, although Natives secured the provincial vote, they are still being denied the federal vote without signing away [their] rights and exemptions on the reserve. Other people come from foreign lands and after only a short period get full rights, but the Indian is still denied his primary rights.[358]

Maisie attended the convention but had to return to Vancouver early for urgent business and so missed the stirring tribute to her and the *Voice* delivered by Paul Mason from Kitkatla.

This paper is one I am very proud of. Why? Because it is going forth and I am sure this little paper is going out into the world and covering the world. A lot of our white people are reading our paper today and many of our problems have been solved through our *Native Voice*. We owe credit to our dear lady, Mrs. Maisie Hurley, who has devoted her valued time towards the efforts of this little paper. God bless Mrs. Hurley.[359]

Brotherhood president Chief William Scow was noticeably absent from the convention for he was on his way to England to witness the coronation of Elizabeth II on June 2, thanks to the hard work of Guy Williams and Tom Howarth of the Brotherhood in procuring an invitation for him. He carried with him an "Indian-cured" spring salmon as a gift to the new queen from British Columbia's First Nations. The chief had been assigned one of the coveted seats in Westminster Abbey to watch the event, but while in London he was also to give several radio interviews and visit the gravesite of Captain George Vancouver.

Reporters covering the coronation gushed about meeting Chief Gla-Whay-Agliss and Maisie collected some of their published comments in time for the June issue of the *Native Voice*:

"In traditional robes and thunderbird headdress he attended the coronation as president and representative of Canada's largest Indian organization, the Native Brotherhood of British Columbia."

"After the ceremony he intends to pay official visits to the principal cities of the British Isles."

"He speaks as polished English as any American professional man. To this American ear he speaks a whale of a lot better English than these Englishmen over here."

"A modern Indian at the coronation, he counters the old-fashioned idea of the red man as an aborigine."

"As Pacific Coast Indians, Chief Scow's people always have preferred lodges to teepees. In London he's settling for a room in the Waldorf at $16 a day."

Chief William Scow (Chief Gla-Whay-Agliss) dressed in his ceremonial costume for Queen Elizabeth II's coronation in London, England, 1953. The Chief was accorded a seat in Westminster Abbey for the event. Photo from the family collection.

"Never have I felt so strongly ties that bind my people to the Commonwealth," Chief Scow told reporters elegantly after being the first First Nations individual from Canada ever to sit in Westminster Abbey for a coronation. It wasn't the glitter and jewels that awed him, he said, but the religion and deep dignity. "As I sat there in the Abbey I felt that there might be hope now for a return to religion. That is what my people need. The Queen's example will be a great help to them."[360]

The next day Chief Scow visited the modest gravesite of Captain George Vancouver in the churchyard of St. Peter's Church in Petersham in the London borough of Richmond-on-Thames. Reporters who followed him described the scene:

> An Indian brave, resplendent in bright cerise robe heavily covered with blue stones and wearing his chief's headdress of ermine tails was an unusual sight in this quiet English churchyard. But to Chief William Scow of Alert Bay, representing the Native Brotherhood of BC, it was fitting that he should pay his respects to the man who gave his name to the land his ancestors roamed.[361]

Chief Mathias Joe of the Capilano band had also been invited to the coronation, although he had not rated a seat in the abbey. Before flying across the Atlantic, he had taken a hotel room in Toronto but couldn't bear to mess up the "pretty bed" so laid his bedroll out on the floor to sleep. Once over Lake Superior he was invited into the cockpit of the Trans-Canada Airlines airliner and for a minute took control of the aircraft, later recounting how powerful it was. He eased back on the controls and the aircraft climbed "5,000 feet right through clouds," he recalled. On coronation day he walked the five-mile parade route in the rain wearing his ceremonial regalia, beating his drum to the obvious delight of thousands of cheering fans lining the streets.

Unfortunately, he arrived too late to join Chief Scow for the trip to Captain George Vancouver's grave, and the missed opportunity was viewed as a slight at home despite the chief's explanation that it had been the result of a simple misunderstanding. Andrew Paull, grand chief and president of the North American Indian Brotherhood of Canada, stated that "British rule in BC began on the shores of the Capilano Indian Reserve and Chief Capilano helped to establish British rule here,"[362] and he demanded that officials take Chief Mathias Joe to the gravesite "in full ceremonial dress, where he could sing an Indian song of peace, because it was with peace his ancestors met Captain Vancouver in 1792."[363]

Several months after Chief Scow's return to BC, he was surprised to receive an invitation to a three-day conference convened in Ottawa by the Honourable

Walter E. Harris, Minister of Citizenship and Immigration, to update the government on how Bill 79, the new Indian Act, was being perceived by the country's First Nations. Scow joined the Reverend Dr. Peter Kelly, and the two arrived in Ottawa for the opening of the conference on October 28. Despite loud protests when the bill was first passed, all nineteen of the inter-provincial First Nations conference delegates now felt that they and the country's approximate 130,000 First Nations people appeared generally satisfied with it.

Scow and Kelly, however, not wanting to waste an opportunity, made several recommendations: 1) that tax exemptions under Section 86 of the Indian Act be broadened to include those First Nations fishermen whose income was derived solely from fishing; 2) that recommendations be made for the compulsory medical treatment of First Nations with infectious diseases; 3) that the federal government leave liquor administration to the provincial governments; 4) that the number of day schools for First Nations children be increased; 5) that the waiver of exemptions in exchange for the federal vote be eliminated; and 6) that more health and welfare benefits flow to First Nations. Unfortunately, Scow, Kelly and the rest of the delegates were informed that any changes would rest with Parliament.

Afterwards, both BC delegates remarked that there appeared to be much more inter-provincial co-operation between First Nations groups now. When representatives from Saskatchewan, for instance, made a recommendation, it was supported by the other delegates. This co-operation was so unexpected that it was suggested that perhaps it was time to establish an inter-provincial body to advocate for all First Nations in Canada, but at the same time it was noted that First Nations groups across the nation had such vastly different problems that any inter-provincial body might be cumbersome. In BC, for example, very few treaties had been signed and the troublesome McKenna-McBride Commission, now some four decades old, was still preventing resolution of land rights problems.

MLA Frank Calder wanted to know why the Doukhobors, who were known to blow up bridges and burn down schools, were appeased and accommodated, while the province's First Nations, who were peaceful and orderly, were ignored, and he expounded on this in the legislature when introducing a challenge to the provincial government to be "bigger" than the restrictive covenants of the McKenna-McBride Agreement. His comments came in response to the situation at the old settlement of Metlakatla where the people were planning to adopt Canadian citizenship en masse. The federal government welcomed their decision, and as a result the people of this modern settlement had thought life would continue there uninterrupted. However, the provincial government, referencing the "extinction clause" that was part of the old agreement made between Premier McBride and Ottawa, refused to forego the right to expropriate their land. Calder, who had considered the

Metlakatla example to be a possible solution to the overall First Nations land question, was saddened by the government's attitude. He said: "The province, therefore, should adopt a more gracious attitude to this problem and aim toward the building of a model Indian community that could be an example for other villages that may wish to make a similar step."[364]

In October 1953, Maisie introduced two new associate editors to the paper: "Kitty" Carpenter of Bella Bella and Chief James Sewid, a fisherman from Alert Bay. Carpenter was a dynamo, having just concluded a term as president of the Native Sisterhood. She was heavily involved with the establishment of teenage groups in her home community to keep young people on the straight and narrow, and she had helped to organize special weekly meetings, one each for the educational, recreational, social and spiritual benefit of her young charges. She was also a tireless advocate for women working in the canneries where economic and social progress had been slow to catch up to mainstream society, evidenced by the discriminatory signs on the women's washrooms at the Namu cannery on the central BC coast that read: "Natives Only" and "Whites Only."[365] Even though Alfred Scow had raised the issue of these signs with the cannery's management a year earlier, nothing had been done about it until he showed up the next year with a member of the union shop steward's committee. At that point, management finally conceded that the signs might very well be discriminatory and permitted them to be changed.

Chief Sewid was formerly the head chief of the village of Alert Bay. He was originally from Gilford Island and a member of one of the four groups that had made the seasonal journeys between Gilford and Kingcome Inlet. A deeply religious man, in addition to serving as the rector's warden of Christ Church at Alert Bay, he led both the senior and junior choirs in their native tongue. In an "open letter" addressed to readers of the December 1953 issue of the *Voice,* the chief extolled the virtues and value of the paper. Then he wrote:

> Without this "Voice" our problems would never have been heard. It has carried on and kept alive the voices of our great leaders who have passed on.
>
> Alfred Adams, our late president, travelled from one end of British Columbia to another bringing hope and courage and unity to our people when they were in danger of dying out. The late Mrs. Constance Cook, the late Chief Calder of the Naas, and many other great founders of the Native Brotherhood of British Columbia, for years worked for the advancement of our people and have given them so much; all this the *Voice* has publicized. This *Voice* is the official Voice of the Native Brotherhood of British Columbia. If we lose it, no one

will know of the work we do and no one will hear of the problems of our people. It is thus our duty to support our *Voice*.[366]

A month later similar sentiments were expressed by Alfred Scow, Native Brotherhood business agent, who wanted to know why, given the tremendous success of the paper, that the Native Brotherhood was not making better use of it. He wrote:

> Associated with the *Native Voice* is always the caption: "Official Organ of the Native Brotherhood of BC." This statement is at times questionable. A closer look at the situation reveals that the Native Brotherhood has not made very much use of its official organ.
>
> *The Native Voice* over the past few years has extended its scope practically around the globe. It has gained recognition as our paper. It has given our people some publicity that we would never have received elsewhere. It might be said that to a certain extent the *Native Voice* has contributed to a better understanding on the part of some people with some of the problems our people are faced with. The paper has been an asset to the Organization.[367]

An article on the front page of the same issue highlighted the importance of the paper in airing discriminatory practices. When the proprietor of an auto court at Fort St. James told the participants at a BC Auto Court and Resorts convention that First Nations hunters were indiscriminately killing moose just for their hides, Maisie was thoroughly incensed and told her readers that the auto court proprietor "must very well know" that when First Nations people killed a moose "every bit of meat is eaten and the surplus smoked for winter use" while "the hide is used for moccasins and coats."[368] And Game Commissioner James Cunningham announced that the country did not have enough moose "to allow them to be killed for their hides."[369]

The story had originated with the discovery of several moose carcasses with just the heads removed, the obvious practice of tourist hunters who had no use for anything but the trophies. The proprietor's comments had likely been in direct response to the amount of money in his pocketbook because trophy hunters spent an average of $1,000 per moose kill, while little of the revenue generated by First Nations hunters—a maximum of $20 from moccasin sales—found its way into the pockets of the local resort industry. This was the likely reason for the complaint. The *Voice* editorial that month, which questioned what the tourist hunter did with the meat and hide of his kill, also assured readers that:

> Mrs. Hurley pledged an all-out fight by the *Native Voice* and the backing of the Native Brotherhood of BC Indians. "If you and your organization start robbing the native Canadian of his aboriginal rights

we are going to fight," she said. "Remember, the days of smallpox blankets and long guns are over."

The editorial ended with:

> The Indian hunts for food, the tourist hunter for trophies—such is the "SPORT" of the white man. Did anyone ever hear of an Indian hunting a wee fox with hounds for "sport"? The question is WHO is the "Savage Barbarian"?[370]

Chief Edward Moise John of Fort St. James was astounded that one of his white neighbours could make such an impetuous statement about his people. The *Voice* quoted him as saying, "We have a right to demand that these charges are thoroughly investigated before further proceedings are undertaken, whether legal or otherwise." It was probably Maisie who added the boldface tag to Moise's piece, angrily declaring: "We definitely cannot and will not forfeit our Aboriginal Rights nor submit to the demand of the white man just to satisfy his greed."[371]

Alfred Scow, who was now partway through his legal studies at UBC, took a more conciliatory approach, perhaps presaging his future as a provincial court judge. He suggested that "the situation should be investigated before either side goes off half-cocked,"[372] but he also said that, given the shortage of food in the Interior, "it would seem highly unlikely that such a practice exists among our people." These accusations, he continued, reminded him of the white man's treatment of the buffalo in the previous century where thousands were shot just for the sake of killing them, despite those vast herds representing vital food, lodging and clothing for the First Nations of the plains. "It was said that the intention of those early pioneers was to do away with all Indians or let them die off, as is shown in one of the surviving slogans of the day, 'A good Indian is a dead Indian.'"[373]

Scow, as business agent for the Brotherhood, also announced the appointment of Chief Edward Moise John to represent the organization at the next Provincial Game Convention where it was hoped the issue would be aired. The Chief, who had just been awarded the Coronation Medal for his superb work on the Necoslie (Nak'asdli) Indian Reserve at Fort St. James, was honoured by the appointment, although he expected it to be a controversial meeting. Afterwards, he reported that to his surprise:

> there was not a word said or a statement made in any of the resolutions presented by any of the delegates representing every district in the province which might in any way jeopardize the aboriginal rights of the Native Canadian.
>
> All through the Convention, at no instance had I occasion or reason to protest any of the resolutions or clauses pertaining same.

All resolutions and discussions were for conservation and proper management of fish and game for the benefit of the general public.[374]

But while Chief John was pleased with the results of the Game Convention, he had another and very different complaint to air in the *Voice*: the BC Young Liberal Federation had brashly proclaimed that they were sending a delegation to Ottawa to convince the Senate and House of Commons to abolish reserves. Chief John's anger had more to do with their interference than it did with their message, and he stated that it was up to the First Nations to manage their own affairs. The Young Liberal Federation's idea, however, was not new. Frank Calder was also in favour of doing away with reserves, which he had stated again in the April issue of the *Voice*. "Reserves breed inferiority complexes and sap individual initiative," he wrote, then added that he was also opposed to any further amendments to the Indian Act. "It simply should be eliminated," he declared, so that First Nations people would get equal treatment with whites by being governed by the same legislation that governs white people.[375] (Maisie disagreed and was fairly vocal about it. In a speech in the Indian Council Hall in Sechelt a year later, she said that she "deplored the idea of taking the Indian off the reserve. She said they were not yet ready for this drastic move."[376])

Of course, Minister Harris was not about to do away with reserves or the Indian Act for that matter. In September 1954, the *Voice* told readers that Lehigh Antone of the Oneidas of the Thames had written to Harris, advising him that in view of the possible amendment of the act during this session, "if there must be an Indian Act for the Iroquois, then there should be provisions that provided safeguarding guaranteed rights in accordance with the UNITED NATIONS CHARTER to which CANADA IS A SIGNATORY."[377] Antone reminded the minister that the Oneida had never accepted the Indian Act nor were they consulted about the amendments prior to the passing of Bill 79. Such a plethora of similar complaints were coming to the attention of the Canadian Bar Association from right across the country that a Regina lawyer, M. C. Shumiatcher, introduced a resolution to have the association's civil liberties section examine whether First Nations civil rights were being trampled upon. Shumiatcher said:

> We've treated Indians as children for so long they are going to remain children forever unless there is a radical change in our attitude toward them… Treaty Indians are badly off… The non-treaty Indians are worse off… The general examination should include voting and liquor laws as they apply to Indians and also property laws.[378]

Meanwhile, although the BC government had taken advantage of changes in the Indian Act to permit First Nations people to drink in licenced establishments back in December 1951, this change had apparently remained one of the best kept secrets in the northern half of the province. At a convention for provincial magistrates held at the Hotel Vancouver in May 1954, Stipendiary Magistrate L. G. Saul told the assembled body that "Indians will be kept out of beer parlor(s) at Burns Lake for their own good." He was challenged during the question period by UBC professor Dr. Harry Hawthorn who asked him how he could do that when it was perfectly legal for First Nations to drink in those establishments. Saul had replied, "What's the difference [between] interdicting them one at a time or all at once?"[379]

Alfred Scow later commented:

> He appears to have been acting as a legislator rather than as a judge. The normal function of a judge is to take every case on its own facts and then to apply the law. On the question of legislation, his function is to interpret it, not to make it... Our people are not asking for special beer parlour privileges and we have no objection to being punished for doing wrong. But to be deprived of a privilege for the alleged wrongs of someone else is beyond all reason and on top of that very undemocratic. We hope the findings of the Attorney General disproves the reports we have read on this case and that the established common law rules are still being applied in every court.[380]

Maisie declared that "there are about 2,250 Indians in the Burns Lake area, and only about 50 of them cause any trouble with their drinking. Why should they all be punished for the deeds of the few who are a disgrace to their tribe?"[381]

When Saul was questioned later by reporters, he dug his hole even deeper when he replied unabashedly that "We have a different brand of Indians up there. They're a lower type than you have around Vancouver. When they were given drinking privileges, it was like taking a person out of darkness and putting him into the light."[382] Saul believed that his solution was justified since it had been endorsed by the RCMP, local hotel-keepers and the town's parish priest. Andrew Paull, who was predictably furious, demanded "that Saul be fired for his statement... I'm going to write to the attorney general, asking that his authority be taken away."[383]

Less than a year later, the topic of First Nations people and alcohol was introduced into the legislature when MLA Irvine Corbett (Social Credit for Yale) stood up to complain that in his riding the current liquor legislation where it applied to First Nations people was causing them to lie down on the railway tracks dead drunk to be killed by trains. Corbett went on to say that he was opposed to selling liquor to them, offering as an example a tour he had taken with a magistrate from the Interior where he had "seen Indians lying in the gutter outside beer parlors." Calder, who was generally calm and rational, became apoplectic and responded that his people were the victims of the government's liquor restrictions. "I don't think you are very proud of your skidroads with dope addicts and God-knows-what-else happening there," he said and added, "Clean up your own backyard!"[384]

Maisie, gathering more information on this topic from Vancouver newspapers, told her readers that:

> The newspaper account headed: "Drunk Indians Commit 'Mass Suicide'—MLA" went on to report that "Mr. Corbett told the House about how little Indian children stand around entrances to beer saloons all evening, no matter how cold it is, waiting for their parents who are inside getting "likkered up." Corbett alleged that one couple left their children at home and went on a three-day bender, returning to find they had died of starvation. On further enquiry, the Indian Department could find no evidence of startling "mass suicides" by Natives from drink and have not been able to trace any family who left their children to starve to death while their parents were away drinking.[385]

Even after Corbett tried to explain himself, Maisie remained furious. She wrote:

> Unfortunately for Mr. Corbett, he found out too late that the Natives were not down-trodden, helpless people whom he could use as a political football to throw at Mr. Calder, our beloved Native MLA who is fighting not for just liquor but for our RIGHT TO MAKE OUR OWN DECISIONS as to whether or not we want liquor.
>
> Brothers and Sisters, we are now on the WARPATH. Come and join us! Protect your lands and protect your rights by UNITING as one strong body, and we will show any... attackers they are up against an unbeatable body of determined people who will fight with the strength of righteousness.[386]

Corbett's story was also refuted by a bartender who told the *Hope Standard* that the MLA's statement was a blemish on the whole community. He said that his First Nations clients were no more inclined towards that type of behaviour than were his white clients. "According to you, it's very common to see a drunk Indian lying on the highway, but I have yet to see one. I serve beer to Indians every day and I found them obedient and orderly so far."[387]

Canada's First Nations were not only battling social injustice at this time, they even had to put up with an attack on totem poles mounted by Harold Weir in his *Vancouver Sun* newspaper column. In July 1954 he wrote:

I had no intention in the world of opening my big mouth again about this abominable totem obsession in British Columbia. I reasoned that if the majority of people wanted to plaster the province with these ugly and meaningless objects and label stadiums with the name, it was not my affair… I have heard it said, with what truth I do not know, that even the legends connected to these things are fakes and have no legitimate place in ancient Indian lore.

He added that he was just reflecting the opinion of his readers when he wrote that:

If these horrible creations have any historical significance at all, it is the significance of depravity, the identification of men with animals, the worship of animals. For that is exactly what totemism means among aboriginal people.[388]

Maisie was livid and fired off a torrid letter to Weir, accompanied by one from Constance Cox and another from Harold Sinclair, the district vice-president of the Native Brotherhood for Skeena. The *Sun* refused to publish any of them, citing space considerations, but Maisie offered space in the *Voice* to air the collective response to Weir's column. Her own letter to Weir made it clear that:

Your article on totems has given great offence to a decent kindly people… It distresses me that you should have taken that unnecessary line re totems offending people who do not, unless attacked, like to hurt anyone's feelings.[389]

Constance Cox set Weir right when she wrote that:

The carving on the totem poles records their history, their courage in war, their disasters, their famines and their legends. Each clan has its own totem pole. Many European countries have hideous carvings to represent their history. Why pick on the Indians, belittling their sacred totem poles?[390]

Chief Harold Sinclair used Weir's own logic when he asked him why animals were so objectionable to him when the "government uses the beaver on its crest, Her Majesty the lion and the unicorn on her crest, and more than half the British crests have animals on them."[391] And Maisie, who could not let the matter rest there, accused the *Vancouver Sun* of restricting freedom of the press for not publishing their rebuttals and then, perhaps to rub Weir's nose in it, chose a photo of the stand of totem poles at the University of British Columbia for the September cover of the *Voice*.

Of course, Weir's columnar rant only served to hoist him on his own petard as references to totem poles began popping up everywhere. Frank Calder, not to waste an opportunity, "charmed the House by presenting a rare totem carved by a Haida Indian, J. Hans, from black argillite to the premier for presentation to Lieutenant-Governor Clarence Wallace."[392] This was just before Maisie presented a totem to Calder himself on behalf of the *Native Voice* for the stellar work he was performing on behalf of the province's First Nations. Calder promised to place the polished yellow cedar thunderbird and beaver totem carved by the renowned artist Ellen Neel on his desk in the legislature for all to admire.

Towards the end of 1954 Maisie accompanied Tom on a trip north to Prince George where he was to defend two First Nations men who had been charged with manslaughter. From there she continued west to visit her adopted son, Dick Patrick, at Vanderhoof. "I had a hard time bringing my Dick down to earth as his wife had just presented him with his first daughter, Maisie. Mother and Maisie are doing well," she wrote of the baby who was named after her. Tragically the child died soon after, prompting Maisie's 12-year-old granddaughter, Moira Kennedy, to write a small poem in her honour; it was printed in the next issue of the *Voice*.

Forty miles north, at Fort St. James, Maisie visited her other adopted son, David Benoit, who had returned safely from Korea and was now hard at work. "It was a happy surprise to see my two dear boys again and they seemed happy to see me,"[393] she wrote. She returned briefly to Vancouver and then was off to the twenty-second annual Native Brotherhood conference, which opened on November 17, 1954, in Bella Bella. As expected, Chief William Scow stepped down as president to make room for Robert Clifton, son of Brotherhood co-founder, Chief Heber Clifton of Hartley Bay, one of the highest-ranking chiefs on the coast. The younger Clifton, having married Comox Chief Andy Frank's sister, had moved there from Hartley Bay. He was an ideal candidate to take on the leader's role because he was fully endorsed by Scow, who reminded the convention that his own "father and Heber Clifton were blood brothers and that he couldn't imagine a finer man to take over than Bob."[394] Alfred Scow also left his position as business agent to resume his law studies at UBC, and Ed Nahanee replaced him in that job.

When Superintendent Anfield took his turn at the microphone at the convention, he spoke about the current state of First Nations education, which was still problematic, he said, because there was a shortage of teachers in white schools, so it was proving even more difficult than usual to sign up teaching staff for isolated reserve schools, and he encouraged young First Nations men and women to consider teaching as a profession. But he did have some good news: tuberculosis was now under control to the point that sanitoriums had many empty beds. "Indian health is one of the bright spots in Canada," he added. Then he told the meeting that there was still one fundamental problem with the Brotherhood: "The individual who does not do his share." The organization, he said, "cannot be strong unless its little branches are strong."[395] It was his opinion that the problem was at the grassroots level and he urged each branch to tackle its own problems.

The new Brotherhood president, who was expected to revitalize the organization, had been listening intently to the calls for greater involvement in improvement of living conditions for Aboriginal people. Robert Clifton, whom Maisie described as "a kindly, humble Christian gentleman,"[396] was well-known and liked in both the northern and southern parts of the province, and he wasted little time in getting involved in his new job. One of his first orders of business had to do with the *Voice*. "Realizing the importance of an official voice, the president intends to build up and really make the *Native Voice* a strong official organ of the Brotherhood," Maisie wrote. Clifton also promised the convention that he would "pay a visit to every branch of the organization and also to the Inland Natives to tell them that their problems are the Brotherhood's problems and that we must unite into one strong organization for the improvement of conditions and the protection of our aboriginal rights."[397]

Before the convention closed, MLA Frank Calder spoke of the need to unite all First Nations organizations across Canada under one umbrella, perhaps to be called the National Congress of Canadian Indians, modelled after the National Congress of American Indians. And he expounded yet again on his belief that only a national body of this kind could produce the united effort, harmony, co-operation, strength and unity that were needed when presenting First Nations problems to the federal government.

In her New Year's 1955 address to her readers, Maisie saw great things ahead for the First Nations and for the *Voice*. Her editorial was headlined: We Look to New Year with Utmost Confidence.

> It is one of the anomalies of our time that while expressions of support for the underprivileged of the world abound in the halls of our legislators, the Native of Canada and the United States must wring even the smallest concession from reluctant governments with the greatest of effort.
>
> In fact, there is not the slightest doubt that in 1953 legislative steps taken in the United States [Maisie was referencing Congress's Termination of Reservations Resolution of August 1953] particularly are directed toward removing the dwindling resources of the Indian people at a minimum cost, despite their protection by treaty.
>
> The best method of defending property and other rights of the Native, regardless of how meagre they are, is to continually seek

better conditions and increased rights. By that we mean such things as the federal vote in Canada, complete protection of aboriginal rights, together with a host of much needed legislative corrections which would place the Native Indian on a footing of social and economic equality with his fellow countrymen.[398]

Early in the spring of 1955, Chief Scow resigned his position on the board of the *Native Voice* as well, and despite Maisie's occasionally testy and sometimes strained relationship with the Chief, she praised him for his many years of dedicated service. "We will always honour Chief William Scow as one of us,"[399] Maisie told readers of the April issue of the *Voice*. She then reminded readers that when he had taken on the presidency, children attending reserve schools had been receiving only two-and-a-half to three hours of schooling a day, and due to lack of funding they had to perform chores during part of that time—girls helping with the cooking and cleaning and boys with the firewood and maintenance. Grade 6 was the best a reserve child could hope for in those days, and high school and university were impossible dreams. Tuberculosis had been rampant and discrimination was especially vile. Aboriginal seniors were receiving just $4.80 a month in government pensions with some of them succumbing to starvation and others to the indifference of officialdom, while allowances for children and pensions for the infirm and the blind were not even on the horizon.

In April 1955, during a meeting in the Nimpkish Hall at Alert Bay, the new Brotherhood president, Robert Clifton, spoke of the vision of the founders of the Brotherhood, men like the late Alfred Adams and his own father, Heber Clifton. According to a story in the May issue of the *Voice*, he also told his audience that:

> he dreamed of an organization that would unite all their people in an effort to secure their rightful recognition... Mr. Clifton listed many of the gains made through the efforts of the Brotherhood in recent years. Family allowances, old age pensions, the right to vote, beer parlour privileges and greatly improved educational facilities.[400]

And yet, he said, in spite of the role First Nations advocates were playing in these improvements, there was little or no recognition of their efforts. This had been dramatically demonstrated when the new integrated Alert Bay School, built to accommodate 100 First Nations children and 80 white children, was opened to great fanfare earlier that spring.

> There was much talk of brotherly love and how "this magnificent new school was one where the two races will live and learn together"... Yet in spite of the majority of Indian children and all the talk of brotherhood and "living and learning together," there was not one Indian on

the platform with the Honorable Ray Williston, provincial minister of Education. The dozen invited to the platform were all simon-pure white... Chief William Scow, the distinguished leader of his people, attended. He had to sit back in the audience.[401]

Despite her earnest endeavours, Maisie's desire for the paper to be larger and gain a broader circulation was being eroded. First Nations papers were popping up in the United States, perhaps in recognition that the pen is truly mightier than the sword. The *Amerindian, Smoke Signals* and *The American Indian Hobbyist* were now in direct competition with the *Native Voice* south of the border, although none of them appeared to be interested in the Canadian market. But far from being worried about the competition, Maisie told her readers that she was encouraged by it:

The more printed about the Indians of the Americas, the sooner the real truth about our fine people will be known. We are tired of the lies and vicious pictures that have been painted in the past about the Noble Race, the first inhabitants of the Americas.

Only by writing and telling the facts will the real truth be known how the Natives, tortured, robbed, cheated, but undaunted, have lived through the black cruel years to come into their own, strong with faith in their Heavenly Father unshaken—the world's most noble people. The greatest story since the world began. Maybe someday they will live to send out Native missionaries to make Christians of the White man.

INDIANS UNITE AS ONE GREAT RACE OF THE AMERICAS.[402]

9—THE RUSH TO INTEGRATE

In July 1955, Maisie and Tom Hurley were feted at a celebratory sit-down dinner at the Ferguson Point Tea House in Stanley Park. The event was totally unexpected for the Brotherhood and Sisterhood executives had organized it without the Hurleys catching wind of their preparations. As Brotherhood President Robert Clifton helped Tom into the "magnificent Indian sweater" with the shamrock design over the heart that had been designed and knit by Mrs. Lena Newman, Tom's eyes brimmed with tears, and for once this eloquent master of the quip was bereft of words. All he could do was kiss Mrs. Newman's hand before he finally found his strangled voice and muttered his effusive thanks. Maisie was equally taken aback. The *Voice* reported that "Maisie Hurley, whose work among the Native people of the province is too well-known to require elaboration, was equally unprepared and almost speechless (but not quite) when she was presented with an exquisite pair of Haida hand-carved raven earrings."[403]

At the Hurleys' request, no notes were taken at this event, but Maisie told those gathered at the teahouse that the celebration was adequate thanks for the decades of hard work on behalf of their friends. "Tom and I feel that you, the Native people, have made us very rich and happy in your loving friendship," she said. "All we can say is that from the bottoms of our hearts we thank you. You have made us very happy. God bless you all."[404]

Ed Nahanee, the Brotherhood's business agent, regaled the guests on this occasion with stories from the recent BC Game Commission convention where he had been invited to speak about the First Nations view of the current game laws. This convention had been a first for Nahanee, so he had wasted no time in accepting the invitation. His audience included people from Washington, Oregon, Montana, Idaho and the three western provinces, and he began by telling them of his childhood:

> I will always consider it a piece of good fortune to have arrived in the world in the late nineties when game was plentiful, and at no time was it necessary for anyone to go too far afield in order to get a good vitamin-enriched food supply, and by using this as our lifeline, there was no need for Salk Vaccine.

Recounting his first hunting trip at the age of 10, on which he bagged a duck with his father's favourite musket—without his permission—he had his audience in stitches. "Game was so plentiful," he recalled, that it was common to see "deer, grouse, ducks and snipe hanging in the market places in Vancouver, for sale at the usual Saturday afternoon bargain prices."[405] Then he had explained that hunting privileges for band families had traditionally been divided territorially and no one could hunt on another family's preserve without their express permission.

> The government does not recognize these age-old customs—that is, the right of every family to hunt and fish in the territories allotted to them originally by the tribe... So the answer lies with you. Are the game being benefitted by keeping the Natives out of the woods and making room for the cougar and wolf? Are game being protected by prosecuting the Native? This is the thought that I am leaving with you.[406]

Nahanee knew that First Nations hunters and fishermen who were still following those now-proscribed traditions were frequently butting heads with fish guardians and game officers. Where once they could hunt and fish at will in their assigned regions, now there were laws and regulations restricting them. The previous year, after a 70-year-old infirm Port Alberni First Nations Elder asked two young men in his community to harvest a few male red spring salmon so that he might enjoy the taste of smoked salmon again, fish guardians caught them red-handed spearing the fish in the traditional manner. Despite arguing that they were just observing their food-fishing right in their own territory, the two young men were charged.

Nahanee had got wind of the case and travelled to Port Alberni to speak with the fish guardians who were, they said, "only acting within the scope of the regulations." Nahanee then reminded the officers of:

> the report made to the Bella Bella and Hazelton conventions of the Native Brotherhood of BC by the representatives of the Fisheries Department. The representatives [had] stated to the conventions that no charges had been made to date regarding Natives catching fish for their own use. In reply to questions by the members, [they had said] the Indians could catch fish in any stream and any amount.[407]

Nahanee requested that the case be postponed—likely until the Brotherhood was better prepared to defend it—but on December 29 it was dismissed due to lack of evidence. This would not be the last incident of First Nations hunters and fishermen clashing with government officials over the exercise of their territorial food-gathering privileges on Vancouver Island; a later incident would have a much greater impact, specifically on the question of treaties and First Nations rights.

In Maisie's August 1955 editorial, she noted that Reg T. Kelly had recently resigned from his job as secretary to the Provincial Advisory Committee on Indian Affairs, a job to which he had been appointed by Labour Minister Lyle Wicks four years earlier. The son of Reverend Dr. Peter Kelly, Reg had worked sincerely and assiduously in this position, gathering facts and making a series of recommendations that were heard but promptly dismissed by the minister. Maisie accused Wicks of using Kelly as "a puppet which could be dangled before the public as 'proof' that the Government does not discriminate against Natives."[408]

Maisie told her readers that in his letter of resignation Kelly had written that:

> he felt the present government had no real program for Indian welfare and equality of citizenship. "I felt it was my duty to bring to the public, the Indians themselves and the various government departments, the Indian point of view. The minister differed with me," Mr. Kelly said... [Kelly] charged that since 1952, the government hasn't really done anything to help the native Indians, [409] perhaps reflected in the reduction of the committee's annual budget from $32,000 in 1952 to $7,000 in 1955.

Wicks replaced Kelly with a retired commerce professor, one of the six unpaid honorary members of the "Indian committee" who, according to Maisie, had no "knowledge of Native problems and his personal contact with these people is virtually absent."[410] To her it suggested she had been correct in accusing the government of window dressing by hiring Kelly. Fortunately, his talents were not wasted since he was offered a position in Ottawa as an administration officer with the Department of Indian Affairs.

The September edition of the *Voice* reported on the two-day meeting held in Vancouver on July 20 and 21 to discuss the Indian Act. Forty-six First Nations councillors from all over the South BC Coast as far north as Bella Bella and up the Fraser Valley as far as Yale and Hope had been invited to the meeting by Colonel Lovell Fortier, the federal deputy minister of Immigration and Citizenship; Colonel H. M. Jones, director of Indian Affairs; and Len L. Brown, the solicitor in charge of Legal Affairs and Trust within the Indian Department. At first blush, it had appeared that the government was prepared to listen to some of the concerns of BC's First Nations, but it soon became apparent that this committee was only interested in speaking to its own agenda. None of the three questions of most concern to the BC First Nations were even introduced, let alone addressed: Canadian citizenship without the waiver of rights and privileges, protection of aboriginal rights, and education—the last being especially urgent, given that 2,000 First Nations children in the province were receiving no education.

When it was Chief Oscar D. Peters' turn to address the meeting, he implored the government to delete the section of the Indian Act that dealt with compulsory enfranchisement because, he said:

> it is not only misleading but would lead our Native People to total ruin, destruction and complete elimination of the Native Race, with deed and title free to sell our lands, get all our monies out of the Indian Department to spend as we please, and with our lands completely sold out, where do we go? We can't retire to China, Japan, Scotland, England or any part of Europe. This country is our Motherland, where our ancestors were the aboriginal inhabitants from far beyond what is defined as the history of Canada.[411]

Chief Peters was referring to Section 110 of the Indian Act, which stated that the reserve land of the enfranchised "may be disposed of by him by gift or private sale to the band or another member of the band." His point about the "complete elimination of the Native Race" was somewhat, albeit sadly, reinforced by a young Bella Bella high school graduate, Wilfred Humchitt, son of the chief, during his valedictory speech to his eleven fellow alumni, when he stated perhaps innocently that: "We leave now because this is 1955 and our age-old ways of life are being replaced, and if our race is to hold its head high, we must sacrifice many things."[412]

Chief Peters was unable to follow up on his request for the elimination of the offending section of the Indian Act because he suffered two debilitating strokes a few weeks after the meeting, leaving him too weak to debate the issue and incapable of writing about it, but Maisie refused his offer to resign from his position as a director of the *Voice*. She was lamenting the passing of the old guard, the men and women with whom she had begun the paper nine years earlier and who were now succumbing to the ravages of age. She was further crushed when she received the news that her beloved Father Carlyle had passed away in Bath, England. She wrote of him that:

> Early in life he had a choice of two roads, one of comfort and security, but he chose rather the unblazed trail, giving his help, his love, and his understanding to the lost ones of the world. He lived as he died, a humble Christian gentleman who walked in the footsteps of his Master.[413]

On November 30 Dan Assu, one of the founders of the Brotherhood and still a vice-president of the organization, died when his car plunged into Burrard Inlet. He was 55. His body was conveyed on his seiner, the *San Jose*, together with his family and friends, to the little church on the Cape Mudge Reserve where he was to be buried. Brotherhood president Robert Clifton played the organ before and after Reverend Dr. Peter Kelly eulogized in glow-ing terms the "unselfish work Dan had done for his people."[414] In December Maisie told *Voice* readers:

> Losing Dan is one of the hardest and greatest blows ever dealt to the Native Brotherhood. He worked for the advancement of his people without personal or tribal gain.
>
> Dan, we miss your sunny happy smile and quick wit, your cour-age and your strength. You always offered encouragement when our spirits flagged. Goodbye, old pal, until we meet again.[415]

For Maisie the passing of these two dear friends was sad, but in typical fashion within a month she had rallied and returned to the task of defend-ing "her people," this time against what she considered a direct attack from Ottawa. Two years earlier Louis St. Laurent had led the Liberal party to its fifth consecutive majority government. Jack W. Pickersgill (MP for Bonavis-ta-Twillingate in Newfoundland) had entered St. Laurent's cabinet as secre-tary of state before being moved a year later to Citizenship and Immigration, a portfolio that automatically made him superintendent-general of Indian Affairs. A subsequent tour of both northern and southern Ontario reserves had convinced Pickersgill of the need to move the members of those reserves beyond their traditional ways of life, which he believed was in jeopardy. Ac-cordingly, he appeared anxious to speed up the assimilation process, and thus became the bane of Maisie's existence.

In the December 1955 issue of the *Voice* she reported that Pickersgill had convened a "hush-hush" three-day meeting in Ottawa to discuss First Nations land issues, but when he sent out invitations, he had bypassed the Native Brotherhood with all its legislative experience and its significant his-tory representing First Nations interests. Instead, he invited six BC First Na-tions leaders: Frank Calder, representing northern BC; William Scow, past president of the Brotherhood, representing Alert Bay and Vancouver Island; Andy Paull, representing the Vancouver Indian Agency; Charlie Johnson, representing the Alkali Lake, Chilcotin and Williams Lake areas; James J. Antoine, representing Stoney Creek and the Fort St. James areas; and Charlie Isaac, representing Dawson and the Yukon Territory. Although all of these men were considered competent, Maisie wondered in print why the secrecy and why the Brotherhood was being squeezed out. She was worried that the six who were invited might commit to signing what was known as a "location ticket," which gave title to a small piece of land in exchange for waiving the right to the disposition of common band lands. And she fretted that this was the way Ottawa was going to force integration.

The executive of the Brotherhood had been incensed and fired off a telegram to Prime Minister Louis St. Laurent under the signatures of the president, Robert Clifton, and the legislative chair, Reverend Dr. Peter Kelly, requesting that representatives of the Brotherhood be permitted to attend this Department of Citizenship and Immigration conference and, if this was not granted, that they would like the option to address Parliament. Maisie's editorial in the December 1955 issue barely masked her seething anger over the affront:

> We cannot help but feel that Minister J. W. Pickersgill is one of the greatest calamities that could befall any government... Perhaps Mr. Pickersgill feels that, instead of helping the Indians to achieve a decent standard of living—and to this he should add old age pensioners and returned men—he thinks that it would be better to help immigrants, many of whom were former enemies, by seeing that they are housed and given money to live on until they go to the jobs that are provided for them. The government takes a paternal interest in them because in five years they will be full-fledged citizens and ready to vote. *Surely this is discrimination against our own Canadians who have to starve and walk the streets looking for work.*
>
> All this makes us wonder just what is in store for our Indians on this coming "hush-hush" trip to Ottawa... A similar plan was forced on the Cherokees and Iroquois in the United States.
>
> We only hope that the six representatives of the Bands who are on their way to Ottawa will not sign papers nor commit the Bands of British Columbia whom they represent. We strongly warn them that the situation is fraught with danger.
>
> The government policy is the age-old one of "divide and conquer" and unity of the Indian people is the answer.[416]

A month after sending their telegram, the Brotherhood was still waiting for a reply, and in the January issue of the *Voice* Maisie continued to express her displeasure:

> The Native Brotherhood of British Columbia is the most representative and democratic organization in Canada. It has been so recognized by the Parliamentary Committee. In all the deliberation leading up to the revision of the Indian Act from 1946 to 1949 and subsequent conferences of 1951 and 1953, the representatives of this organization took a leading part.
>
> In convening the conference presently held in Ottawa, Hon. J. W. Pickersgill has deliberately ignored this organization. On December 9 the minister was quoted in a press release from Ottawa that this conference was called to "discuss a stepped-up program for integrating Indians into the Dominion's economic and social life."

The method of calling the conference was undemocratic and much too hasty for such an important conference.

For reasons unknown to us, there has been undue haste exercised to deal with matters affecting the future of a whole race. Mr. Pickersgill was quoted that Indians are not citizens and not subject to taxation and also exempt from game laws. This is not true to facts.[417]

It is possible that Maisie was right about Pickersgill and that his intent was to destabilize the Brotherhood, which had become a powerful organization, one that wielded immense influence over the province's First Nations. Furthermore, by refusing the *Voice*'s request to publish the conference proceedings, the government was effectively controlling the message as well. In the January 1956 edition of the *Voice*, Guy Williams also editorialized on the Brotherhood's past successes—winning old-age pensions, pensions for the blind, improvements to health and educational standards as well as improving housing and reserve conditions. And then he pointed out:

These are just a few of the many gains fought for and won by our great organization, the Native Brotherhood of British Columbia. We have always played the game courteously and democratically. We see no reason now why the present government should openly by-pass an organization on which they have depended so heavily in the past.[418]

John Laurie, a frequent contributor to the *Voice* and the only white member of the Indian Association of Alberta, put Minister Pickersgill's initiatives into perspective when he told the *Calgary Herald* that First Nations people:

do not oppose integration in principle—indeed, it is our contention that that is the most desirable long-range goal—but we dislike anything which might be interpreted as coercing the Indian into accepting an empty and barren form of citizenship in exchange for the special privileges and protection which he now enjoys.

Laurie further argued that many of the changes that were being made by the federal government in the regulations that governed Aboriginal affairs "inevitably lead to loss for Indian reserves, health services, education facilities for both adults and children, all of which would only result in displaced persons roaming about as did the Metis." The final thrust of his argument was that, although integration was inevitable, the timing was wrong and the First Nations must first be provided with adequate "training which is necessary for them to survive, let alone prosper, in the white man's world on the white man's terms."[419]

Frank Calder returned from the conference in Ottawa with a list of the items discussed, but noticeably absent from that list was any meaningful dialogue on the federal vote. He couldn't discuss any of the details because the government had put a "gag order" on all the participants, so they would have to wait until the government report was released before they could speak about it. Calder had probably been invited to the conference because of his political experience as well as his prominence in the north but more importantly, perhaps, because of his public stance on reserves, which he had stated should be eliminated altogether because they "breed inferiority complexes and sap initiative."[420] Although he was also on record stating that he was against any further amendments to the Indian Act and that it too should be abolished, he was buoyed by the concurrent amendments, which he said were leading the First Nations to become "self-determining, self-supporting and self-governing."[421]

In February 1956, Maisie was still questioning the secrecy behind the conference: "We want to see public exposure of its aims; we want to see public discussion; we want democracy. We fear those who wield the heavy hand of censorship,"[422] she said. In fact, it took Pickersgill a full year before he finally met with the Brotherhood executive in Vancouver and admitted that excluding the organization from the Ottawa meeting "was not in the best interests of all concerned."[423] He said he planned to make sure that future events would not only include the Brotherhood but would also be widely publicized well beforehand.

The December conference in Ottawa was one of the subjects that garnered much discussion at the 24th annual Brotherhood convention held in May 1956 at Cape Mudge on Quadra Island, the home of the late Chief Dan Assu, although the gathering appeared to be more of a housekeeping convention than anything else. There was one notable exception, however; the Sisterhood finally exercised their right to vote in Brotherhood affairs, a right they had won in 1951. Robert Clifton's position as president was reaffirmed, as was Reverend Dr. Peter Kelly's as legislative chair, George Wilson's as secretary, Reginald Cook's as treasurer and Ed Nahanee's as business agent. But although the meeting lacked excitement, it was, according to Maisie: "One of the most beautiful conventions attended," especially when Vice-President William Pascal, a cowpuncher from Lillooet, got up to relate in his deadpan voice his hilarious adventures while travelling to various Brotherhood conventions by boat. Pascal had the crowd in stitches as he relived several agonizing journeys through rough seas. That he had attended despite his discomfort was evidence that the Brotherhood was growing beyond its fishing roots in its endeavour to represent all of the First Nations in the province.

Also in attendance at the convention was Sir Michael Bruce, the eleventh Scottish Baronet of Stenhouse and Airth and a descendent of the first king of

Scotland, Robert the Bruce. He was there in his capacity of reporter for the *Vancouver Herald*, in which he subsequently wrote that he "heard speeches that might have emanated from college professors or skilled politicians and dined at a feast that would have done credit to any of Vancouver's first-class hotels."[424] One of those accomplished speakers was Calder's nemesis, provincial Labour Minister Lyle Wicks, who implored the men in attendance to take advantage of vocational and technical training and the women nursing and teaching courses. George Wilson, however, pointed out that, although Ottawa was "stepping up the pace to integrate the Natives of Canada into Canadian society,"[425] discrimination was still a huge barrier to their progress. He related the case of a young man who had received sufficient technical training to qualify for a mill job but was declined because "the mill was not hiring Native Indians."[426] Wilson had just resigned from his position as treasurer of the United Church at Bella Bella because the church had refused to let him handle the books by himself, although the minister stated that it was because he wanted two people responsible to protect the integrity of the position as well as for coverage when one was away. Wilson described himself as treasurer in name only. Reverend Dr. Peter Kelly also criticized the churches for treating First Nations as minors; this was no small complaint given that he had just been elected president of the BC Conference of the United Church.

In June 1956, as the House of Commons was recessing for the summer break, MP John Diefenbaker (Progressive Conservative for Prince Albert) told the press that "the tremendous problems at stake in the administration of the Indian" would never be resolved by "a piecemeal, haphazard amendment to the Indian Act from time to time." His speech followed closely on the heels of yet another debate in the House of Commons about amending the Indian Act in order to give First Nations people "liquor rights approximating those of the white man—provided his province and his band agree." According to a story in the July issue of the *Voice*, Diefenbaker had argued that:

> a royal commission should be appointed that would sit in all parts of Canada at appointed times and places so the Indian's point of view could be placed before Canadians as a whole "rather than through the narrow conduit pipe of the administrative services within the department itself."
>
> "The Indian Act," he said, "should be made an instrument of justice for the Indians of our country rather than in some cases, as it is, an agency of tyranny in its present form."
>
> Mr. Diefenbaker said the rights of Indians under treaties should be maintained and guaranteed. There should be more expansion of the

rights of Indians towards self-government, including an opportunity to take up administrative positions in the field and in the department in Ottawa. There should be provision for appeals by Indians to the courts against administrative orders affecting their individual rights."[427]

When the House resumed sitting in September 1956, E. Davie Fulton (Progressive Conservative for Kamloops) suggested that the right of First Nations to appeal in the courts should be enshrined in the Indian Act, and he moved an amendment to the act that "would have given Indians the right to appeal any government decision affecting band funds, reserve lands, real and personal property and the enfranchisement or disenfranchisement of Indians and bands."[428] Minister Pickersgill responded that there was no need for the amendment because Indians already had that right. Fulton's motion was subsequently defeated by the majority Liberal government.

But more MPs from the Opposition side of the House of Commons were beginning to comment on this issue in a way designed to embarrass the government. Ambrosh Holowach (Social Credit for Edmonton East) called the First Nations reserves "glorified concentration camps" and R. R. Knight (CCF for Saskatoon) told the house that reserve land "wouldn't maintain a gopher."[429] Minister Pickersgill admitted that conditions on reserves were not what he desired, but because the population was growing so quickly, it was becoming urgent that "new ways be found to enable Indians to make a living."[430]

Meanwhile, in July 1956, Maisie reprinted an article written by Andre Renaud for the *Indian Missionary Record*, a creation of the Missionary Oblates of Mary Immaculate. The headline was: No Longer Indian?

At this time when they are given greater educational opportunities than ever and they sense a renewed interest for their future on the part of the Canadian people, Indians are raising the question: How much do you want us to change?

These are the words used not so long ago by an Indian in addressing his fellow teachers and principals from the federal Indian schools in Ontario. His message was this:

Is it completely wrong to be born an Indian? Is everything that we have inherited from our ancestors totally opposed to the Canadian way of life that you want us to share? Isn't there something in our own history as well as in our way of thinking, feeling and behaving which is worthwhile preserving for the whole nation and of which our children can be justly proud? Can you train children for life in your competitive society without acknowledging and cultivating their self-respect, their pride in being what they are?

What a pertinent question to ask of Indian school teachers and all those who are concerned with the future of the Canadian Indian. At the same time what a paradox that it should be raised in an "immigrant-receiving" country that boasts of being officially bicultural and that invites all newcomers to contribute the best from their cultural heritage to the building of a new nation... Can the oldest immigrant to this country... not become a Canadian whilst preserving from his cultural heritage what he feels is comparable, if not superior, to what the newcomers have brought to his country?[431]

In the midst of all this turmoil, detractors began attacking Maisie and the *Native Voice*, prompting a terse reply from President Robert Clifton who happened to be out fishing at the time but who felt that an immediate response was necessary.

I, as president of the Native Brotherhood of British Columbia, in consequence of malicious and ill-founded rumours and actions circulated by enemies and false friends of our people, find it necessary to make this announcement concerning the *Native Voice:*

The *Native Voice* is the official organ of the Native Brotherhood of British Columbia. It was founded 10 years ago by Mrs. Maisie A. C. Hurley and members of the Native Brotherhood and has run steadily ever since... It has proven a valuable instrument in the great work of the Native Brotherhood in the fight for better conditions and advancement and defence of the aboriginal rights of the Native people, not only in British Columbia but in other parts of Canada and the United States.

Neither the publisher nor the associate editors have ever received any money for their services. The Native people should wake up to the value of this paper and appreciate the great work which is being done by the paper, and they should give their support.[432]

On September 15, 1956, Maisie was invited to Skeena Crossing to attend a great celebratory feast in her honour. Chief Haklgout (Arthur McDames) had invited over 200 people, including the Indian superintendent and the commissioner of the RCMP to whom he had to apply for permission to hold the event. Chief Negwa (Ken B. Harris) explained to the gathering that:

Maisie Hurley came to consolidate a name bestowed on her several years ago, the legendary name of Shim-clux (Spouse of the Sun) who was allegedly the first mother of the nation of Dahmlakamat. Shim-clux allegedly by the power of God gave birth to three children. By this token the nation of Dahmlakamat claims divine origin.

According to the October 1956 issue of the *Voice*, the name "Dahmlakamat" at one time referred to an immense village on the Skeena River that was devastated by a large snowstorm in June "causing the run of fresh salmon to disappear. The result was a great famine in which many families died. Those who were left migrated to Kitseguekla, so the House of Chief Haklgout is called Dahmlakamat."[433] The story in the *Voice* continued:

> Touched by Maisie's sincerity in her effort to consolidate a legendary name in the proper traditional manner, Chief Negwa on behalf of Chief Haklgout bestowed on Maisie Hurley a hereditary title, Chief Men-glug-um-kee-pikee, meaning, "the Eagle that could not fly from the ground." [Maisie later spelled her new name Min-klux-cum-ge-pikee.][434]

This thousand-year-old "Man-Name," which was higher than that of a chief and which was rarely conferred upon a white person, gave Maisie power over fourteen villages. The *Voice* story concluded:

> "There is so little one can say of appreciation for this trust and faith of a kindly, godly people," Maisie stated. "Only that I promise I will to the best of my ability and humbly strive to be worthy of their trust. I want nothing from them, just to be allowed to serve them faithfully with God's help—and to fight for their hunting grounds, their traditions. For as the chiefs told me, 'Never forget, Maisie, God is Chief, and God made chiefs to help guide the people.'[435]

Chief Andrew Frank, hereditary chief of the Puntledge First Nation at Comox, wrote to the *Voice* to express his delight that Maisie had been so honoured.

> There was no mistake in selecting Maisie Hurley as one of our people and making her a chief with a Man-Name; Maisie Hurley is properly privileged and entitled to her name now.
>
> I say this as I know Mrs. Hurley well myself and know the great good she has been doing for our people. She surely deserves to have this high recognition.
>
> It is a privilege to have her among the chiefs of the Coast, and Maisie Hurley will be recognized by all the hereditary chiefs of the coast."[436]

This new honour bestowed upon Maisie only reaffirmed her resolve to defend "her people."

In January 1957, a few weeks after Maisie's return from Skeena Crossing and other northern stops, the *Voice* published an editorial written by Ruth Gorman in which she told how Minister of Citizenship and Immigration Pickersgill, without informing Parliament, had some time earlier begun to register all First Nations people with a view to applying Sections 11 and 12 of the 1951 amended Indian Act. These sections allowed the government

> to remove from the register, Indians who have been signed to Treaty for the following reasons: 1) They or their ancestors did not technically properly join the tribe they now live with; 2) There is illegitimacy in their background somewhere; 3) They have the "taint" of white blood in their veins; 4) Their ancestors applied for an allotment of scrip after the Riel Rebellion.[437]

According to the story in the *Voice*, this move by the government especially affected the 103 descendants of 118 predominantly Cree men of mixed heritage (historically known as "half-breeds" by the government) of the Samson Band at Hobbema, Alberta, who had accepted scrip (land valued at $120) under the auspices of Treaty Six (the Treaties of Forts Carleton and Pitt signed in 1876). Subsequently, this scrip had been purchased from them for $10 by the very man who later reported them to be receiving scrip as well as benefiting from treaty rights. Their descendants were now about to pay the price for their action by being "booted off their reserve."[438] It apparently meant little to the present government that the men who had received and then sold their scrip had later been permitted to return to their reserves by the authority of the Department of Indian Affairs.

With no education or training, their descendants were now destined for a life of poverty and deprivation off their reserve, and were they to present their case before a judge, which was their legal right, the court could only act within the narrow confines of the Indian Act. Gorman's editorial demanded that "the Act must be changed before, by this subtle way of breaking Treaty, all our Indians are driven from their reserves. It is now apparent that this is Ottawa's intent."[439]

MP George Hees (Progressive Conservative for Toronto-Broadview) accused Pickersgill of harbouring a "Fascist attitude,"[440] and Dick Snell, a *Calgary Herald* staff reporter, "charged that the "Hobbema case has a frightening resemblance to the methods used by Nazi Germany where a finger pointed to someone suspected of Jewish blood resulted in a loss of status (and property) and imprisonment."[441] Maisie agreed with Snell when she wrote:

> That, in our opinion, is not too harsh an accusation, and in our opinion, too, the finger must be pointed directly at Mr. Pickersgill, and particularly his predecessor, Mr. Harris, for having brought this vicious policy into effect.
>
> We are sick and disgusted with this sham. The federal government must halt its policy of discrimination against a people who have

sacrificed much for Canada in two world wars and before that. Surely there can be no justification for giving them any less consideration than people from another land, who not so many years ago were at war with Canada.[442]

In his 1994 memoir, *Seeing Canada Whole*, Pickersgill tried to set the record straight by explaining that it had been the "registrar of Indian bands, a senior official in the department, whose duty it was to maintain a complete list of all persons in Canada with Indian status," who had made the call to register all First Nations people, based on the latest revisions to the Indian Act. Pickersgill's memoir continued:

> To bring the lists up to date, the registrar was required to post the existing list of members of each Indian band in a prominent place on the reserve or reserves. For six months after the list was posted individuals could apply to have names added or removed from the list. Applications to have names removed were called protests... The registrar's decisions were final, subject to an appeal to the Courts... Some Alberta newspapers and some Conservatives in the Opposition, led by Diefenbaker, took up the hue and cry... When I persisted in urging those who were dissatisfied to appeal to the courts, I was portrayed as arbitrary, arrogant and inhumane. The abuse was hard to take because I believed that the registrar had made a mistake, and that if the case was taken to court, the decision would be reversed. [443]

Meanwhile, the marked members of the Samson Band, facing eviction within three months, prepared a petition that they forwarded through the governor general directly to the Queen. In part, it read:

> If any of our ancestors had white blood in their veins, or if our marriage customs varied from the white man's, or if any of our ancestors at any time signed for scrip, or if they did not properly join the tribe in the technical sense, we, their descendants, are now deemed to be non-Indians and are being ejected from our ancestral homes, the reserves.
>
> We feel that we are not as yet prepared or trained to enter the world of our pale-face brethren. It is our eventual hope that we may do so, but we do not wish to be forced out of treaty until we are ready. We fear for our children, whom we feel we cannot support and maintain at this time if we must leave our reserves.[444]

But their petition was not passed along to the Queen by the governor general and instead was placed directly in the hands of Minister Pickersgill. Carl Nickle (Progressive Conservative for Calgary) demanded to know "by whose authority was the Indians' petition to the Queen transferred from the office of the governor general" to Mr. Pickersgill. Prime Minister Louis St. Laurent confessed ignorance as "he had received no advice on the subject," although he later said that he believed "the definition of who is or who is not an Indian entitled to be on the reserve has remained unchanged over the whole time since that reserve was set up." Minister Pickersgill responded to the question of why he had not forwarded the document with "I was seeking advice on this subject."[445] At this point in the debate, Mr. Diefenbaker, now leader of the official opposition, interjected:

> Is it not a fact that one of the vestigial rights which Indians enjoy by reason of the fact that they entered into a treaty with the British Crown is the right to direct petitions to the Queen and that it cannot in any way be interfered with regardless of the relationship which Her Majesty's Government in Canada bears to her?[446]

The prime minister then admitted that he had not read the treaties, and although Diefenbaker conceded that the rights of the original treaties had probably been watered down over the years, he said he still believed that the right to petition the Queen was extant.

On March 1, 1957, the government eviction action at Hobbema was quashed by Chief Justice Nelles Buchanan of the Northern Alberta District Court who declared the eviction notice null and void and ruled that "the affected Indians be given full treaty rights, including payments from oil revenues on the reserves from oil rights it holds."[447] Maisie was ecstatic, thanking the court and the myriad of people, both First Nation and white, who had stood behind the protest.

> That inspiring movement, in which the *Native Voice* was proud to play a small part, is proof positive that when the Canadian people get the facts, they are most certainly on the side of those who are being discriminated against.
>
> The light of publicity must be thrown on similar instances and certainly on the Indian Act itself and any further changes contemplated by that most unpopular cabinet minister, J.W. Pickersgill.[448]

After Parliament was dissolved that spring, John Diefenbaker visited Vancouver where Maisie interviewed him on April 12 for the next issue of the *Voice*. She was most impressed and wrote:

> Although I have never been a Conservative, I left Mr. Diefenbaker with a feeling of confidence that his way was the middle decent way of security. He has a great concern for the Indians—and a determination to see that all treaties and rights made with the Indian are respected and unbroken.[449]

And Diefenbaker after his return to Ottawa sent Maisie a letter in which he said in part:

When I spoke to you last week in Vancouver, I promised to let you have the three points which I had set forth as the policy of the Progressive Conservative Party towards our Canadian Indians.

These points are:

1. The repeal of Sections X, XI, XII of the Indian Act.

2. The appointment of a royal commission to investigate and make recommendations on the entire field of Indian affairs.

3. The appointment of an Indian to the Senate of Canada with special responsibility of speaking for Indians in the Parliament of Canada.

I was very pleased indeed to meet you and delighted to hear something of the excellent work you are doing to set before the people of Canada the particular problems of the Indians, especially those in the province of British Columbia.

With kindest regards. I am

Yours sincerely,

John Diefenbaker.[450]

In the beginning, Maisie's work with her First Nations friends had probably been performed out of a sense of obligation, the *noblesse oblige* that she had been taught by her parents. That, however, had quickly evolved into feelings of abiding love and deep respect. First Nations people had little to offer her in return for her years of hard work, but their respect for her materialized in the form of naming ceremonies. She was already carrying the Man-Name Men-glug-um-kee-pikee from her Skeena friends, as well as the name Maithla, the Dancer, conferred upon her in 1951 by the Squamish people. In May 1957 it was the turn of a special friend, Chief Andy Frank, hereditary chief of the K'ómoks (Comox) First Nation to honour her. This time she received the name of "Gwie-molas," meaning "Her Door is Always Open to Welcome and Very Generous"[451] during a totem pole raising ceremony at Lewis Park on the banks of the Puntledge River at Courtenay on Vancouver Island. It was a historic moment, made all the more important by the fact that the poles were carved by Mungo Martin, the iconic leading Fort Rupert carver, with his two assistants, Dave Martin and Henry Hunt. This naming ceremony, according to Andy Everson, a noted First Nations artist who was named "Nagedzi" after his grandfather, the late Chief Andy Frank of the K'ómoks First Nation, had great significance and meaning: "When you give someone a name they become part of the family and are therefore addressed in this fashion at ceremonial gatherings. It is a very significant honour and is much like an adoption."[452]

Following the dissolution of Parliament in April 1957, Prime Minister Louis St. Laurent, confident of winning another Liberal majority, dropped the election writ. But the Liberals had been in power for twenty-two years,

Chief Andy Frank, hereditary chief of the K'ómoks (Comox) First Nation, honoured Maisie with the name of "Gwie-molas" during a totem pole raising ceremony at Lewis Park on the banks of the Puntledge River at Courtenay on Vancouver Island. In a 2002 ceremony, the poles were replaced by replicas carved by Island carver Calvin Hunt. Photo credit to William Mathis.

Maisie holding Mary Frank at the trailhead of Moose Falls above the Campbell River on Vancouver Island, while her husband, Tom, and their friend, Chief Andy Frank, look on. Photo from the family collection.

which was more than enough time for complacency and arrogance to seep into their policies, positions and procedures. As a result, in the June election the Progressive Conservatives won 112 seats to the Liberals 105. The CCF party managed 25 seats, Social Credit 19; four independents were also elected. Diefenbaker, though now prime minister, headed up a minority government, and even if he could count on some of the Social Credit members to vote for his legislation, they would not be enough to push through the radical changes he was planning, including changes that would enrich the lives of the First Nations across Canada. He would have to bide his time until he could call another election to gain the majority he needed. But Maisie editorialized her delight as well as her caution in the *Voice*'s July issue:

> For 22 years the government of today was seated in Opposition, and during that time advanced many important and constructive proposals. Tax cuts, higher old age pensions, a Canadian Bill of Rights, and fair play for Native Canadians were among its recommendations... The real test of the new government's sincerity will come when it brings down its program of legislative action.
>
> We as a newspaper will neither praise nor condemn until we see concretely what that program will include, but we feel very strongly that the Native policy of full citizenship rights with retention of all aboriginal rights cannot long be overlooked by any government sincerely interested in justice for the first people of Canada.[453]

10—The Federal Franchise at Last

After the federal election of June 1957 the Honourable Minister Pickersgill became simply the Liberal member of parliament for Bonavista-Twillingate, but he was now heckling Diefenbaker's government from the Opposition benches at every opportunity. Maisie's beef with Pickersgill and with Harris, who had held the Citizenship and Immigration portfolio before him, had been neatly summed up by a *Calgary Albertan* newspaper reporter when he wrote that they had "seemed to be saying; 'I will decide what's best for the Indians. I am their guardian. They aren't capable of making important decisions.'"[454] It was this attitude that Maisie hoped would disappear under the new government. The First Nations in Canada were anxious to become citizens but on their own terms.

That First Nations represented a potentially significant voting bloc, given that they were one of the fastest-growing demographics in the country—the population had increased 7.3 per cent in the previous three years to approximately 163,000—was not lost on Diefenbaker's Progressive Conservative Party as well. The prime minister, speaking to the civil liberties section of the Canadian Bar Association convention in Banff in late September, announced that the changes to the Indian Act they were requesting would begin during the next session of Parliament, which was due to commence October 14. He also mentioned that, although no decision had yet been made about appointing a First Nations individual to the Senate, he believed that an appointment "in due course is certain." On his way back to Ottawa he took time out of his busy schedule to meet with reporters in Calgary where he informed them that the Indian Act would be revised to prevent a repeat of the Hobbema incident. He went further, stating that those sections of the act used against the Hobbema people "cannot be used against any person accepted as a reservation Indian when the act came into effect" in 1951.[455] It appeared that Diefenbaker was taking his election promises seriously.

When the House of Commons resumed sitting that fall, Frank Howard (CCF for Skeena), sensing a shift in thinking, introduced two private member's bills to amend both the Indian Act and the Election Act to grant First Nations people in Canada what he felt was long overdue, an unencumbered federal vote. Referencing the race riots that had occurred in Little Rock, Arkansas, following the May 17, 1954, ruling by the US Supreme Court that segregated schools in the US were unconstitutional, Howard stated:

This does make us think about our own attitude and approach towards our Native Indian people. We must certainly look into that part of our social structure and take immediate steps on the Native Indian question. For years we have been paternalistic and segregation-minded towards these people. For over a century we have made them feel inferior and as a consequence they *are*—as a race, that is.

He then unveiled his platform of reformation:

1. Establish a gradual system for developing self-government among Indian bands. 2. Generally and gradually reduce the authority of Indian agents, to the end of eliminating agents entirely. 3. Transfer educational jurisdiction to the provincial government with a concomitant payment by the federal government towards education. 4. Grant the vote in federal elections without waiving or eliminating hereditary or aboriginal rights. 5. Encourage our Native Indians to accept responsibility. 6. Establish a House committee or commission to continually evaluate the progress being made and recommend legislative and administrative changes accordingly. 7. Apply liquor laws on an equal basis with "local option" applying to Indian reserves as voting units.[456]

In the second week of October, Robert Clifton and Reverend Dr. Peter Kelly travelled to Ottawa once again to press the Brotherhood's case for enfranchisement at a meeting with the Minister of Justice, E. Davie Fulton (he was also acting Minister of Citizenship and Immigration at this time), Minister of Agriculture Douglas Harkness (the member for Calgary North) and a few other Progressive Conservative MPs. Afterwards, the Brotherhood's brief was forwarded to select ministers and department heads, including the director of Indian Affairs, H. M. Jones, who was wary of the Justice minister, given Fulton's past criticism of the department. On their return Maisie wrote about the meeting for the *Voice*:

Weary of the evasive methods of previous "buck-passing" governments, and knowing the friendly determination by the present government to do the right thing by the Indians, they decided that the Brotherhood brief was solely for the absorption of the present Conservative government and the Opposition and not as it has been in the past for the Department of Indian Affairs alone, so they started by giving every minister a copy of the brief.

Their demands were fully dealt with in a concise and to-the-point brief asking for the federal vote for Indians with full citizenship and with protection for all aboriginal rights; a royal commission on Indian rights to investigate the legality of all Indian claims and treaties; a senator from British Columbia, and more power for our people in handling their affairs.

They also asked that no Indian should be tried by any officials of the Department of Indian Affairs and that they be tried and dealt with in the ordinary courts of the land. Unfortunately, on too many occasions our people have found themselves appearing before tribunals which acted as police, prosecutors and judges, men not even trained in the law.

President Clifton stated that it is up to British Columbia Indians to get behind the Brotherhood solidly and organize and show their strength in a united voting body with only one objective: namely, protection of Indian rights and justice... Mr. Clifton announced that from now on he is "giving them both barrels," not even Marquis of Queensbury rules, no holds or punches barred. "We are on the march to victory. It is a case now for the governments, both federal and provincial to put up or shut up; we now know our strength."

Maisie finished the account of the Ottawa meeting with a pep talk for her readers:

No more pats on our backs. As August Jack Khatsahlano says, "They only pat dogs on the back." No more gold-washed pens and pencils as gifts so that we can sign away our rights.

United we stand, divided we part.

We demand our full rights and that the governments, both federal and provincial, past, present and future, grant us our full rights. Tempus Fugit (time passes). We have been a long time starting; we have no time to lose.

Native Canadians March to Victory.[457]

Clifton and Kelly had arrived in Ottawa for their meeting on October 13 and the next day had sat in the gallery of the House of Commons to witness Queen Elizabeth opening the first session of the 23rd Parliament. Afterwards, they attended a reception for the queen, mingling freely with the cabinet ministers of Diefenbaker's new government. Days later, when they appeared at the Brotherhood's silver anniversary convention at Bella Bella, President Clifton could not stop talking about "his Queen." But he admitted that, although he had stood a mere five feet from her at the reception, he didn't get the opportunity to tell her that "she is Queen of our hearts. Queen of our Canada."[458]

When it was Reverend Dr. Kelly's turn to speak at the convention, he recalled the vision of Alfred Adams and told the meeting that "the organization is stronger today than it ever has been." However, he was frustrated with the roadblocks set up by the Department of Indian Affairs, which he felt had bypassed the Brotherhood so that:

they could deal separately and divide [First Nations] so the Indians could be controlled in dealings with them. We will not submit weakly. I serve notice on you now we are going to take it to a higher authority. We have among our leaders in this organization the best-informed men on Indian problems.[459]

One of those "best-informed men" was Guy Williams, who had just been appointed public relations officer for the Brotherhood. He was already heavily involved in Brotherhood business, being a current member of Kelly's Legislative Committee, a director of the *Voice* and having served as the organization's business agent in the past. He was also the captain of his own seine boat and lent his expertise to numerous committees negotiating on salmon fishing issues. Maisie was particularly fond of Williams, and together they had planned to make political waves with their Indian Non-Partisan Political Party, although since its inception in 1951 they had done little to promote it. It had also been Williams, teaming up with the late Tom Howarth, who had arranged for former Brotherhood president Chief William Scow to attend Queen Elizabeth's coronation and to be given a seat in Westminster Abbey.

In January 1958, Maisie went on the rampage in the *Voice* after twenty or thirty armed Ku Klux Klansmen had showed up for a cross-burning rally in Maxton, North Carolina, aimed not at black people this time but at the local Lumbee tribe of Indians. However, the Klansmen were quickly surrounded and vastly outnumbered by about a thousand Native Americans brandishing weapons and shooting into the air over their heads. Maisie, always ready to provide lessons on solidarity for her readers, wrote:

Ah, it warms the ancient corpuscles in my blood to hear of those fine Red Men scattering the rats and "shooting them up" like the old Westerners of my youth—no bloodshed, just plain scaring them and putting them on the run, their bedsheets trailing behind. When the leaders of the Klan were finally brought to justice, they faced a jury of "three Indians, two negroes and 13 whites..." [To add to the irony] the judge—Lacy W. Maynor—was himself a Lumbee Indian, although his mild penalties were in sharp contrast to the cruelty and injustice of the Ku Klux Klan... [But he] also urged his fellow tribesmen to "learn to use the ballot, the most powerful weapon of the 20th century." Indians must become politically active if they are to protect their lands and preserve their cultural heritage.[460]

On February 1, 1958, Prime Minister Diefenbaker met privately with Governor General Vincent Massey at his residence in Quebec and informed him of his desire to dissolve Parliament. He then made haste for Ottawa where he entered the House of Commons and announced that Canada's 23rd Parliament was no more. In the election of March 31, 1958, the Progressive Conservatives were returned to office with the largest majority in the entire history of the nation.

About a month before dissolving Parliament, Diefenbaker had fulfilled the third promise he had set out in his letter to Maisie: "the appointment of an Indian to the Senate of Canada with the special responsibility of speaking for Indians in the Parliament of Canada." In his memoirs, published in 1976, he explained that:

> Believing, as I did, that it would be a long time, if ever, before an Indian could be elected to the House of Commons because of their numerical minority in any one constituency, I appointed Chief James Gladstone, an outstanding and devoted servant to his people, to the Senate.[461]

James Gladstone had not been the only First Nations person considered for the position. Andrew Paull had also been on the short list, but Paull was too well-known for his activism—and his hair-trigger temper. In addition, he had recently been unwell. Another candidate was Dr. Gilbert Monture, a respected government scientist, originally from the Six Nations Reserve, who had been recommended by the Ontario Conservatives. But Gladstone had been recommended by John Laurie, Ruth Gorman and Diefenbaker's minister of agriculture, Douglas Harkness, and it didn't hurt that the prime minister was personally acquainted with him and knew his views were moderate. He was considered the safe choice.

In an interview with Maisie nearly a year later, Gladsone, whose tribal name, Akay-na-muka, means "Many Guns," recounted how he had learned of "this great honour":

> We had been planning, my wife and I, to go to San Francisco where we have a daughter, and at that time we were staying with our other daughter in Calgary, waiting for her husband to return from a trip. I was sitting having a cup of tea when the phone rang, and I heard Mr. Diefenbaker's voice calling me from Ottawa, saying he wanted to appoint me a senator. I very nearly dropped the receiver I was so surprised and excited, and by that time my wife and daughter were by my side and were just as excited as I.
>
> One of the requirements I had to have to accept this appointment was to own property to the value of $4,000. My house and property are on the reservation, which is tribal land and of course did not count, so I asked the prime minister how much time I had in order to do what was required. He was speaking to me on Tuesday morning and said he must know by Friday morning.

We didn't bother with breakfast but got into the car and went down to Cardston and hunted around and finally found a house that suited us and bought it. It took a little time to get the cash, but on Thursday morning I completed the deal and got a wire off to the prime minister and returned to Calgary. On Friday morning Mr. Diefenbaker acknowledged receipt of my wire and asked me, "Would you accept this appointment?" I couldn't say anything for a minute or two, but then I said, "I would be happy to accept it because the people who have written to me and those I met when I was in Ottawa last October when the Queen was there all hoped I would be the one chosen, and therefore I am happy to accept on their behalf.[462]

When Maisie formally interviewed him for the paper, he said:

My work in the Senate will be aimed at improving the position of Canada's Indians, obtaining gradually for them better conditions as they want them and are ready for them and without changes being forced upon them.

Maisie's story continued:

[Gladstone] told his interviewer he is intensely proud of his Indian background. His mother was a full-blooded Indian, a member of the Blackfoot tribe. His father, William Shanks Gladstone, a Scot, was born in Montreal in 1830 and came west at 18 to work for the Hudson's Bay Company as a boat builder. The Senator attended industrial school at Calgary to become a typesetter, a skill which he employed in the composing room of the *Calgary Herald* before becoming an interpreter on his reserve and a local ranch hand. He was then hired by the Royal Northwest Mounted Police as an interpreter and scout. During the First World War he was engaged in increasing the crop production on the Blood Reserve, an interest that eventually led him to purchase an 800-acre ranch where he and his two sons were raising 500 head of Hereford cattle.

"I am thinking of making my first appearance in the Senate in my formal dress if that is permissible," he said today. That dress would include buckskin jacket and chaps, beaded moccasins and colorful Indian headdress.

The Senator planned to get right to work, one of his first pronouncements having to do with:

the lack of education being the main problem of fitting Indians into a changing society. Amazingly, though, in the last 10 years Indian parents have wanted their children to receive a full education. And there is a growing demand that they be taught in public schools where they can grow up as equals with whites.[463]

The first First Nations individual appointed to the Senate, James Gladstone, said to Maisie after accepting Prime Minister Diefenbaker's invitation: "I am thinking of making my first appearance in the Senate in my formal dress if that is permissible." Photo courtesy of the Glenbow Museum Archives.

Gladstone was not alone in recognizing education as the key to progress. At a four-day conference in May hosted by the Department of Indian Affairs and presided over by H. M. Jones, director of the department, MLA Frank Calder delivered a brief on its vital importance, but he wanted the province rather than the federal government to oversee the future education of Aboriginal people. In addition, he requested that teachers in Aboriginal schools "be certified, qualified and receive similar salaries to those employed in regular schools under the Department of Education. Employment of unqualified persons and persons who have absolutely no teacher training must stop."[464]

While Guy Williams agreed with Calder and Gladstone that education was the key to progress, he lamented that discrimination was still haunting the employment path. Dr. Stuart Jamieson, a professor in the Department of Economics at UBC, felt that a solution to that problem would be for First Nations to leave the resource industries, where jobs were declining in number, and educate themselves to become small businessmen.

In June 1958 the *Vancouver Sun* published a series of very disturbing articles on the plight of First Nations in the province, and having read them, Guy Williams demanded a federal royal commission to investigate "all aspects of the Indian problem in British Columbia." Maisie, reporting on his concerns, wrote in the *Voice*:

> Mr. Williams proposed that the royal commission deal mainly with the administration of Indian affairs, the educational facilities, the housing and living standards. He also suggested that it investigate making the federal franchise available immediately to all Indians. "We must have this if we are to have equal status," he said.
>
> Mr. Williams said the *Sun*'s series "left a very black picture" of the Indian situation in BC. "It left the reader with the impression that the Indian himself is responsible for the state of 'poverty and squalor' that he is in," he said. "To a certain extent this may be true. But he (the Indian) did not bring this on himself. You (the public) and your government brought this squalor and poverty on us. The Indians' plight here is your problem."[465]

On June 30, depressed by the *Vancouver Sun*'s stories of stolen Aboriginal lands and traplines, Maisie wrote to the prime minister:

> I feel so helpless to help these dear Native Canadians. I seem to have no defence against the money grabbing robbers who steal the aboriginal rights from [them]... Those white robbers have cheated them for years over their trap lines and land. What can I do? It makes me feel a

failure and helpless, and I love these dear good Canadian people who own this land... The Indian department has it in hand, but I am afraid they are helpless against these big money grabbers.[466]

Maisie had not mentioned enfranchisement in her letter to Diefenbaker, but her editorial in the July issue of the *Voice* let the prime minister know she had not forgotten about his promise:

Full democracy with retention of all aboriginal rights for Canadian Indians has long been advocated by the *Native Voice* and a good many leaders of Canada's Indian people.

For that reason, we are more than a little disappointed that the Dominion Government has so far failed to see the issue and come up with a program that will meet the needs and desires of Canada's Indians.

She pointed out that the provincial vote had been offered on similar terms to that of other voters and had proved successful, but that the First Nations people were still waiting for "the federal vote and election of federal candidates."

It is not enough to have an appointee in the Senate, even though we think that in itself is an important advance for our people. The very fact that Prime Minister John Diefenbaker has seen fit to place such a fine representative as William [James] Gladstone in the Senate is, in fact, an admission that the Indians should have representation in the high councils of government.

Having made that admission, however, Mr. Diefenbaker can do no less than take the next step: enfranchise the Indian people of Canada. And again we stress—there can be no strings attached to the ballot. The Natives have already lost too much. Let them have their full rights as Canadians.[467]

In the same issue, Maisie was able to report that Frank Howard's private member's bills to amend the Indian Act and the Elections Act in order to provide First Nations with an unencumbered federal vote were being "talked out'" on the floor of the House of Commons. However, Erik Nielsen (PC for Yukon) told the House that the bill had the right idea but was "premature." His experience indicated many Indians did not want the vote. Douglas Fisher (CCF for Port Arthur) countered that Nielsen's argument for withholding the bill was "specious," given that he had lauded "the appointment of an Indian to the Senate." In fact, Nielsen was right in some instances; the chiefs of the Six Nations of Brantford, Ontario, who believed that their Confederacy was a Nation unto itself, had made it plain that "voting as ordinary Canadians would be a denial of their heritage."[468]

❈

At the end of July 1958, Maisie published a special edition of the *Native Voice*, her primary purpose being to celebrate First Nations history on the hundredth anniversary of the establishment of the Crown Colony of British Columbia. The edition was filled with traditional narratives, some that had been recorded by Maisie's mother and father when they were staying in First Nations communities in the north, and enriched with warm messages from government. However, she reserved page one for a special event. Princess Margaret, the queen's younger sister, had been invited to BC to help celebrate the occasion, and one of the last events on her tour was a huge potlatch held in her honour in Courtenay arranged by the Brotherhood president, Clifton. Unfortunately, he had been taken ill and was convalescing post-surgery in St. Joseph's Hospital in Comox when the event took place. But he was totally surprised and humbled when the princess appeared at the hospital to greet him and wish him well. The centennial edition printed his grateful thanks to the princess:

> I do not think there is any other man in this great Commonwealth of Nations who has had the honour which today you have bestowed upon me. I could not express the words, and I don't know what words to use. As long as life will inhabit this body, I will never forget it personally, but it will be down on our Record Book of the Native Brotherhood of British Columbia.
>
> I am quite sure Sister Superior and the sisters and staff at St. Joseph's Hospital join me in a little prayer that the richest blessings of God be bestowed upon you as you travel through this our great Country until you arrive safely at home.[469]

The next two pages were filled with photographs of H.R.H. Princess Margaret at various events throughout the province. Page three contained a message from the prime minister, which said in part:

> It is indeed fitting that in British Columbia's Centennial Year the *Native Voice* should be publishing a special edition. Its appearance adds a special note to the occasion, a reminder of the long centuries of Indian association with the province... How interesting and how euphonious are such names as Salish, Athapasca, Kootenay, Nootka, Kwakiutl, Haida, Bella Coola and Tsimshian! They add individually to the nomenclature of the province... I am proud of my connection with the first citizens of this country, have a warm sense of solidarity in their aspirations, and rejoice that an Indian representative now sits in the Senate of Canada.[470]

Page seven of the celebratory issue carried a message from BC Premier W. A. C. Bennett:

> I am confident that the world will learn, as time goes on, of other outstanding achievements of our Native Indians, and I welcome the occasion of this Centennial Greeting to commend you on your preservation of the rich Indian heritage which you as the Native Brotherhood of British Columbia hold in trust.[471]

Bennett was especially proud of the hundred-foot totem pole that had been sent to the queen in honour of the celebration. It had been carved by Mungo Martin with assistance from his son, David, and son-in-law, Henry Hunt, and now stood proudly in Windsor Great Park in London.

The euphoria Maisie experienced over the centennial celebrations and the princess's visit quickly evaporated when she learned of a riot and alleged police brutality that had occurred in Prince Rupert on August 3, 1958. It had begun with two First Nations women

Recovering from a recent surgery, Brotherhood President Robert Clifton was humbled when Princess Margaret visited him at St. Joseph's Hospital, Comox, Vancouver Island. "I do not think there is any other man in this great Commonwealth of Nations who has had the honour which today you have bestowed upon me," he said. Photo courtesy of Mary Everson.

engaged in a hair-pulling match, and it might have ended peacefully with a charge of drunkenness, except for the actions of local police who allegedly beat the women with flashlights to separate them. Their friends had intervened, and the ruckus had ended with a total of thirty-five people arrested.

For the September edition of the *Voice*, Maisie wrote:

> The people and the Prince Rupert press appealed to Attorney General Bonner for an impartial investigation as he is the head law enforcement officer for British Columbia. Mr. Bonner REFUSED.
> WE THE NATIVE CANADIANS DEMAND EQUAL RIGHTS SUCH AS ARE GIVEN TO THE MOST RECENT IMMIGRANTS TO OUR COUNTRY.
> One of the grievances of the Non-Treaty Indians of British Columbia is that, although they OWN British Columbia, never having

surrendered same knowingly, [and] although they are punished [and] taxed under the laws of Canada, they have no voice in the making of such laws. Their Aboriginal Rights are not protected and their status is confused and ambiguous. WE DEMAND A ROYAL COMMISSION TO CLARIFY AND INSURE TO US OUR ABORIGINAL RIGHTS AND TO GRANT TO US DIGNITY WHICH IS OURS AS THE ORIGINAL OWNERS OF CANADA.[472]

Harold Sinclair was incensed at the riot charge made by the RCMP and Prince Rupert's mayor, Peter Lester, especially when within hours the story had been picked up by CBC radio and various stations in the US. One of Sinclair's friends, Barney Goode, had been among those charged and promptly sentenced to six months in Oakalla, while twenty-two others awaited sentencing. Fortunately, the mayor granted Sinclair's request for a public meeting to air the incident, which Sinclair believed would not have escalated had it not been for the actions of the local police. At the meeting a witness told of seeing a man sleeping it off in the lobby of a local hotel when the police grabbed him by the wrist and twisted it. Sinclair told the *Voice* that the witness said they took the man

> to the police wagon, kicked him in the back and threw him in the wagon. Upon arriving at the police station, they unloaded him with another kick in the back, using a police club and at times a flashlight over the man's head... This is pure ill-treatment, definitely ill-treating Indian people, which is not in the law books of Canada. And it is pure racial discrimination. This has been proved in the past number of years by various reliable people who saw these very actions.[473]

At the conclusion of the public meeting, it was agreed that the mayor and the RCMP would work closely with First Nations in the future to avoid a repeat of the incident. The police suggested that they hire a First Nations policeman as a liaison officer and that a committee be established to "work hand-in-hand with the committees and the authorities of the city each year."[474]

Homer Stevens, secretary of the United Fishermen and Allied Workers Union, "laid the blame for the riots in Prince Rupert on discriminatory legislation such as the liquor laws and Indian Act and the application of such laws and discrimination against Natives in general."[475] The new senator, James Gladstone, stated that "most of the Indian troubles" were caused by "the Indian Act and [he] encouraged delegates to foster the desire for more education."[476] It took a three-man investigative team a whole year to issue a final report, but they determined that the riot had been partly caused by "white persons who capitalized on discrimination against Indians and incited them to acts of defiance." The investigators concluded that many First Nations people felt they were subject to "various forms of discrimination" and described the BC Liquor Control Act as "the most obvious form of discrimination," since the act permitted them to drink beer in parlours but forbade them to drink at home.[477] However, although the solutions to these problems were obvious, the political will to correct them was still missing. In the meantime, Maisie and a friend, Wing Commander LeRoy Brown, had appealed to E. Davie Fulton, the minister of justice, for the release of Chief Barney Goode of Kitwancool, who had been arrested in the melee for interfering with a police officer. Having made the case that he had actually been trying to explain things to the police, they achieved his release from Oakalla in time for him to be home with his family for Christmas.

The December 1958 *Voice* covered the 26th annual convention of the Brotherhood, which was held on December 2, 3 and 4 in Prince Rupert, and Maisie told readers how, on the night before the convention officially opened, she and the executive of the Brotherhood had met over dinner at the Broadway Café with Mayor Peter Lester and his council so the Brotherhood could state its case informally and seek ways to prevent a recurrence of the August riot. The next day, Reverend Dr. Peter Kelly told the conference that he had met with the prime minister and the new minister of Citizenship and Immigration, Ellen Fairclough, and attacked the set-up of the Native conference held in Vancouver early in 1958 where the Brotherhood had been ignored in favour of band councillors, some of whom "were not well versed in legislative matters, and many lacked experience in dealing with the government."[478] Kelly also reported that Prime Minister Diefenbaker, although desirous of providing the vote to First Nations people, thought that the "greatest problem is the indecision of the Indians," the barrier being the age-old fear of having to relinquish their rights for what Andrew Paull had called "the dubious privilege of marking a ballot every four years." The First Nations, he said, had come a long way, and it was a tribute to their ingenuity that, despite fierce competition and continued discrimination, they were managing to make a living for themselves, but "if the government believes there should be integration, then it should begin a vigorous move in that direction by helping the Indian to help himself."[479]

The convention was considered one of the best in the Brotherhood's history, with representatives from forty-two branches in attendance. The attendees included one of the founding members, the elderly Chief Heber Clifton, who had the pleasure of seeing his son, Robert, reaffirmed as president. Senator James Gladstone also came and was made an honorary member and his wife an honorary president of the Sisterhood. Two white men, James Sinclair, former Liberal Fisheries minister and now president of the Fisheries Association of BC, and Dr. R. G. Large, alderman of the City of Prince Rupert and author of *Skeena, River of Destiny*, attended and were also awarded honorary memberships. Sinclair, who ten years earlier had told the House of Commons that if First Nations were to "move out of the reserve and live as other Canadians live, [they would] get the vote," now said that in his eighteen years as an MP and five as a cabinet minister, he had never seen such a well-organized convention. Dr. Large told the conference that he had been born in the village of Bella Bella and had been "given an Indian name and was proud to be a member of such a fine organization as the Brotherhood."[480]

One of the resolutions passed was that the executive should prepare a brief for the provincial government under the signatures of President Clifton and Legislative Chair Kelly, to seek a number of concessions:

1) to have a representative on the Provincial Advisory Committee on Indian Affairs;

2) that roads through reserves used by the public should be maintained by the province;

3) that the First Nations of the province should receive the same sales tax rebate as that accorded municipalities;

4) that foreshore rights be recognized as part of reserve land;

5) that provincial sanitation regulations should apply to reserves;

6) that First Nations children, although advancing educationally, should be included in all the health and welfare programs in the province;

7) that regulations with respect to trapping licences be rewritten to remove ambiguity, since the regulations in place stated that First Nation trappers do not need trapping licences, yet the game department insists they do;

8) that the right to cut timber in the forest for personal use as well as the right to hunt and fish be granted in perpetuity;

9) that First Nations be given equal rights for liquor purchase and use.

Maisie was able to tell *Voice* readers that Premier Bennett had responded immediately to the last item by stating that he had already applied to the federal government for approval to give full liquor rights to First Nations people within the province. Under the revised Indian Act, federal approval of provincial requests was required in the form of an order-in-council, although permission would be automatic upon request. The only remaining barrier to implementation was that each First Nation had to hold a referendum to permit its members to decide whether or not they wanted liquor to be consumed on their respective reserves.

Maisie's editorial for the December 1958 issue was reflective and cautiously hopeful: "We look to 1959 for great and new achievements in the life of Native Canadians,"[481] she wrote before reflecting on her own life. She had just celebrated her 71st birthday, although the celebration had been marred a few days later by the death of an old friend, Gabriel Moody of the Squamish First Nation. She concluded her end-of-centennial year editorial with the caution that:

> much remains to be done. It is still a matter of deep concern that Native Canadians do not have the federal vote and our long-standing efforts to achieve this objective while retaining Native aboriginal rights must be continued and accelerated.
>
> There are too many other ways through which Natives have been relegated to second-class citizen status. These injustices and inequalities must be removed.[482]

But this issue of the paper also contained an appeal for more advertising dollars. The paper had moved to a larger format—double its original page size—but that issue had been restricted to four pages instead of the usual eight because of a lack of funds. Desperate for advertising revenue, and despite the unresolved question of liquor equality for First Nations people, the *Voice* now began hosting ads from Carling's Breweries to hawk its UBC (Union Brewing Company) Bohemian beer.

In February 1959, Maisie's editorial was entitled "Let Us Not Forget: The Fight Goes On." Never one to be lulled into a comfortable sense of satisfaction over small victories, important though they were, Maisie always kept her eye focussed on the distant horizon, on the bigger prize. And this time the prize—besides an unencumbered franchise—was the resolution of the "Indian Land Question," which was now coming before the federal Parliament. Aboriginal peoples had an ally in the leader of the British Columbia Progressive Conservative Party, Deane Finlayson, also known as Chief Straight Tongue, a name given to him by the Shushwap First Nation because of his honest dealings. He now vowed to support the province's First Nations in securing a judicial hearing on the land question.

Maisie devoted several pages of this edition to revisiting land rights history in the province, even publishing the entire Royal Proclamation of 1763 and describing the efforts of the Allied Tribes before that organization's dissolution in 1927. She quoted a letter from James Douglas, written while he was governor of the whole Colony of British Columbia, to the speaker and gentlemen of the House of Assembly and delivered to them on February 5, 1859. He had written:

> When the settlement at Victoria was formed, certain reservations were made in favour of the Indian Tribes.
>
> First: They were to be protected in their right of fishing on the coast and in the bays of the Colony, and of hunting over all unoccupied

Crown lands; and they were also to be secured in the enjoyment of their village sites and cultivated fields.

Those rights they have since enjoyed in full, and the reserves of land covering their village sites and cultivated fields have all been distinctly marked on the maps and surveys of the Colony, and the faith of Government is pledged that their occupation shall not be disturbed.

For that reason the Government will not cause them to be removed because it is bound by the faith of a solemn engagement to protect them in the enjoyment of those agrarian rights.[483]

All this was Maisie's round-about way of introducing the contentious issue of the $100,000 that had been granted annually by the federal government since 1927 to the First Nations of the province in lieu of treaty rights. Although the grant had been rejected by the Allied Tribes, it had been legislated nevertheless. Now the Department of Indian Affairs had announced a plan to hire First Nations individuals to help distribute these funds, and Maisie feared this might jeopardize the position of BC's First Nations with respect to their lands. Once again she addressed herself directly to the prime minister—although she also printed her words in the *Voice*:

> I feel that the forthcoming discussions on the hundred thousand dollars given to the Non-Treaty Indians of British Columbia in lieu of annuities and refused by the Non-Treaty Indians (Allied Tribes) of British Columbia in 1926 and 1927 should be adjourned until the forthcoming investigation re the valid claims of the Non-Treaty Indians of British Columbia have been heard.
>
> Many old Indians feel that the appointing of Indians to help the Department in the distribution of the hundred thousand dollars might jeopardize their valid claims to the ownership of their lands and might be construed as an acceptance in full settlement of their valid claims. As this would result in a miscarriage of justice, I ask you, who loves Indians, to adjourn the hearing.[484]

The land rights question came up again on April 26 at a special meeting arranged by George Manuel and his councillors at Kamloops. There the Reverend Dr. Peter Kelly revived the issue by stating that "the BC Indian land case has never come up for hearing and has never been settled, therefore aboriginal titles to British Columbia lands have never been extinguished."[485]

On April 28, 1959, the *Vancouver Sun* followed up with an editorial that explored the same points the Reverend Kelly had raised:

> Discontent of BC Indian chiefs over their land rights and their claims to treaty violations cannot be shrugged off. It's not something to be kicked around gleefully and chuckled over, as Indian

claims so often are. It's something rather for mature and generous consideration.

When men of the calibre of Dr. Peter Kelly are party to the rising chorus of Indian demands for reconsideration of our treatment of the Native peoples, it is a cry that defies being ignored. Not that we should wait until a Dr. Kelly speaks up. For if there has been injustice to the Indians, there should have been a way to right it regardless of the oppressed's status in the community. The need of a Dr. Kelly is in itself one of the chief injustices our Indians suffer under.

There is no denying, however, that Dr. Kelly's association with the people's protests adds to the air of legitimacy surrounding their cause. The land problem and treaty rights are important to these people, displaced in their native country. They are dissatisfied. Superficial reading of their evidence suggests they have at least some reason to be.[486]

These were also the reasons why MP Frank Howard (CCF for Skeena) was promoting yet another private member's bill—his third in three sessions of Parliament. But this one was designed to repeal the section of the Indian Act requiring First Nations to sign away their tax exemption for income earned on the reserve in exchange for enfranchisement. He told the *Native Voice* that "the Indian has a psychological attitude—in which he was fully justified after his shameful exploitation—that he is surrendering important rights in signing away tax exemption."[487] This time Howard had the support of a member of government, George C. Fairfield (PC for Portage-Neepawa), who as a physician had been treating people from two reserves within his constituency for many years.

On July 2 and 3, 1959, Reverend Dr. Peter Kelly and Brotherhood president Robert Clifton appeared before yet another Special Joint Committee of the Senate and the House of Commons on Indian Affairs in Ottawa. Kelly told the twelve senators and twenty-four members of parliament that "the petty tyranny by Indian Affairs administrators" was a grave problem among First Nations cultures and he "pleaded for a "more humane attitude" from the department, which was still holding tightly onto its veto power over First Nation decisions. He asked that "Indians be given more responsibility in dealing with band funds and affairs—to make mistakes and perhaps profit by them" and said that Indians "are placed in an inferior position because of the attitude of the Indian Affairs administration."[488]

Maisie told *Voice* readers that the lengthy Brotherhood brief had also "covered Indian education, housing, loans, health and welfare," but when it came to the subject of Aboriginal title claims by the non-treaty Indians of British Columbia, the committee had decided to hold a closed meeting to hear Dr. Kelly's brief.

Dr. Kelly submitted the history of the land claims of the non-treaty British Columbia Natives and went back to the days when the government before Confederation and after Confederation took over large areas of lands in the province... He demanded a judicial decision, claiming that the BC Indians hold aboriginal title to the lands of British Columbia.[489]

The joint committee was especially interested in also receiving a brief from Andrew Paull, president of the North American Indian Brotherhood, but asked that he forward it by mail prior to his appearance; it dealt "with the fundamental legal rights of the Indians as guaranteed and preserved for them in the British North America Act." Through his brief, Paull advised the committee "that the constitutional advisors for the Indians have taken the position that the Indians of Canada are entitled to elect Indians by a separate Indian vote to the parliament of Canada, as is exercised by the Maoris of New Zealand..."[490] and he asked the committee to change the laws to make this happen. In fact, the British North America Act had made very little reference to Aboriginal people except where the words "Indians" and "lands reserved for the Indians" had been tacked onto a list of items that came under the purview of the federal government. As well, later amendments to the act made no mention of such a voting/election privilege. Paull's stand was also contrary to the position of the Native Brotherhood, which had discarded the "vaguely understood Maori Plan,"[491] almost a decade earlier when they were negotiating the provincial vote. It was now considered a non-issue.

Paull also requested a judicial inquiry to investigate land removed from reserves following the 1913–1916 royal commission and another into BC Order-in-Council No. 1036, which permitted the government to expropriate reserve land for public highway use. BC Labour Minister Lyle Wicks, upon hearing this, advised that two federal judicial inquiries into the issue of Aboriginal title had failed to resolve it, and he didn't hold out much hope that a third would do any better.

Andrew Paull never got to Ottawa to present his brief in person. He had been gravely ill while preparing it, but declared that he would "go on a stretcher"[492] if he had to. However, on July 28, 1959, only days after mailing his brief to the committee, he succumbed to a heart ailment. He was 67. He had been a fierce advocate for his people, defending them both in the courts and the legislatures, and any hint of the rancour that had followed him throughout his career evaporated on the day of his funeral service. A thousand people came to Reserve No. 1 on the North Shore to say goodbye, slowly accompanying him on the last few steps of his mortal journey, past his home and on to the burial grounds that cradled his ancestors.

The fall months of 1959 dragged on with no action by the federal government on either the land question or the franchise, but in mid-December, a *Toronto Telegram* editorial stirred up fresh interest among the general public. Referencing Minister of Citizenship and Immigration Ellen Fairclough's recent tour of western Canadian reserves, it read:

> The record is bad. These original inhabitants have been encouraged to segregate, to lead inferior lives barely touched by modern education and medicine and economic prosperity of the mass of Canadians.
>
> Even the law sets these people apart. The Indian Act gives Indians separate status. It should be abolished. Indians, says James Gladstone, Canada's first Indian senator, want only "equality of opportunity" and "equal status," not much to ask in a democratic society.

The *Telegram* article concluded that:

> Proper recognition of the discrimination meted out to Canada's Indians and Eskimos is in itself a move towards solving it. Canada's policies should ensure that these people can live where and how they please, with the security of life that belongs to any Canadian. [493]

While in Calgary, the minister had been presented with a six-page petition from Ruth Gorman, past chair of the Civil Liberties Committee of the Canadian Bar Association, which had been signed by forty bands, churches, labour unions and other First Nations advocates. It requested that an appeal process be instituted so that the First Nations could challenge ministerial decisions and that "treaty Indians" not lose their status.

On January 18, 1960, the first day of the third session of the 24th Parliament, Prime Minister John Diefenbaker honoured the pledge made to Canada's Aboriginal population by the "Great White Mother" Queen Victoria that her ministers would respect and uphold their rights "as long as the sun shines, the grass grows and the waters flow." He gave the First Nations people of Canada the federal vote with no strings attached. In Maisie's editorial in the February 1960 Special Edition of the *Voice*, she wrote:

> It remained for Canada's greatest son, John G. Diefenbaker, to implement the great Queen's assurance. By doing this, he has erased the blackest stain on Canada's escutcheon. This country can now face the world with a clean conscience. This is a voluntary measure without barter or bargaining or waiver of aboriginal rights.[494]

Prime Minister John G. Diefenbaker in headdress with his wife, Olive. Maisie said of the granting of the federal franchise to Canada's First Nations: "It remained for Canada's greatest son, John G. Diefenbaker, to implement the great Queen's assurance." Photo courtesy of the University of Saskatchewan, University Archives & Special Collections, John G. Diefenbaker fonds, MG 411, JGD 4859.tif.

The prime minister, in the course of his speech in the House of Commons, said:

> The provision to give Indians the vote is one of those steps which will have an effect everywhere in the world—for the reason that wherever I went last year on the occasion of my trip to Commonwealth countries, it was brought to my attention that in Canada the original people within our country, excepting for a qualified class, were denied the right to vote. I say that so far as this long overdue measure is concerned, it will remove everywhere in the world any suggestion that color or race places any citizen in our country in a lower category than the other citizens of our country.
>
> I say this to those of the Indian race, that in bringing forward this legislation, the minister of Citizenship and Immigration—Mrs. Fairclough—will reassure, as she has assured to date, that existing rights and treaties, traditional or otherwise, possessed by the Indians shall not in any way be abrogated or diminished in consequence of having the right to vote. This is one of the things that throughout the

years has caused suspicion in the minds of many Indians who have conceived the granting of the franchise as a step in the direction of denying them their ancient rights.[495]

Diefenbaker could now rest assured that his criticism of the apartheid regime of South Africa would be on solid ground and that he could with all confidence usher in his Canadian Bill of Rights without excluding Canada's First People.

Minister Ellen Fairclough assured First Nations people that they would "have the right to vote on an equal basis with other citizens irrespective of whether they reside on or off a reserve." She also advised BC First Nations that the offer of the federal franchise would in no way alter the terms of the McKenna-McBride Agreement "or the status of the reserves as they exist at the present time."[496] Two bills would be required, one to amend the Indian Act and the other to amend the Elections Act, the amendments to come into force on proclamation so that they would take effect simultaneously.

An elated Reverend Kelly was quoted in the *Voice*'s Special Edition as saying that the next step would be to prepare:

men of the calibre to stand among the worthy lawmakers of the country. The way to the highest position in the country is now open to us. The place at the top is open to persons of training, stability, unselfishness and brotherly spirit.[497]

And Brotherhood president Robert Clifton was overjoyed that:

After years of "wardship," years of hardship and suffering caused by the neglect and indifference of white governments to those who were first in the land, Native Indians at last stand as full citizens. I am proud of my people, proud of what the Native Brotherhood has accomplished and confident that out of their splendid heritage the Native Indians will make an even greater contribution to the progress of their country.[498]

But there was sadness, too, for those who had worked for this day but died before it came. Chief Bill Wilson recalled that "my Dad died the year before he became a citizen of this country. He had two or three hundred white employees and couldn't vote, but he controlled their lives by his efforts to pay them."[499]

Maisie's euphoria lasted for months. In September 1960 as she strolled down Hastings Street in Vancouver with *Province* reporter Roland Wild, she told him:

"Darling," (she calls most people darling)... "It took the Tories to give justice to my people! If I could get an inquiry going into what happened 50 years ago, I could stop the PGE trains running! But at least the Indians have got full citizenship at last! Canada has 60,000 new voters!"[500]

11—The Defence Rests

As elation over the granting of the federal vote subsided, sober reflection spawned a range of emotions that quickly filled the vacuum. Big White Owl cautioned that:

> Many Indians in Canada look upon the granting of the federal vote with suspicion, skepticism, distrust and fear. The Indian cannot be blamed for taking this attitude.
>
> The white man has consistently failed to keep his word with the Indian. Not so many years ago he went so far as to embark on a program of destroying Indian cultures, history, arts, crafts, and the whole ethnic structure of the Indian was undermined.
>
> The Indian has been cheated, robbed, fleeced, despised, trampled upon so often (and for so long), how in the name of Heaven can you expect him to trust the white man now?

His argument was that, although in time the vote would be advantageous, not until sections 108 to 112 of the Indian Act were repealed would Aboriginal people be confident in expressing their franchise. And he warned that:

> Under Section 112 of the Indian Act of Canada, the minister of Indian Affairs can compel the Indian—even a whole tribe or band—to be removed from an Indian Reserve, if a three-man committee agrees the Indian or the Indians in question are capable of fending for themselves in the competitive white man's world.[501]

Ruth Gorman, legal counsel for the Alberta Indian Association, had arrived at the same conclusion and expressed "some doubt about using the vote while the Indian Act remains unchanged in certain sections."[502] She mirrored Big White Owl's sentiments that the vote would be a valuable instrument if those offending sections were removed. Maisie, too, received some fallout downstream of the vote—although this had more to do with her editorial on that subject than the subject itself. It was a rather nasty phone call from the president of the BC Liberal Association, taking umbrage at her reference in the special edition of the *Voice* to John Diefenbaker as "Canada's greatest son." He demanded, "What about the Honorable Lester Pearson?" To which Maisie later responded in print:

> I managed to squeeze in a few words between your terrible barrage of abuse. I admitted that Mr. Pearson was a nice man, although he

irritates me beyond words, and I find his views more destructive than constructive... Our Prime Minister will always hold a warm spot in our hearts for what he has done for the Indians of Canada. God bless him.[503]

The Liberal Association's president followed up his telephone call with a letter requesting the opportunity to publish a Liberal Special Edition of the *Voice*. Maisie's reply was terse: "We regret that an exhaustive perusal of the Liberal record has revealed nothing to justify a special "Liberal" issue of the *Native Voice*."[504]

Meanwhile, Chief Rising Sun (Carl Lewis), a successful Toronto businessman and sometime contributor to the *Voice*, was skeptical that the vote would change much. "If the privilege to vote in federal elections is put as an invitation to Indians to participate, I am afraid it will be declined," he wrote. "Why? Because the red man is not yet ready for it."[505] This was perhaps, also the view of a group led by George Manuel, chair of the Aboriginal Native Rights Regional Committee of the Interior Tribes of BC, which had prepared a twenty-two-point brief that proposed "sweeping legislation to improve their living standards and fit them into the province's industrial development."[506] They were asking for basic things that other Canadians took for granted—adequate community planning, proper water, electrical and plumbing systems as well as recreational facilities—but they were all barriers to advancement and came far before any thought might be given to the vote.

Meanwhile, the old question of Aboriginal title to the land, which had been simmering in the background while First Nations fought for the vote, was coming to the fore again. Land was especially significant to BC's Interior tribes since much of their arable reserve land had been expropriated in the wake of the McKenna-McBride Commission. But Manuel and the Interior First Nations had an unlikely ally in their court; ex-minister Pickersgill now appeared to be supporting First Nations initiatives, even voting in favour of Minister Ellen Fairclough's proposition to grant the vote, something his government had consistently denied them while he sat in that chair. Now he was championing their rights by telling the provinces that:

> The Indians are Canadian citizens like any other Canadian citizens, and the provincial governments have exactly the same responsibility towards them when they move off a reserve as they have towards any other citizen of the provinces.[507]

MP Frank Howard (CCF for Skeena), who had been pressing the government to grant the unconditional vote to First Nations people for three years, was ecstatic that it had finally come to fruition, but now he urged the government to "move quickly in correcting some of the abuses that have been heaped upon the Indian by the so-called white man."[508] It was these "abuses" that were keeping First Nations from gainful employment, he explained, although BC's minister of Labour, Lyle Wicks, had told the Brotherhood convention in December 1959 that the province was leading the country in First Nations education, proven by the huge increase in school enrolment in the last ten years. And, he said, he didn't think there was discrimination against First Nations in the employment sector. His elation had been crushed by Godfrey Williams, the Masset delegate, who told the conference that: "Unemployment is the greatest problem on the reserves. There is a terrible waste of manpower, and ways should be found to give employment to Native people."[509] In answer, Wicks offered the oft-repeated solution that there were plenty of opportunities in the small business sector for First Nations individuals with the right training and education.

According to Assistant Indian Commissioner F. E. Anfield, education was certainly a priority. He said that $4,000,000 was being spent annually on First Nations education in the province, although of the 9,000 First Nations children attending school, 70 per cent were not in the public system. This was because children were still being removed from their homes and shipped off to residential schools in what has been described as an attempt to "kill the Indian in the child," an expression attributed to Duncan Campbell Scott, deputy superintendent of the Department of Indian Affairs from 1913 to 1932. Furthermore, 15 per cent of the teachers at these residential schools were unqualified to teach.

The Brotherhood urged that residential schools be closed except in isolated circumstances, that music and dancing be taught, and bursaries and scholarships awarded for university and vocational training. Closing residential schools, however, was not the wish of every First Nation in the province. At a meeting of the Upper Stó:lō and Lower Thompson First Nations chaired by Oscar Peters in October 1960, it was resolved to petition the federal government to allow "all parents who are now sending their children to residential schools that they permit them to complete their schooling there." Peters believed that the residential schools "are properly disciplined to the faith of obedience, religion, intelligence, and the high standard of characteristic ideals and will help those who will urge that these schools be maintained always."[510]

His opinion was in direct contrast to the Department of Indian Affairs' evolving perspective on residential schooling, which would culminate in a conference for Indian agency superintendents and regional supervisors at Harrison Hot Springs a year later. At that time Robert F. Davey, chief of the education division of the Indian Affairs branch, told the gathering that integration of First Nations children into mainstream schools was the only way to advance their educational needs. He said that:

reservation schooling is authoritarian... It has no significant impact on the Indian people as a whole and its influence is largely superficial. The attitude of parents will not change as long as the Indian school remains aloof from community life, a trespasser on the reserve, intruding in family life, alienating children from parents, disturbing old folk ways and hampering the freedom to roam.[511]

Education was also one of the themes highlighted by the new Senator James Gladstone in October 1960 when he accepted the award for Outstanding American Indian of the Year granted by the All American Indian Days Committee in Sheridan, Wyoming. He told his audience that Canadian and American Aboriginal peoples shared common problems in educating their children.

We want them to learn how to make a good living in this fast-moving world. We want to hold onto our reservations and keep them for the people who can make a living from the land. And, most of all, we want to assure for our children a bright future in this America that once was ours... Those who speak of ending government responsibility [for Native people] in a few years cannot fully understand the great change which must take place in our lives. Let us first have education and understanding. Then we can seriously consider our own responsibilities and those to our country.[512]

With the federal vote taken care of, it appeared that the federal government was becoming more accommodating towards First Nations issues in other ways. On April 8, 1961, Minister Fairclough announced that enfranchised First Nations women and children forced to return to their reserves due to economic circumstances would be granted the same welfare and educational benefits as if they had full status. It was a compassionate move, historically uncharacteristic of the federal government, but in keeping with the recent policies of Diefenbaker and his Progressive Conservatives. Even Liberal MP Jack Pickersgill joined CCF MP Frank Howard in support of the motion.

But while the federal government was spreading its largesse to First Nations, the provinces were lagging behind, especially with respect to liquor privileges. In the Northwest Territories, Aboriginal peoples had the same liquor rights as their white neighbours, while the governments of Newfoundland, Prince Edward Island, New Brunswick, Saskatchewan and Alberta had failed to progress beyond total prohibition, although within a few months Saskatchewan would remove all restrictions subject to the approval of each First Nation. In Nova Scotia, Manitoba, the Yukon and British Columbia, Aboriginal people were still restricted to licenced premises, although in BC, there was pressure from unexpected allies for restrictions to be lifted. The Anglican Diocesan

Synod of British Columbia was advocating unrestricted liquor rights, and the New Westminster Legion would shortly request that First Nations veterans be permitted to drink in their establishment as well. The subject was also part of the brief presented by George Manuel of the Interior Tribes to the joint committee at Ottawa. He pointed out that:

> Nothing can be accomplished in Indian integration until Indian liquor restrictions are removed. An Indian who does well in business and attends a dinner as a guest of white men is immediately segregated because he cannot accept a social drink. This has happened many times.[513]

In July 1960, when Alderman Gordon E. Carlson was delegated by the Prince Rupert City Council to write to Attorney General Robert Bonner to request full drinking privileges for First Nations people in that area, he received the reply that "no special announcement of policy is available at this time."[514] The council's request had been prompted by both financial and moral considerations. The town was experiencing higher policing costs during the summer fishing season, which placed an unnecessarily heavy burden on local taxpayers; granting full liquor rights to First Nations people would make this extra policing unnecessary. The mayor was also concerned that "as it stands, the Indian Act has to be enforced. It is enforced with difficulty, but it is morally wrong and should be changed."[515] His continuing efforts to promote that change included an offer to support the Nisga'a Tribal Council's "Indian plebiscite on the question of permitting Indians equality under the terms of the Indian Act regarding liquor."[516] On September 17, the mayor followed up his colleague's letter to the attorney general with one of his own, requesting equal liquor rights be granted to First Nations in the entire province. He wrote:

> We feel the law, as it presently stands, is not only unjust but unenforceable. We think that a law such as this, which denies social equality to any group, is a form of Apartheid that has no place in Canada.[517]

A month later he was still waiting for a reply. Meanwhile, Frank Howard had waded into the debate, calling the provincial law "asinine, over-strict and foolish."[518] He accused Bonner of failing to understand the Indian Act. Once again Liberal MP Jack Pickersgill sided with Howard, although he saw the liquor rights solution in terms of Indians being "completely integrated with the rest of the population."[519]

But while liquor laws were capturing the headlines, one of the greatest barriers to equality and integration remained the unresolved issue of Aboriginal title to the land. On May 26, 1960, at a meeting of the Special Joint Committee of the

Senate and House of Commons on the Indian Act, Frank Calder, representing the Nisga'a people, pressed the case for a court judgment to force settlement of Nisga'a Aboriginal title. He told the committee that the provincial government was gradually chipping away at the 6,400 square miles of the Nass River basin that the Nisga'a claimed under their "aboriginal rights."[520] George Manuel of the Interior Tribes followed him, telling the committee that "the People of British Columbia want this question settled once and for always. The best place," he said, "was before a judicial committee of the Privy Council."[521] Unfortunately, the Privy Council had ceased to be Canada's highest appeal court in 1949.[522]

In the June 1960 issue of the *Voice,* Maisie weighed in on the topic, too:

> It seems impossible that a request for a court settlement, [which] the Natives say (and history validates) is their right, to a large piece of British Columbia can be refused...
>
> Mr. Frank Calder has, according to a Canadian Press report, complained that the British Columbia provincial government won't meet his group on the issue of the 6,400 disputed acres (sic).
>
> That is most unfair since the tribe also charges that it is the BC government which has sold or leased large portions of the vast land area in dispute...
>
> At the barest minimum, the issue must be settled in the manner requested by the Nisga'a.[523]

With a provincial election set for September 12, 1960, Frank Calder, who had lost his seat in the legislature in the 1956 election, was once again campaigning on the CCF ticket and laying plans to badger the government over the Nisga'a land issue if he was successful at the polls. He had First Nations company in this election because Guy Williams had finally put his name forward for the Progressive Conservatives in Skeena district, as had Horace Kelly—the son of Reverend Dr. Peter Kelly—in Prince Rupert. Kelly, a World War II veteran, was pushing plans to develop Prince Rupert as a northern rail and shipping terminus. Although Calder was returned to the legislature, neither Williams nor Kelly was elected.

Meanwhile, Frank Howard remained a strong representative for his First Nations constituents in the federal arena, and in August 1960 he announced that in the next session of Parliament he was going to introduce yet another private member's bill, this one to repeal Section 112 of the Indian Act, which empowered the government to enfranchise Indians against their will.

> This section is one of the most obnoxious and objectionable sections in the entire Act and has been opposed by practically every Indian in Canada. In fact, the Joint Committee on Indian Affairs

unanimously recommended on July 6, 1960, that at the first opportunity the government introduce legislation to remove the compulsory
enfranchisement provision from the Indian Act.

Even though private member's bills have little chance of passing
at the best of times, and even though this bill will appear at the bottom of the agenda, I hope that the minister will accept the bill and ask
that it be transferred to government orders, thus bringing our Indian
people one step closer to equality.[524]

When the joint committee finally released its report on this issue, recommendation 1c was to delete the word, "enfranchisement" from the "ob-
noxious and objectionable" section of the Indian Act that had accumulated
so much distrust among First Nations people. In March 1961, Senator James
Gladstone had the unique privilege of moving second reading of the repeal of
this draconian bit of legislation. Howard, who was justifiably pleased, decided
that all his badgering for equality over the years may have had an impact.

Equality was such a powerful mantra to the effusive MP for Skeena that
it must have come as a shock when BC's Department of Highways expropriated a four-mile-long 200-foot-wide stretch of land through the Kitwanga Reserve, which was within his constituency, to construct a road from northern
trans-provincial highway 16 to the ferry landing on the Skeena River. Although
Highways Minister Philip Gaglardi's representatives had attended a meeting
on the reserve in the spring of 1960, they had responded to all the questions
raised by the people of Kitwanga by saying they would have to defer to the minister for answers. The representatives never did get back to the Kitwanga people, and that summer when road crews showed up to begin work, it became
obvious that the government was going to proceed regardless of their concerns.

The chiefs and councillors of the band retaliated by demanding payment
for the full value of the destroyed property, "and if there is no payment, the
chiefs and councillors will install toll gates and charge motorists using the
road. Free passage will be granted members of other Indian bands as well as
Kitwanga residents." Band members also erected a sign that read: "Sorry to
embarrass you, Mr. Gaglardi, but you haven't paid for this four miles of Indian reserve land."[525]

Maisie was predictably furious with the government and editorialized
that: "The action of the British Columbia government in bulling its way
through Indian reserves without advance arrangement with the people affected or their leaders is callous and deplorable."[526] She went even further when
she gave an interview to reporter Hugh Watson in October. His subsequent
article in the *Vancouver Province* was headlined:

SORRY FOR THE INCONVENIENCE, BUT IT'S WAR!

War! That's what Maisie Hurley calls it. And as the only white woman life member of the Native Brotherhood of BC, Maisie should know what she is talking about.

She says the next conflict between the white man and Indian will be a "cold hot war," fought on a battlefield four miles long through the Kitwanga Village near Hazelton.

The weapons? Toll gates at 10 paces...

The government originally offered the Kitwanga Indians $482," says Maisie. "They've since raised it to a more respectable $6,538. But what we really want is a judicial inquiry establishing the aboriginal rights of BC Indians. We've never signed a peace treaty with any government. (One tribe did but Maisie doesn't like to mention it.) We want our rights firmly established and we'll go to John Diefenbaker—again—if we must."[527]

In November the Hazelton Indian agent, A. E. Fry, offered that he thought that the Kitwanga First Nation had some rights, given that the government had proceeded without their approval. Kitwanga Chief Harold Sinclair stated that he had received a letter from the Highways Department and that they were "very much disturbed by our toll gate plan." When Maisie was asked how much they should charge at their toll gates, she replied: "I think about two bits should cover it."

"I can't understand why they are acting this way," Highways Minister Gaglardi complained. "Someone must be agitating them. Sounds like it's all politically inspired."[528]

Maisie, who was indeed one of the agitators, stated that the expropriation of Kitwanga land was simply the straw that broke the camel's back. She said:

It isn't just this issue. We want a full judicial inquiry into all aboriginal rights, including social assistance, fishing rights, land infringements by the provincial government and logging companies. We're getting sick of it all. Our only hope is to force Mr. Diefenbaker to give us the inquiry.

These men are the true owners of this country and are asking to negotiate like gentlemen.[529]

Although Maisie appeared to be in fine fighting form, she had recently undergone surgery at the insistence of her doctor and was recuperating at home. She thanked her friends for their best wishes and concerns and advised them that she might be a bit slow in answering their letters. She was now approaching her 73rd birthday, but she launched herself from her sickbed in time for the Brotherhood's AGM in Prince Rupert in mid-December.

Mayor Peter Lester welcomed the delegates to Prince Rupert with the contrite and sincere comment that "We've made mistakes here, but we will attempt at all times to understand your problems." Robert Clifton stepped down from his role as president to make room for Guy Williams, a natural-born leader who had been heavily involved in Brotherhood business for so many years. Williams, who had been born at Kitimat but now resided in Steveston, told the convention delegates that he would do his utmost to fulfill the role with dignity and courage, always keeping their interests before him.

When Maisie rose to speak about the Kitwanga road issue, she informed the meeting that pages ten and eleven of the Indian Act clearly spelled out the procedure with respect to trespass on reserve land. She said that only the governor-in-council in Ottawa could decide on the disposal of Aboriginal land and that "the Indian Act supersedes the BC Highways Act both in regard to trespass or taking land for public purposes."[530] While she conceded that there was provision in the act for a province, municipality, local official or corporation to take or use reserve land for public purposes when necessary, it could only be at the consent of the governor-in-council, and it was restricted to a small percentage of the land. Gaglardi, she pointed out, had failed to get this consent. "We would suggest that Highways Minister P. A. Gaglardi adopt as his personal coat of arms a bulldozer rampant with Indian superintendents couchant," Maisie said before promising to watch "closely the moves and squirms of the Victoria government."[531]

This was not the end of the Kitwanga story, however. It was revived by a comment made by an unnamed official in the Indian Affairs Department in Ottawa to the effect that the province did not have to pay for the land it had expropriated from the Kitwanga Reserve. His comment had been prompted by a letter Maisie had written to the Minister of Justice, E. Davie Fulton, in January 1961 "in which she asserted the reserve land was held in trust for the Kitwangas and the BC government had absolutely no right to tamper with it."[532] She had supported her letter with a plethora of references to historical documents including the Indian Act, then she added:

And furthermore, I feel the dust and mildew on the federal trusteeship and guardianship of Indian rights and lands should be cleared off and the whole matter thoroughly reviewed.

I feel that the federal government should search and find some of the ancient documents to determine what belongs to the Crown in trust for the Indians and just where this provincial grab of land stops.

It all boils down to this—statements from the Indian Affairs Department notwithstanding—we want a judicial decision on the non-Indian lands which were never surrendered to anyone. In all fairness, this action must be taken.[533]

Weeks later she was still awaiting a reply to her letter, but this did not stop her from editorializing about the land grab again in the February 1961 issue of the *Voice*.

An important point in the campaign is the legality of provincial actions taken since 1938 when, by virtue of Minute 1036 of the executive council, [the province] over-rode the McKenna-McBride agreement. By this agreement the provincial government vacated all rights in lands transferred to the federal government for non-treaty Indians in British Columbia.

Minute 1036, adopted in July 1938, empowered the province to resume unimproved land to the extent of five percent of the area transferred to the Dominion for roads and other public works without compensation. The province relied on this power when it cut a road four miles long and 200 feet wide through the Kitwanga Reserve without Native approval. But the Kitwanga Indians are standing firmly by their rights and demanding $100,000 as compensation for land and timber lost.[534]

(The band had earlier rejected both of the province's offers of financial settlement, claiming that the timber alone was worth $27,000.)

In a debate in the House of Commons on February 17, Minister Fairclough offered vaguely that whether "an individual band received compensation for the land it lost I cannot say... but over the years undoubtedly things were done that should not have been done." Later in the debate she mentioned the right of the province to expropriate up to 5 per cent of reserve land for such purposes as roads, then added, "Of course, they have taken more than that and we agree the situation is not what it might be..."[535]

MP Frank Howard's response was "Obviously, the Bill of Rights means nothing as far as [the people of Kitwanga's] land is concerned."[536] His reference was to Prime Minister Diefenbaker's brand new Bill of Rights, introduced on August 10, 1960; this first attempt at human rights legislation in Canada had made no specific mention of Aboriginal peoples. As well, it was restricted to having only quasi-constitutional powers at the federal level, a shortcoming that would not be corrected until the passage of the Canadian Charter of Rights and Freedoms twenty-two years later, a constitutional agreement that would cover the application of both federal and provincial law in Canada.

However, despite the new Canadian Bill of Rights making no specific mention of Aboriginal rights, it was employed successfully for that purpose only a month after Howard had condemned it for failing to protect the Kitwanga people from land expropriation by the provincial government. When Hector MacDonald of the Pavilion Indian Reserve near Lillooet was arrested for unlawful possession of beer while away from his reserve, the police charged him under Section 94 of the Indian Act. A local magistrate, Ed Angman, decided that this section of the Indian Act was discriminatory and that it had been superseded by the Bill of Rights. He ruled that Section 94(a) of the Indian Act, which prohibited Indians from being in possession of alcohol or being intoxicated away from their reserves, was invalid as it violated section 1(b) of the Canadian Bill of Rights, which provided "the right of the individual to equality before the law and the protection of the law." Angman's ruling was "believed to be the first in Canada since the Bill was made law,"[537] and as a result, Attorney General Bonner appealed the case for "clarification" of the ruling."[538]

A couple of months later Police Magistrate A. D. Pool disagreed with Angman's judgment when he found Harvey Jerome Gonzales, a respected member of the Squamish band, guilty of a similar offence. Tom Hurley, Gonzales's lawyer, had defended him using Section 1(a) of the Bill of Rights, which guaranteed "the right of the individual to life, liberty, security of the person and enjoyment of property, and the right not to be deprived thereof except by due process of law." In his "reasons for judgment," Poole wrote that:

> the Canadian Bill of Rights seems to be popularly thought as ensuring, in the widest terms, that there can be no discrimination in any regard between different races, colours, religions or sexes. That is far too sweeping a thought to be practical... Discrimination is not necessarily adverse; it implies nothing more than observation of a difference and can be equally favourable or unfavourable in its effect... The Canadian Bill of Rights was enacted with full knowledge of the existence of the Indian Act, and it would be an extraordinary thing if Parliament was to be held by implication to be condemning its own existing, exclusive, specific legislation in any of its details. The Canadian Bill of Rights, in fact, does not express any intention to change the law. On the contrary... this wording can only be construed logically as confirming existing legislation and authoritative interpretations of it.

Then, with respect to Tom Hurley's defence of "enjoyment of property," Poole declared that "property refers to a thing of substance, a man's estate, his material worth... It does not give unfettered freedom in transient contracts."[539] Hurley appealed the case to the BC Supreme Court, citing the Bill of Rights and contending that it superseded the Indian Act, and when Mr. Justice H. A. McLean confirmed the conviction, Hurley decided to appeal the ruling to the BC Court of Appeal. Maisie, who had appeared with her husband at the Supreme Court hearing, declared that, "We'll fight this to the Supreme Court of Canada."[540] And Tom added that if "whites are permitted to possess liquor, then so are Indians if the new bill is to have any real meaning."[541] But Maisie was becoming disillusioned and she later wrote:

It is an ugly black thought, but could the passing of the Bill of Rights and the granting of the federal vote to the Indians have been for the sole purpose of saving the face of Canada when appearing before the United Nations and the Commonwealth of Nations? We're waiting for Ottawa to prove otherwise.[542]

The unfair laws surrounding First Nations purchase and use of liquor were considered of such significance—not only due to the equality issue but because the penalties for abusing those laws were so harsh—that it was discussed at almost every Brotherhood AGM. This had also been true of the AGM in Prince Rupert in December 1960, but on that occasion it had been the Chiefs who spoke up, in one case taking charge of their own emancipation. The Ulgatchmo Band at Anahim Lake wanted equality with their white neighbours and simply requested "equal liquor rights with whites... [as] the present law obliges people to resort to homebrew." (In her report in the *Voice*, Maisie wrote: "And they might have added [that] the latter is illegal if it is made or possessed by Natives."[543]) MLA Frank Calder, who was also president of the Nisga'a Tribal Council, representing four northern British Columbia villages along the Nass River—Aiyansh, Canyon City, Greenville and Kincolith—resolved to obtain full liquor rights for his band by bypassing the provincial government altogether. He told the conference that:

> Under section 96A of the Indian Act, resolutions [requesting permission to hold a referendum on the reserve re liquor privileges] must be sent to the [federal] Department of Citizenship and Immigration, which advises the provincial attorney general's department of their receipt. Unless the province enters an objection within 60 days, the federal government then directs "that the wishes of the band with respect thereto be ascertained by a referendum of elections of the band."

> If every Indian village in BC were to forward a resolution to the federal minister, Attorney General Robert Bonner would have no choice but to amend the BC Liquor Act, thus granting equal liquor privileges for Natives.[544]

George Manuel told the conference that he had already convinced twenty First Nations in the Interior to complete and forward resolutions and he was just waiting for his legal advisors to prepare the documents. This ploy, he said, had recently worked in Ontario.

Attorney General Bonner, however, in an attempt to sidestep the issue, had passed the buck to the federal government by inserting a small item into a lengthy housekeeping bill, which said in effect that "if the federal cabinet requests it, BC Natives will be able to consume liquor in full accord

Magistrate Roderick Haig-Brown, in his study at his home in Campbell River, commented on the unfair legislation involving First Nations and alcohol: "It brings them into court when they shouldn't be there—it is the rankest kind of discrimination..." Photo courtesy of the Campbell River Museum Archives.

with provincial law."[545] This prompted the Nisga'a Tribal Council to issue the following statement:

> A bold and forward measure must be taken now because the Social Credit government has refused to acknowledge its responsibility to consider full and equal rights to liquor for the BC Indians, and it failed to recognize the legal procedure by which Indians may secure such privileges as provided in the Indian Act, when at the spring session of the BC Legislature, the government passed a motion which in effect referred the Indian liquor question to the federal jurisdiction.[546]

The province's attempt to place the responsibility on the shoulders of the nation backfired when Minister Fairclough responded negatively. Meanwhile, the parliamentary joint committee, which was considering yet another complete overhaul of the Indian Act, recommended that:

> In view of the fact that the possession and consumption of intoxicants off reserves by Indians is dependent on a request by the

province, [this] committee recommends that all existing liquor restrictions in the Indian Act be deleted; and that the same rights extended to non-Indian citizens of the various provinces be applicable
to Indians, except that the right of possession and consumption on
the reserve be granted only after the approval by a majority vote of
the band.[547]

This wasn't about to happen any time soon as Campbell River Magistrate
Roderick Haig-Brown discovered several months later; when he raised the
issue with BC's attorney general, that gentleman "replied by trying to pass the
buck to Ottawa."[548] Reporting on this impasse the *Campbell River Courier*
told its readers that:

The result of these restrictive regulations has been that liquor has at-
tained an importance far greater than it deserves or would otherwise
have had. It has become, to the Indians, a symbol of inequality... Everyone knows what happened when an attempt was made to prohibit
the use of liquor in Canada and the US. Almost the whole population
deliberately set out to flout the law, with many people drinking just
to show their independence.

Among the Indians, as Mr. Haig-Brown says, the same thing has
happened, but in their case there is the added need to prove that they
are just as good and just as grown-up as white people. Many will say,
from cursory observance, that Indians are not able to handle liquor, but
it has been proven by scientists, social workers and others that there
is no physical reason for an Indian to be less able than anyone else to
handle liquor properly. They just haven't had the chance to show it.

Haig-Brown stated that: "It brings them into court when they
shouldn't be there—it is the rankest kind of discrimination... The provincial government since 1956 has had the remedy right in its hands"
through section 95 and 96A of the Indian Act. The government has
done nothing...

"In social legislation we're similarly backward," Mr. Haig-Brown
stated. "There is no probation officer in the province specifically
trained for Indian work. There is, in fact, no one at all at such Indian
points as Alert Bay or the Prince Rupert area. For want of this kind of
services, Indian young people are sent to jail and industrial schools
when white children would not be."[549]

Besides liquor rights, one of the major discussions at the Prince Rupert
convention in December 1960 had been the calamitous salmon fishing season—"the worst in 50 years,"[550] according to Brotherhood president Guy Williams, himself a fisherman—and he expressed his worry that the Federal Winter

Works Program was proceeding too slowly for effective relief. The poor fishing season combined with the slow winter work program meant that people were being forced away from their reserves in order to find employment. In March, President Williams told a meeting of the Vancouver Kiwanis Club that: "Natives need encouragement, understanding, sympathy and assistance... It takes a lot of courage to move off a reservation... The future is completely unknown to them."[551]

Maisie's respect and admiration for the man who had given "her Indian friends" the federal vote had made her shy of overtly criticizing his government, so when she wrote her editorial for the April 1960 issue of the *Voice*, she signed it simply "A Pioneer Friend of the Indians." Unfortunately for Diefenbaker, it wasn't enough to appoint an Indian to the Senate and give First Nations the vote. The plethora of ills that had been affecting First Nations since the previous winter prompted her to take his government to task in very plain language. In reference to Gladstone's appointment she wrote:

> Here [you will] find an otherwise commendable sense of pride tinged with a hypocritical piece of window dressing. The long-overdue appointment of Senator Gladstone does not compensate for the neglect of his Indian brothers nor does it indicate any promise of a constructive policy toward the betterment of the original occupiers of this great land.
>
> Included earlier in Mr. Diefenbaker's humanistic vision is a "Colombo Plan" for Africa, but what in the name of justice is needed is a "Canada Plan" for Canadians, with earnest consideration given to a measure which will raise the Indian peoples to where they can take their places in the economic life of this country.

The "Pioneer Friend" then advised the prime minister to reduce his African aid by $25 million and invest it in his own country's Aboriginal peoples. "Here, unlike the Congo," she wrote, "there is no raw savagery, fanned by 'the winds of change,' but in contrast, a too patient docility in awaiting a share of the largesse we hasten to give to others."[552]

She also criticized the federal government for the $125 million allocated to the Canada Council:

> which yearly provides lucrative hand-outs in the name of culture to many who are not in need of such assistance, as well as to those of the avant garde whose writings, music, paintings and other phantasies the world could do without. This is truly the blue mink coat that hides our ragged underwear. It is a sad commentary in the face of the truth that our Indian people are forced to shuffle as best they may.[553]

Maisie Hurley was a talented artist, rendering many a pastel portrait of her First Nations friends. Photo from the family collection.

Given that Maisie was an artist herself, having produced many well-crafted pastel portraits, she was being a little harsh on the arts, but her frustration at the slow pace of progress in improving the lot of First Nations was making her even less tolerant with the government than usual. At the same time she recognized that the arts represented an important aspect of First Nations peoples' life, their history and spirituality manifested in the magnificent totems, masks, weavings, ceremonial clothing and beadwork that she so prized. She had even established a fan club for Jay Silverheels (who played Tonto in the "Lone Ranger" series) and gave regular updates on his career in the *Voice* in order to showcase this remarkably humble Mohawk actor while at the same time drawing in a younger readership for the paper. Further evidence of her appreciation of the arts was the dedication of the entire July 1961 edition of the *Voice* to the poet and performer Pauline Johnson (1861–1913) to celebrate the centenary of her birth.

On the day of the memorial celebration, a group gathered at Johnson's gravesite and memorial in Stanley Park to hear Chief Mathias Joe Capilano, son of Chief Joe Capilano who had been the source of the stories in her book, *Legends of Vancouver*, sing a song of his own composition in the language of the Squamish people. This was followed by prayers and dances performed as a "stirring tribute to the memory of this revered Canadian."[554] Although the celebration took place a long way from Johnson's birthplace near Brantford, Ontario, Dr. Richard Pilant, co-chair of the Institute of Iroquoian Studies, wrote that:

> the pilgrimage seems to us a way of bringing a large number of the alert Indians of Canada into official contact and as a way of generating favorable publicity for Indian achievements... Until the white people know more of the Indian contribution to Canadian history and their potentialities, little progress can be made."[555]

In June 1961, Alfred Scow learned that he had just become the first First Nations person to graduate from UBC's school of law. He was out fishing halibut at the time and only learned of his success between trips. "I am sure," he told the *Voice*, "that in future many more will follow me through university." Maisie's tribute to his success in the June issue of the *Voice* was effusive:

> We are indeed proud of Alfred Scow, son of Chief and Mrs. William Scow of Alert Bay. Alfred will soon become the first Native Indian lawyer in British Columbia following his graduation last month.
>
> How many other boys, regardless of race, would have put up Alfred's long, brave fight to achieve his goal? Alfred, confronted by lack of funds, his problems increased because he is a Native Canadian,

Alfred Scow was the first First Nations individual to graduate from UBC's Faculty of Law, later becoming a Provincial Court judge. Photo credit to Chris Wheeler.

worked as a fisherman, saved, studied, and finally won his degree... Alfred's achievement recalled to my mind that brilliant man, the late Andrew Paull. Although trained in the law by the late Judge H. S. Cayley and with a talent for criminal law, he was unable to practise because of discrimination against him...

May success and the blessings of Our Father in Heaven be with you to the end of the long trail; that is the wish of your friend, Maisie.[556]

The remaining news in the June issue of the *Voice* was not as encouraging. When MP Frank Howard had stood in the House of Commons on May 20 to ask Minister Fairclough for the results of a June 25, 1959, commission of inquiry into treaties 8 and 11 in the Mackenzie District, her reply had been so shocking that Maisie's report in the *Voice* was laden with bold print and capital letters:

[The minister] named fifteen reserves under study by a commission which held meetings two years ago and apparently, in her words, "recommended against the establishment of reserves IN THE PROPORTIONS PROVIDED FOR IN THE TREATIES..." The next step, as stated by the Hon. Minister, is that the government [will] "open negotiations with the various Indian bands with a view to ascertaining whether IN LIEU

OF THEIR LAND RIGHTS UNDER TREATIES, they would be interested in monetary compensation, a combination of both, or some other form of compensation."

This suggestion, Maisie wrote indignantly, flies in the face of the minister's promise following the granting of the federal vote that:

EXISTING RIGHTS AND TREATIES, TRADITIONAL OR OTHERWISE, possessed by the Indians shall not in any way be abrogated or diminished in consequence of having the right to vote.

While Mrs. Fairclough notes that the matter is "under study by an interdepartmental committee," we are alarmed that such unthinkable policies could merit a moment's consideration... May we ask an oft-repeated question: Are Indian treaties merely scraps of paper or do Canada's Indians really have rights? We would appreciate an answer unqualified by the kind of action indicated in the reply to Frank Howard's questions.[557]

Maisie got her answer when on July 14, 1961, the Vancouver Sun reported that the National Harbours Board—which reported to the Minister of Transport—had leased the foreshore rights on reclaimed land immediately in front of the seventy-five-year-old twin-spired St. Paul's Catholic Church on North Vancouver's Mission No. 1 Reserve to Deeks-McBride Ltd. for the construction of a cement plant. The Sun, shocked by this event, told its readers that:

The Indian community rightfully is up in arms. It calls the transaction an illegal land grab. It claims to have proof that the reserve extends to low water—not high water as claimed by Ottawa... Federal authorities claim the reclaimed waterfront property belongs to the National Harbours Board, not the Indians who've had ownership since the reserve was designated. But worse, they neither consulted nor informed the Squamish Band of their interpretation or the impending industrial leases. And the bureaucrats seem hell-bent on making their interpretation stick. Machines have already been on the site, readying it for construction.

Where does the Native turn when faced with such tactics?... The Indians asked Mrs. Fairclough to intercede. They'll go to court if she won't... Certainly it appears the Indians have a strong case. How would any private waterfront owner feel if the federal government could reclaim property in front and lease it for a cement works? Canadian treatment of original Canadians—Native Canadians—has never been noted for its enlightenment. North Shore Indians mean it when they refer to white tyranny over them... This is a strange period in Canadian history for a government not only to defy the principle that justice must appear to be done, but seemingly to bypass a court ruling on justice itself.[558]

Maisie reprinted the *Vancouver Sun* story in the August issue of the *Voice*, and followed it with the rest of the story. It seems that:

> Native Band members, incensed by what one of their leaders, Cliff Paull, brother of the late Andy Paull, described as an attempt "to steal a million dollars' worth of foreshore rights from the Squamish Indians," reacted rapidly. They quickly massed before the ancient church and marched across the Pacific Great Eastern Railway tracks—men, women and children—in a public demonstration of their opposition to the work proceeding on reserve property.
>
> Not stopping at this action, the band sent wires to Minister Fairclough and the Director of Indian Affairs, H. M. Jones... quoting a resolution passed by a meeting of the Band Council on July 3: "This council refuses to consider any application for property fronting on any of our reserves situated on Burrard Inlet... We are definitely opposed to any lease being granted to Deeks-McBride by the Harbours Board," and they demanded an immediate stop to construction work.[559]

The protest and telegrams to the minister found their mark when the National Harbours Board cancelled the lease and within a week Deeks-McBride withdrew their construction equipment and dismantled the site. "This whole issue," Maisie wrote, "it is felt in some quarters, might well spur demands for a full judicial inquiry into Indian land rights in British Columbia, long urged by the *Native Voice* and Native leaders."[560]

The same sentiment was expressed by Percy Paull, Squamish Band Council member and son of the late Andy Paull, when he was a guest speaker at a meeting in North Vancouver attended by Mayor William Angus, MP William Payne and various representatives of the Department of Indian Affairs. "We will fight for our lands right up to the United Nations if necessary," he said. After requesting the appointment of a tribunal to investigate the band's foreshore rights, he asked for a judicial inquiry.

> We call upon the government as our self-appointed guardian to prove they really have our interests at heart to establish not only our rights but to give an accounting of our monies for all transactions for the past 100 years. After this judicial inquiry has established our rights, we will sit down with the representatives of the Crown at the bargaining table to negotiate a treaty for our protection... We Indians have always been loyal to our kings and queens and have always believed in the policy of British fair play. But in turn we want to be treated justly—give us justice first.[561]

Justice and Aboriginal rights were the subject of protests in other parts of the country as well, and it was becoming apparent that a body was needed that would speak for all First Nations people in Canada. William Scow and the Reverend Dr. Peter Kelly had first suggested such an integrated body at the Native Brotherhood's annual convention in 1953, but finally eight years later it appeared that its time had finally come. On August 17–19, 1961, a founding convention was held in Regina of the new National Indian Council, which would later be known as the Assembly of First Nations (AFN). William Wuttunee, the first First Nations lawyer to be called to the bar in Western Canada, was appointed national coordinator.

A hastily arranged executive committee of seven was struck to comment on the recently released Special Joint Committee of the Senate and House of Commons report regarding amendments to the Indian Act. In the September issue of the *Voice* Maisie reported that this committee had found the report

> sketchy and disappointing... They charged that the findings [had been] based on recommendations made in camera by senior officials in the Department of Indian Affairs and on briefs presented by "white organizations."
>
> They said not enough time and concentration was given to thoroughly examine evidence in briefs submitted by Indians. The report merely tidied up the Indian Act rather than giving us what we requested in our briefs.[562]

Two months later the Indian Association of Alberta (IAA) made similar criticisms, stating that the parliamentary joint committee report failed to deal with:

> some of the most important problems of the Indian people. No mention was made of hunting and trapping or general employment, both on and off reserves. No action was taken on the request for appeals to the courts against the decision of the minister of Citizenship and Immigration or on a number of other questions raised by Indian groups from all parts of Canada.[563]

As well, they were alarmed at the amendments to the management of their land. Lawful title was being recommended for people living on the reserve for twenty years or more, and band councils were empowered to lease land, a right also given to individual members on the reserve. The implementation of such a policy, the IAA felt, would see the eventual disintegration of their reserves.

Native Brotherhood President Guy Williams supported the new national organization, although he wondered publicly whether other provinces would be ready to support such a co-operative venture. He was right. The IAA, which had sent observers to the Regina conference, decided not to join, stating that "the IAA still feels it should remain a provincial organization where it has a strong and independent voice."[564] It would take time before the advantages of speaking with one voice would become obvious to all.

In October Maisie was happy to tell her readers that she had just conscripted Percy Paull as an associate editor for the *Voice*. Friends and family had been urging him to carry on the important work of his father, and in an interview with publisher Maisie Hurley, he laid stress on the land question and the need for recognition of Native claims. "Our rights must be fully protected," he declared.

> Mr. Paull said he thought one of his projects would be the formation of a study group with the aim of uniting all interested groups. Purpose will be to strengthen the Indians of British Columbia in their efforts to save their lands and to stiffen their fight against "extermination and assimilation."[565]

That same month Maisie had to admit that the paper was once again in financial trouble, and her editorial was yet another cry for help. She had struggled to publish even four pages, subscription numbers were down, and she had to plead for advertising revenue. She reminded readers that the *Voice* had been publishing for fifteen years and that, although it was "not always robust and healthy in a material sense," it was "always fearless, outspoken and ready to do battle on behalf of the Native people."[566] Her plea resulted in many subscription renewals and letters of concern that the paper's "honest publicity" would disappear. In the November-December edition, which reached an acceptable sixteen pages—eight pages per issue—after thanking her subscribers for stepping up to the challenge, Maisie wrote that "With this type of help, we know we will not only survive, but grow stronger. We must if we are to serve our people effectively."[567]

The November-December 1961 issue also reported on a meeting of the North American Indian Brotherhood at Lillooet on November 24 where its president, George Manuel, had conferred upon Maisie an honorary membership in the organization. Reporter Paul Orth wrote about this event:

> I cannot claim—as so many white people appear to do—that I have lived in this country before the Indians nor that I know everything about them. But I know with certainty that such honors as were received by Mrs. Hurley are not easily bestowed upon non-Indians. Although she must be aware of the fact that no material rewards await her, she has taken up the sake of humanity and speaks her mind courageously

and vitally that many younger people must quietly muse and wonder whether they will possess the same power of conviction if ever they should reach the same point in life.[568]

At the 29th annual Native Brotherhood convention held at Alert Bay in November, the entire executive slate was reaffirmed. These positions were voluntary and unpaid, and it took significant dedication and resolve to stay the course through the constant controversy, funding issues and personal sacrifices. None of the men who took them on were wealthy, but they placed the needs of their First Nations brothers and sisters before their own.

Minister Fairclough attended the convention and after her address she was queried by President Guy Williams about the "equality of liquor rights for Natives." He explained that most First Nations people were in favour of being granted these rights, although he himself had reservations on this matter because of the difficulties he could foresee. The minister ducked the question by saying that this was "a provincial issue." On this topic at least, Ping-Pong still appeared to be the game of choice between the two levels of government.

The rest of the question-and-answer session was equally unsatisfactory, to say the least. When the Reverend Kelly asked her about the "less than adequate educational opportunities for children in Indian schools," he received the response that it was all caused by a teacher shortage. Kelly persisted, asking when did "an Indian become a non-Indian?" He was referring to First Nations people who had been away from their reserves for five years or more and had no way of financing their children's higher education. The minister stated that there were forty-four national scholarships available and that "the Indian affairs department was doing all it could."[569] When Haida vice-president Godfrey Kelly informed her of the lack of employment on reserves and that fishing was now only a seasonal occupation at best, the minister replied that the winter works program introduced by the federal government would take care of their needs.

A month after the convention, Christmas 1961 came with a profound life-altering shock for Mazie. On Christmas Day her husband, confidant and soul mate, Thomas Francis Hurley, collapsed while walking their dogs. He died later in hospital. He was 77.

On December 29, at the Guardian Angels Church at Broughton and Pendrell streets in the West End of Vancouver, Thomas Francis Hurley was eulogized in glowing terms, flowers banking his coffin, which was draped in an Irish flag. Requiem high mass was celebrated by Monsignor F. A. Clinton, who had officiated at Tom and Maisie's wedding in the same church on almost the same day ten years earlier. A full police escort preceded the funeral cortège to Forest Lawn Cemetery where the burial took place.

Honorary pall bearers included judges, magistrates and lawyers, a senator and a police chief, as well as First Nations chiefs August Jack Khatsahlano, Dominic Charlie, Andy Frank and Clarence Joe. The actual pall bearers were his old friend and fellow lawyer Isaac "Ike" Shulman; his former law partner Angelo Branca; friend, associate and mentee Thomas Berger; friend and fellow lawyer Harry Rankin; and lawyers William Bell and Sean Stapleton.

That night Maisie went back to the offices that she had shared with her husband in the Standard Building and sat down to write a letter to Prime Minister Diefenbaker:

> I am sitting in an empty office—just a few hours ago my darling was buried. He left me on Christmas day... I am so alone—but I am going to fight on until my call comes. Everyone is so kind and wonderful. I am enclosing cuttings—The tributes are great...
>
> My darling used to stand on the steps rain or shine waiting for me. He never left me without a kiss. We were one—Now he has gone.
>
> God, how can I stand the ghastly silence...[570]

12—The Voice Falls Silent

Maisie's grief at her beloved Tom's death was muted somewhat by the outpouring of accolades and offers of support she received from family, friends and associates. Many of them were reprinted in the January 1962 edition of the *Native Voice*. They included the *Vancouver Sun*'s announcement of his death:

> He was a spellbinder but he knew his law, a leprechaun with gifts that contributed to changing laws, a bon vivant, a classic Irish fighter with a golden tongue and big heart. A rich, rich character cast in the mould of Ireland's greatest, including Shaw and Behan, with a Churchillian mastery of phrase-making thrown in for good measure.[571]

Tom's long-time friend and associate Ike Shulman proclaimed that "He was probably the greatest criminal lawyer Canada ever had. He was a great lawyer in the traditional sense—a fighter for the downtrodden. He defended just about everybody who needed help." But as well as his compassion, Shulman said, Thomas Hurley was so skilled in the law that

> a number of decisions that Mr. Hurley won on points of law were upheld by the Supreme Court of Canada and thereby established precedents as effective as amendments to the laws. For example, until Mr. Hurley established that provocation could be long-term—as accepted by courts in the United Kingdom—the law of provocation was interpreted differently in Canada. [And] the procedure in bootlegging cases was altered when Mr. Hurley successfully argued that when bottles were found on the premises, the onus should be on the Crown rather than the alleged bootlegger to explain their presence. As a result of a successful Hurley argument, cross-examination procedures were changed, giving defence counsel greater latitude in cross-examining witnesses. He broke the city's padlock law and he almost got the habitual criminal law thrown out on a technicality.
>
> The theme that runs throughout Hurley anecdotes is threefold: his mastery of criminal law, his unparalleled courtroom oratory and wit, and the fact that fees never entered his mind when he was convinced that an underdog needed defending... For 50 years he graced our courts. And his knowledge was ever available to the young lawyer seeking guidance. It's trite but true that an era in Vancouver's court

history ended Christmas Day when Tom Hurley's number came up for the black coach. We hope BC's Law Society and Bar Association will, in some way, pay him the lasting tribute he earned. If they need an excuse, we offer this: in his practice, Tom Hurley was years ahead of his profession in recognizing that free legal advice is an essential service to society.[572]

Maisie singled out Ike Shulman and Thomas Berger for special thanks in the *Voice*, along with a bevy of First Nations friends and colleagues, a senator, judges, the police chief and his officers, Law Society staff and Fisheries officers—among others. It was an impressive list, a list that corroborated the value of and love for this simple Irishman with the "golden tongue and big heart." In her grief Maisie wrote: "There are many more whose names should be mentioned but who I know will forgive me for omitting their names and accept instead my heartfelt gratitude for their kind and thoughtful consideration."[573] And, amid her grief, she remembered to post a change of address for the *Voice*. Tom's office at 325 Standard Building was no longer affordable so she moved the paper's headquarters to her Denman Street apartment. "*The Native Voice* will not only carry on," she wrote, "but with your continued support, will grow in strength and influence."[574]

After the BC Supreme Court had failed to overturn Magistrate Pool's verdict in the Gonzales "possession of liquor" case, Tom Hurley had appealed it to the BC Court of Appeal, but he had been too frail to continue, and the task of presenting his arguments had fallen to Thomas Berger. In early January 1962, Appellate Justice C. W. Tysoe released his written judgment, and the *Voice* reported on his findings. In his reasons for refusing to override the previous verdicts, he wrote that "equality before the law, as provided in the Bill of Rights, means that the law as it exists be applied equally and without fear or favor to all persons to whom it applies" in its enforcement. But he pointed out that the key phrase was "to whom it applies." He said that:

> Indians are a particular group who, by the Indian Act, have particular rights, privileges and disabilities. If the Bill of Rights does not affect their rights and privileges, it cannot affect their disabilities such as the law governing liquor.[575]

It was a disappointing outcome, but the tide was beginning to turn with respect to liquor rights for the BC First Nations. On January 5, the four Nass River villages that had applied to the federal government for a plebiscite to overturn liquor restrictions voted overwhelmingly in favour of full liquor rights. On February 28, MP Frank Howard, now a member of the New Democratic Party (formed in 1961 from a merger of the CCF and the Canadian Labour Congress), issued a statement regarding BC First Nations liquor rights:

> For some time now we have been promoting moves towards equality of treatment and equality before the law for our Native Indian people. One of the moves relates to the question of liquor rights and responsibilities.
>
> There is an involved procedure in the Indian Act which allows for Indian Band Councils to start into operation the machinery which would bring such equality. Several bands have taken the first step in passing resolutions asking for referendums to be conducted on the question of whether or not it is desirable to be legally in possession of liquor on a reserve. The governor-in-council takes the final step by declaring formally by way of a proclamation that such a right will be conferred upon the reserves which vote in favor of having the right to be in possession of liquor.
>
> The first such proclamation for British Columbia was issued on February 16, 1962, affecting 11 Indian Bands and covering 92 reserves. Of these Bands, four are in the Federal Skeena Riding—Aiyansh, Canyon City, Greenville and Kincolith.[576]

Outside of Ontario, the Nisga'a was the first Nation to successfully apply the plebiscite to overturn the provincial government's denial of this fundamental right, but MLA Frank Calder said he was confident that other First Nations throughout the province would be holding similar plebiscites soon. He was right. By May 6,000 First Nations people, representing 15 per cent of the 40,000 First Nations population in BC and the Yukon, had voted for full liquor rights. And within a month so many First Nations had applied for plebiscites that the provincial government could not distinguish which had agreed and which had not, finally forcing Attorney General Bonner's hand. His solution to the problem was exactly what they had asked for all along: he announced that liquor vendors throughout the province had been advised they could sell liquor to First Nations people without restriction.

Calder told the *Voice*'s readers that the government's decision had just "proved conclusively" that the interpretation of the Indian Act put forward by First Nations leaders had always been correct: "The final action of extending full liquor rights rested absolutely with the provincial government." But he cautioned First Nations that equal liquor rights also meant equal levels of punishment: "Today, if a law officer encounters an intoxicated white man and requests him to go home and cool off, he must say the same thing to an intoxicated Indian."[577]

Prince Rupert Mayor Peter Lester wrote to Maisie to express his delight that full liquor privileges had now been granted to all First Nations people in the province. "Many, like myself, have been urging this for years. While we all realize that liquor, if improperly handled, can be more of a curse than a blessing, still we felt there was no justification for discrimination."[578] Four months later Maisie was able to tell the *Voice*'s readers that:

> Despite the prophets of doom, the new privileges have provided no new nor startling developments among the Native people of the province. We have seen no examples of physical or spiritual disintegration.
>
> The fact of the matter is that granting of liquor rights has merely proved our repeated contention that there is no significant difference between the races when it comes to the effect of liquor. Individuals may have varying levels of resistance but groups don't...
>
> Yes, we're satisfied that the end of prohibition among BC Natives has wiped out another mark of discrimination and moved them along the road to Canadian citizenship, first class, which must come without any loss of aboriginal rights.[579]

With a federal vote looming on June 18, 1962—the first that Canada's newest citizens could participate in—Maisie began advising her friends to question the candidates in their ridings about what they were going to do for them. In the May issue of the *Voice* she told her readers to ask:

> What is their minimum program for Native people? What about their position on employment? On educational opportunities? The general rights for Native people to such benefits as welfare in comparison to other voters? What about the land question in BC and the long-standing, still unsatisfied demand for a full inquiry into the matter and correct settlement of the land issue?[580]

As Maisie had always accorded Frank Howard space in the paper whenever he needed it, he used it now to remind his First Nations constituents of their voting responsibilities and how to register to vote. Some readers, however, perceived his frequent articles as messages from the CCF party itself, while the paper's guiltless support of Diefenbaker and his Progressive Conservatives prompted others to question the paper's political leanings in that direction—despite Howard and Diefenbaker being on opposite sides of the House of Commons. There was, of course, no question that Maisie was very political, but she always aligned the paper with those politicians who supported Aboriginal peoples causes, and in defence of that position she wrote that:

> Our politics, to state it as simply as possible, are pro-Indian. To put it another way, we have no politics.

The Native Voice has no political affiliation and intends to have none. We are free to praise or criticize, and we do, with our sole guide [being] what we, our associate editors, and the organized Natives themselves think is best for the Native people of Canada and the United States.

We may sometimes be wrong in our opinions, but we are not prejudiced by this or that political faith in drawing our conclusions.

We believe neither in racial, religious, political, nor any other kind of bigotry. We feel certain our readers will agree that the sort of honesty (sometimes considered foolhardy or rash) that has been associated with the *Native Voice* is the policy they want to see continued.

We reserve the right to criticize or praise anybody, and frankly, we're a lot happier praising than criticizing. We only pass along praise to people and groups who are seeking justice for the Native people.[581]

Among those seeking justice for First Nations people that spring were several young men from the next generation of activists. Following his graduation from UBC's school of law, Alfred Scow was quickly becoming a leader like his father. In March 1962, as the keynote speaker at a leadership conference at the Grosvenor Hotel in Vancouver, he told his audience that it was important for the First Nations to develop their own leaders. "This in spite of the fact that many people have their own ideas of what they think Native people want." Then tackling the reserve question, he said that one of the easy solutions was to abolish reserves, but "we do not want abolition of the reserves. We consider them our home. They represent the only thing we have left of the country we used to consider our own." But, he continued, the First Nations person today was not content merely to remain on the reserve: "He is getting out and establishing himself in his rightful place in society."[582] To facilitate that transition, Scow emphasized that education was vital and warned that co-operation must come from the First Nations themselves if they were to succeed. A month later, he was guest of honour at the Buckskin Varieties, a boxing tournament, and this time he spoke about having a fighting spirit: "Some of you may ask what do we need a fighting spirit for? The answer is simple: we are going to have to fight for our place in Canada. We have to do it now. We have to do it together. And we must enlist the aid of our non-Indian friends.[583]

Percy Paull, the *Voice*'s newest associate editor, agreed that education was the key to a smooth integration and offered that:

It is my feeling that the Indian people should not be pushed into integration by law or pressure or propaganda. Rather, we should be educated into the pros and cons of such a move and let us be the judge.

We are aware that integration is coming, but we also have our pride and therefore would like to know just what is going on [in] this realm of integration. It is true we wish to be honest and true Canadians, but we also wish to have the freedom of rights to remain as Indians and still be a help to our great country.[584]

On the eve of the federal election scheduled for June 18, 1962, Prime Minister Diefenbaker told the press that it was his "intention to establish an Indian Claims Commission, which will go fully into all claims of Indian bands or tribes and will then make recommendations in keeping with justice, fairness and good faith."[585] This was not a new idea. It had been suggested as early as 1948 by the Special Joint Committee of the Senate and House of Commons before the Liberal government introduced Bill 267 to amend the Indian Act. However, the amended bill had borne little resemblance to the committee's recommendations and the Claims Commission idea had disappeared entirely. In resurrecting it now, Diefenbaker reasoned that:

Various Indian tribes and bands in all parts of Canada have claimed over the years and still claim that some of their treaty rights have been unjustly restricted or abrogated and that lands have been taken from them without proper compensation for their aboriginal interest. They have advanced their claims from time to time, some dating back almost one hundred years.

The reading of the minutes of proceedings and evidence of parliamentary committees on Indian Affairs will show that these claims continue to give rise among Indians to feelings of injustice... Whatever the merits of the claims may be, it is clear that there has been a continuing sense of grievance amongst Indians for years that no action has been taken to have these claims determined upon with finality and, if found to be valid, settlement made.[586]

Frank Howard welcomed the prime minister's announcement but commented, "I have campaigned for such a commission every session since I have been a member of parliament. Last session I introduced a bill to set up such a commission. I can only hope, at this stage, that the government's bill sets up effective machinery which will operate fairly and justly."[587] In fact, Howard had introduced three private member's bills over the years to establish a Court of Indian Claims, all to no avail. MLA Frank Calder, on the other hand, favoured direct access to the courts to redress injustices. He said, "BC Indians no longer accept the methods of negotiation or a royal commission to settle the land question. The only acceptable course is to the courts for a judicial decision on the case." And when BC's attorney general failed to respond to his suggestion, Calder asked, "Are you afraid to meet us in court?"[588]

Maisie, meanwhile, was occupied with another worry. With the election only two weeks away, she contacted J. A. Macaulay, chairman of the Minorities Committee in Ottawa, to advise him that she and a great number of her First Nations friends were harbouring the strong suspicion that the amendment to section 14 of the Canada Elections Act—an act that had, among other things, disqualified First Nations people from voting in the past—had actually destroyed the special rights they enjoyed under the Indian Act. She was particularly concerned "over the effect of this amendment... on Indian's rights pertaining to lands forming Indian reserves."[589]

The Minorities Committee consulted Leroy Brown, a geologist well-known for his interest in and acquaintance with many BC Coastal First Nations, and Alfred Scow, who was soon to be called to the bar. Both "confirmed the fact that there is a widespread fear among the Indian bands that exercise of the franchise in the federal election will somehow destroy the individual Indian's status under the Indian Act."[590] All were aware that until this time only First Nations people who had served in His Majesty's Forces in World War I or II or had foresworn their special privileges (tax exemption) by waiver were eligible to vote federally. But having accepted the franchise, they were "deemed not to be an Indian within the meaning of [the] Act or any other statute of law" (Section 109 of the Indian Act.) But especially troubling to Maisie was the fact that the reserve land upon which the newly enfranchised resided would, under Section 110 (2) of the Indian Act, and by order of the Governor-in-Council with the consent of the band council, "cease to be Indian reserve lands." The enfranchised person was then permitted to purchase his—at this time, it was most likely to be a man and the language of the act reflected this bias—land over a ten-year period, at which point title would be transferred to him or his legal representative. So ultimately enfranchisement meant that the land would be transferred to him personally, thus reducing the size of the reserve—a perfect recipe for the dissolution of a culture.

Maisie feared that the 1960 amendment to the Canada Elections Act would have "the same effect as if an enfranchisement order had been made under section 108 [which applied to individuals] or section 111 [which applied to Nations] of the Indian Act." Therefore, the wise course for Indians to follow was "to abstain from exercising this franchise so that they may be in a position to repudiate or deny that they have been enfranchised."[591]

Although Macaulay wrote back to say that this did "not seem logical," it was nevertheless the belief of many First Nations people in the province, especially following the BC government's recent confiscation of land at Kitwanga. As a result, Macaulay suggested that the prime minister "consider making a short and simple statement" to the effect that the amendments to the Canada

Elections Act giving First Nations people the right to vote in federal elections do not constitute enfranchisement within the meaning of the Indian Act and that none of the rights and privileges granted under the Indian Act would be affected either by the amendment to the Canada Elections Act or by the act of voting.

Maisie printed the prime minister's letter in the June issue of the *Voice:*

> I welcome the opportunity of reminding the Indian people of Canada that as a result of the amendments to the Indian Act and the Canada Elections Act introduced by the government which I have the honour to lead, the Indians of Canada now have the right to vote in federal elections without any restrictions whatsoever, and we have thereby for the first time equalized the rights of the Indians with those of all other Canadian citizens. The right to vote is the greatest right of citizenship in a democracy.[592]

Maisie then restated the non-political policy of the paper and reminded her readers to educate themselves about the issues and candidates. She finished with: "Make your vote count for Native progress,"[593] which would seem to suggest a vote for Diefenbaker. On June 18, however, only 116 Progressive Conservatives were returned to Ottawa to face 99 Liberals. Diefenbaker would be leading a minority government, while hoping for the support of the Quebec Social Credit party, which held 30 seats, or the NDP, with 19. Worse still, many of Diefenbaker's cabinet ministers no longer supported his policies. For the Native Brotherhood, looking for progress on Aboriginal title to the land, it was now a matter of wait-and-see what the fall session of Parliament would bring.

At the end of August 1962, George Manuel, president of the North American Indian Brotherhood (NAIB), headed for Toronto to meet with the recently formed National Indian Council (NIC) and present five resolutions that he and his committee had drawn up. His aim was to get the NIC's backing so that when he presented his resolutions to the federal cabinet, they would carry the full support of virtually all First Nations organizations in Canada. The NAIB resolutions, none of which were novel or new, had been on the wish lists of many other First Nations organizations over the years, although the government had not chosen to act on any of them. They called for a separate Indian Affairs Department with its own cabinet minister and personnel; a standing committee on Indian affairs, which would meet annually to review and update the Indian Act; decentralization of the Indian Affairs Branch with some authority passing to provincial governments; more grants provided to First Nations associations with organizational abilities; and a more equitable social welfare system.

Maisie contacted Big White Owl to ask him to attend the NIC meeting in Toronto for the *Native Voice*. His subsequent report centred on the NAIB's first resolution—that First Nations still did not have their own ministry. "Now is the time for action," he wrote. "Let us have a Department of Indian Affairs... and let it be headed by a Native Canadian Indian." But most of the article he wrote for the September issue focussed on a new problem for First Nations people:

> This nasty business of integrating the North American Indian people into slum communities of the big cities is shameful, unfair and utterly disastrous. It is a plan of extermination by assimilation. It is plain legalized genocide.
>
> Why do I make this claim? Because Indian people who migrate to the cities, minus a skilled trade or good education, are doomed to slowly rot away on welfare handouts, and drift with the lowest sector of white and Negro peoples, where alcoholism, crime and social disease are rampant.[594]

As the opening day of the fall parliamentary session neared, Frank Howard told the *Voice* that he intended "to take steps during this present Parliament to have the basic human rights of the Indians of Canada reviewed by Parliament and protected where such protection is found necessary." He expected to introduce a bill to "consolidate the Indian Act and its various amendments." The minister of Justice would be required to study this "re-enactment of the Indian Act" to see that it was "in accordance with section 3 of the Bill of Rights as to its compatibility with the Bill of Rights. Our Native Indians, above all other ethnic groups, have had these rights and freedoms regularly infringed on by succeeding governments. The Indian Act is a straitjacket for them. Its bonds must be loosened."[595] But Howard was well aware that Diefenbaker's government would have difficulty pushing its own agenda through parliament, let alone taking on his private member's bill.

On October 1, 1962, Alfred Scow, having finished his articles, was called to the bar at a ceremony attended by his beaming father and mother, Chief and Mrs. William Scow. He had come a long way from his birth at St. George's Hospital at Alert Bay thirty-five years earlier where "there was one ward for the Indians, one ward for the Chinese, one for the Japanese and one for the white people."[596] Like his father, he was no longer involved with Brotherhood business, although Maisie had named him special correspondent to the *Voice* some months earlier.

The new lawyer moved into an office in the Ford Building because it was close to the courthouse and because the Brotherhood also had their offices there and he hoped to do legal work for them. However, the Brotherhood required more senior counsel, and although his sincerest desire was to spend his life defending his people, the first client through his door was not someone looking for justice under the Indian Act but a white man seeking a divorce. Three years later, however, at the Nanaimo Assizes of the Supreme Court of British Columbia, he would successfully defend a First Nations woman charged with murdering her young daughter.

The 30th annual convention of the Brotherhood was to have been held in Prince Rupert's Civic Centre in December, but a scheduling conflict shifted it to the Civic Centre in the nearby town of Terrace—where Frank Calder had wanted it all along. The stage there was large enough to accommodate the Greenville Concert Band and the Aiyansh Philharmonic Band and the floor spacious enough for a grand ball to which the public would be invited on the final evening. To mark the thirty years since the Brotherhood's founding, the special guests would be three of the men who had represented the Allied Tribes of British Columbia decades earlier in their first efforts to settle the "land question." The Reverend Dr. Peter Kelly, still the Brotherhood's Legislative Chair, was one. The others were Chiefs William Pascal and Peter Calder. The latter, now 87, had helped to set up committees in the late 1880s and was still involved in the struggle to resolve the "land question." Another important guest was the lieutenant-governor, the Honourable George R. Pearkes, who was taken completely by surprise at the opening banquet when MLA Frank Calder bestowed upon him a chieftainship of the Nisga'a First Nation. The December *Voice* reported that his chief's name was "Ogit" and "according to ancient custom, the name means big chief, a good leader and a wise councillor."[597] Calder explained that it was the first time a hereditary chief's name had been granted to anyone outside of the Nass River Valley.

President Guy Williams' opening remarks spoke of the struggle by his predecessors against men "who were set up by the government of Canada to fight issues against the Indians." Included among them had been two future prime ministers, R. B. Bennett and William Lyon Mackenzie King. Williams also recalled how, as a young man, he had attended a meeting with Alfred Adams in the office of Indian Commissioner D. M. McKay; in a heated exchange, McKay had blurted out, "I want you to know that I am here to represent the interests of the government, not your interests." Williams told the conference, "That attitude—that dictatorial attitude, I am most happy to say—the Native Brotherhood is being instrumental in changing to an attitude of co-operation between the government and the Native Brotherhood." And he quoted the statement made by the current minister, Ellen Fairclough, that "when the Native Brotherhood of BC speaks, the government listens because

the government knows that it is the voice of the BC people." In this environment of co-operation, Williams offered that "this convention, brothers and
sisters, will make and deliberate very firmly requests and demands to the government on an immediate program of action. This convention will set forth
on a trail of definite objectives."[598]

Some of those objectives were to strike several new committees to address
issues such as education, employment, fisheries, organization, credentials
and resolutions. Perhaps the most important of all was a claims commission committee that would be chaired by Reverend Dr. Peter Kelly. Williams'
speech continued:

> This organization has been instrumental in making the government
> of today see the necessity of appointing an Indian Claims Commis-
> sion. It has been mentioned by the prime minister in the speech from
> the throne. While that committee has not been appointed yet, the
> extent of its powers of reference we do not know, but we will set up
> in this convention a committee of our own to deal with this matter.
>
> The fire of the noble men is now already kindled. It is for you
> and for all your band members at home, and all of the Natives in
> this province to make a definite stand that we will get across to the
> government a just and a very equitable conclusion. When this claims
> commission is over, possibly five years, ten years, twenty years [from
> now], it is our aim that we will have acquired the results of what the
> Allied tribes had started out to accomplish. This will be a big job, it
> will require time; it will require research; it will require the support
> of every Native in this province.
>
> Now may I say this, the Native Brotherhood of BC—I'll put it in a
> slang way—the Native Brotherhood at this time will not chicken out.
>
> You have a serious problem before you. You have got to bear in
> mind the dictatorial and militant attitude of a decade ago is gone...
>
> We cannot afford at this time to quibble, we cannot afford to be
> petty. We seem to at times get into petty problems and make them
> more serious than we should. You have heard that there was a lack of
> unity at that time. At this time there will be no lack of unity. To some
> of the passing generation, it is now or never.[599]

In a narrow victory over the polished and charismatic Frank Calder, Guy
Williams was returned as president to lead the Brotherhood for another year.
He was also nominated to chair the organizational committee in concert with
the Nisga'a Tribal Council and the North American Indian Brotherhood. He
would be paid to travel the province to garner support for the committee, which
would promote unity "in building a stronger Indian provincial group." This
committee, Frank Calder had stated earlier when he was affirmed as president

at the 5th annual Nisga'a Tribal Council's AGM, "would unite the North American Indian Brotherhood, Native Brotherhood of British Columbia and Nisga'a Tribal Council to speak unitedly on BC Indian land claims."[600]

At Lytton, which was one of Williams' first stops on his organizing tour early in the new year, he implored his audience to have a "united front on the BC Indian land question before the forthcoming Indian Claims Commission." Recalling the division that had taken place between the Interior and Coastal tribes in 1926 when the Allied Tribes had failed to make their case at Ottawa, he emphasized that this was their "last ditch stand.[601]

Maisie celebrated her 75th birthday while at the Brotherhood conference in Terrace, and as usual in the last few years a wave of intense nostalgia swept over her. Adding to her melancholy this year was the fact that her birthday fell close to the anniversary of Tom's death. But back home again, she overcame her lassitude by digging out one of her father's old mining journals in which he had written: "I am that Indestructible and Omnipotent Universal Law which is all and within all here and everywhere, Now and Forever, Amen."[602] He had penned these words while standing atop a mountain near Khutz Inlet, and the words reminded Maisie of an editorial she had written for the *Voice* in 1949 following an arduous prospecting trip she had undertaken up Mount Donaldson on the Sunshine Coast with August Jack Khatsahlano. Now she resurrected part of that editorial for the December issue of the *Voice*. It ended with the words:

> When you are in the mountains, you are as much a part of nature as the leaf that falls from the tree, the water in the creek, the rain from the sky. You are no greater than these, only part of it all: "As in the beginning, world without end!" Death is all around you, thousands of years of death, unmourned dead things absorbed into the making of new life...
>
> Much water has flowed under the bridge since I wrote the above. Many of our loved ones have since gone to their eternal rest. Our time too is short so what matter the paltry things of life, only Our Father in Heaven. For thine is the kingdom, the power and the glory for ever and ever. Amen.[603]

One of her frequent correspondents, *Vancouver Sun* columnist Elmore Philpott, was so moved by Maisie's "cry of faith from the mountain top," that he wrote:

> I always understood what you were doing, or at least I imagined I did. That was to help our originals to recover their racial self-respect,

which had been so shattered by circumstances beyond their own control... No wonder you love the Indians and no wonder they love you. For in that confession of faith you are pure Indian.[604]

Once recovered from her December "blues," Maisie was ebullient in her year-end remarks, editorializing on the gains the Brotherhood and First Nations had made over the past few years—the provincial and federal votes, liquor rights and the promise of an Indian Claims Commission. And she told her readers that "We of the *Native Voice* see the land question as paramount to the immediate future and intend to do all we can to bring the matter to a favourable conclusion."[605] By the January 1963 issue, it was obvious that she was in fighting form again when she announced that:

> An independent tribunal must be established by Canada to review and decide on Indian land claims, but its members must be outside mediators—men of high standing from both countries [the US and Canada].
>
> For 100 years, the people who have taken over Indian lands in this province have made billions of dollars from the lands themselves, the timber, fish, minerals, and other rich resources... All the Indians of the province must unite as one to demand their rights and to fight for them through the medium of an impartial tribunal.
>
> *The Native Voice* will do its part in this great struggle for justice by carrying background material as well as current developments in an effort to make the issues known and understood.[606]

Maisie pressed her First Nations readers to be aware of the issues and to lobby all the political parties to make sure that the tribunal commissioners would be truly impartial. She reminded them of the sacrifices made by their forefathers who had sold all of their assets in order to attend the important conferences where they could advance the First Nations case:

> The old leaders worked for years to establish this tribunal for our British Columbia Natives, yet no concrete steps have been taken as yet by our Indians to assure the type of hearing that will be acceptable and fair to our Indian peoples... For instance, in the past debates over Indian land title in British Columbia, no one appears to have bothered to bring up the matter of Indian concepts of right in real property. Opponents of the concept of aboriginal rights repeatedly stated that the Indians had simply roamed randomly over the land, never claiming particular and specific areas. Ethnographic information has made clear, however, that the Coast Indians, at least, had very concrete concepts of land ownership.[607]

On February 4, 1963, Diefenbaker's Progressive Conservative minority government fell after only seven months in office, and another federal election was slated for April 8. This was an enormous setback in the drive for an Indian Claims Commission, but at the AGM of the North American Indian Brotherhood in March the participants resolved that "a Canadian Indian Claims Commission composed of unprejudiced and unbiased commissioners, with a majority chosen from within the British Commonwealth of Nations but outside Canada,"[608] was an absolute necessity. Experience had taught them that the government of Canada was far from impartial and would make a poor adjudicator.

On April 8, 1963, the federal election delivered the Progressive Conservatives just 95 seats to the Liberals 128. Although Lester B. Pearson's Liberals had actually taken 41 per cent of the vote, they were 5 seats short of a majority government. Diefenbaker clung to power for a few days, hoping that the 24 Quebec Social Credit MPs would join him, but they were split when six of their number signed a petition stating that Pearson should form the government, thus forcing Diefenbaker to resign on April 22. Although the Quebec MPs would later retract their statement, Pearson had momentum on his side and formed a government that was backed by the 17 NDP members elected.

Maisie remained largely silent on the change of government, perhaps adhering to her recent statement on the paper's non-political policy. But she probably recalled her heated exchange with the president of the BC Liberal Association when she had said that Pearson "irritates me beyond words, and I find his views more destructive than constructive." But there was one bright spot: during the election campaign both Diefenbaker and Pearson had promised to set up an Indian Claims Commission. In fact, "the Liberals [had] distributed 15,000 pamphlets before the election promising an unbiased and unprejudiced Indian Claims Commission."[609] The question was: would they do it now that they were in government? Maisie didn't have long to wait for an answer. George Manuel, president of the North American Indian Brotherhood, had also been impatient to know and had sent letters and telegrams to both Prime Minister Pearson and his new minister of Citizenship and Immigration, Guy Favreau, requesting a response to his organization's resolutions, one of which called "for an unprejudiced and unbiased Claims Commission with wide terms of reference."[610] At last the minister responded with the following telegram:

GEORGE MANUEL

CHASE, BC

GOVERNMENT IS NOW CONSIDERING METHOD BY WHICH INDIAN CLAIMS MIGHT BE SETTLED STOP AN ANNOUNCEMENT WILL BE MADE IN HOUSE OF COMMONS WHEN DECISION REACHED STOP REPLY TO RESOLUTIONS OF NORTH AMERICAN INDIAN BROTHERHOOD WILL REACH YOU IN NEAR FUTURE

GUY FAVREAU, MINISTER[611]

It was an ominous sign that there was no mention of an Indian Claims Commission in the Liberal's throne speech, which prompted a frustrated Frank Calder, writing on behalf of the Nisga'a Tribal Council, to press the minister for a date when it would be established. Although he stated that the council preferred a judicial decision on the land question, he said he was willing to wait and see what the commission had to offer. He warned the minister, however, that he and his colleagues had not forgotten earlier Liberal platforms and their failure to give First Nations the vote.

Maisie too was blunt in her advice to her readers:

> *The Native Voice* urges that all Indians in British Columbia be prepared to send representatives back to Ottawa to ask for [an] unprejudiced and unbiased commission tribunal. Funds will be necessary for this. Indians must start giving what money they can at once to finance their representatives.
>
> This is the last chance on the Indian land question. Every one of the 40,000 Indians of British Columbia must now, to put it frankly, "put up or shut up."[612]

One representative who had beaten a path to Ottawa, but who wouldn't be going this time, was Reverend Dr. Peter Kelly who had suffered a heart attack and was recovering in Prince Rupert General Hospital. Fortunately he made an excellent recovery and was soon released to rest at his Comox home, but it was hard for him not to be involved in such pivotal negotiations after representing his people at the council table for fifty years.

The first good news came on August 15 when Minister Favreau, speaking at a conference of the National Indian Council in Winnipeg, stated that the Indian Act would be revised "in accordance with the principles of justice, freedom of choice and human dignity." He promised that a bill to establish a Claims Commission would be introduced before the end of the year and that other policies affecting First Nations peoples would be "pursued vigorously."[613] Education, said Favreau, was to be given special attention. "Experience has showed convincingly that education is indeed the key to the Indian's future." No Indian boy or girl, he said, need be deprived of an education for lack of financial resources, and he encouraged parents to support their children when pursuing that goal beyond the elementary level. Then, referencing the Indian Act, he said he recognized that "an appreciable degree of distrust and resentment on the part of Indians is rooted in the act itself," and with "the passage of time and rapidly changing economic and social conditions, some of its provisions have come to appear harsh and oppressive..." In analyzing the deep causes for distrust on the part of the Indians, he said it had become apparent that "a rankling feeling of injustice among the Indians at the lack of action with regard to the adjudication and settlement of their long outstanding claims was one of the roots of this evil." While "two parliamentary committees had previously recognized this fact and recommended that action be taken to assess and settle all Indian claims and grievances in a just and equitable manner,"[614] none of these recommendations had survived the political gauntlet of the House of Commons.

However, even though First Nations organizations had been united in calling for an unbiased tribunal composed of adjudicators from outside the country, Minister Favreau told the meeting that the chair would likely be someone with judicial experience assisted by two commissioners. And while the tribunal would not "be bound by strict legal rules of evidence... it should have the powers of a court for the purpose of summoning witnesses and the production and inspection of documents."[615] He finished by saying he hoped this tribunal would go a long way towards relieving First Nations grievances. But given the Liberals' tenuous grip on power, his audience wondered if his government would survive long enough to establish a commission.

On Friday, September 13, Maisie Hurley collapsed at home and was rushed to Vancouver General Hospital for examination. At first it was suspected that she had suffered a gall or kidney stone attack, and she was confined to her hospital bed for a week while further tests were done; in the end it was diagnosed as a stroke, the first of the many she was soon to experience. She was ordered to set aside her *Native Voice* and mail duties until such time as she had fully recovered. This worried her since one of her greatest fears was that the paper would fold if she was not there to guide it, but it did carry on as if nothing had changed, albeit without the verve and panache that it had enjoyed under her watch. Following her release from hospital, however, she refused to sit around feeling sorry for herself and instead threw herself into yet another cause.

Just two months before her collapse, an incident had occurred that would dramatically change the course of First Nations justice in the province. On July 7, two Snuneymuxw men, Clifford White and David Bob, accompanied by White's teen-aged son Leonard and Leonard's friend, Jerry Thomas, went hunting on the west slope of Mount Benson near Nanaimo in an effort to feed the hungry White and Bob families. White had nine children and Bob four. The two men shot six blacktail deer but were stopped by a game warden on Old Nanaimo Lake Road while they were transporting the carcasses home. Hunting season had closed nine days earlier so they were arrested and charged with being in possession of deer during the closed season contrary to the Provincial Game Act. It was a summary conviction, meaning that it was less serious in nature than an indictable offence and therefore could be heard by the local magistrate.

On September 23, White and Bob appeared before Magistrate Lionel Beevor-Potts in Nanaimo and on September 25 were each fined $100 or forty days' imprisonment; Bob paid his fine, but White could not raise the funds, so he was transported to the Oakalla Prison Farm to serve out his forty-day sentence. Maisie, fresh out of hospital, learned of his predicament and paid his fine, thus setting him free.

In his book *One Man's Justice: A Life in the Law*, Tom Berger recalls how he then became involved in this case:

> Maisie Hurley appeared at my office, leaning on her cane. She was in her seventies but still a commanding figure. She announced, "Now, Tommy, you will have to defend the Indians." She was not a woman to argue with.[616]

Maisie and her friend, Irene Rogers, explained to Berger that he had two new clients, Clifford White and David Bob, who were planning to launch an appeal of their conviction for hunting deer out of season. Because their case had been heard by a magistrate, Berger determined that "they had the right to a new trial in the County Court."[617] However, appeals cost money, so the "South Vancouver [Island] Tribal Federations organized by Wilson Bob, Dave Elliot, Eddy and Joe Elliot, Fred Miller, Philip Paul and Mike Underwood"[618] together with the Native Brotherhood, offered to finance the case, though at the time it is unlikely that any of them had an inkling of its ground-breaking significance.

Berger travelled to his clients' reserve, wondering what sort of a defence he could possibly mount considering their obvious infraction of the provincial game laws. Expecting to interview just his two clients, he was surprised when virtually the whole community turned out to the meeting. It was there that he learned from the Elders that there was a treaty in place that gave them the right to hunt on "unoccupied lands" during the closed season. As far as Berger knew, the First Nations in the province had never been treated with the exception of Treaty 8 in the Peace River district, signed on June 21, 1899, but this was generally regarded as just an extension of the treaties signed with Prairie First Nations. And since Aboriginal law had not been taught at his alma mater, UBC (the only law school in the province at the time), he was unaware of any other agreements. Obviously he would have to conduct some basic research to determine his next move.

In Victoria he discovered that the treaties the Elders referred to were fourteen land conveyances that had been negotiated by James Douglas in the 1850s with First Nations on Vancouver Island. They were not treaties in the traditional sense, especially when compared to Treaty 8, which was a thirty-page legal document signed by John J. McGee, clerk of the Privy Council. These land conveyances, handwritten on a single page with a subsequent page of Xs made by the chiefs, beside which a clerk had transcribed their names, didn't look much like treaties nor did they read like treaties. They did, however, serve the purpose for which they were intended, that is, to convey land from the various First Nations to the Hudson's Bay Company, which in 1849 had been given the whole of Vancouver Island by the British Crown. The Nanaimo "treaty" to which the Elders referred was transacted on December 23, 1854, and had paid the Saalequum people the sum of 636 white blankets, 12 blue blankets and 20 inferior blankets in exchange for their land.

Thomas Berger, barrister, of whom Maisie wrote, "This young man obviously believes most sincerely and thoroughly in the aboriginal rights of the Native people of British Columbia." Photo courtesy of Thomas Berger.

"But were these conveyances treaties?" Berger wondered, then concluded that "they had to be treaties within the meaning of the Indian Act if the hunting rights they guaranteed were to take precedence over the Game Act."[619] When Willard Ireland, provincial archivist, showed him the conveyances in the archives in Victoria, Berger observed that James Douglas had signed them as chief factor of the HBC and not as governor of the Colony of Vancouver Island, which was his other role. Although Berger knew that treaties are not made with companies but with Crowns, he also knew that Douglas's roles had been interchangeable, and that even though he had negotiated the land conveyances as chief factor of the HBC, he was also acting in his capacity of governor of the Colony of Vancouver Island in that the land he had procured was for the benefit of all its citizens, not just the HBC.

There were other problems, too. The Nanaimo "treaty" consisted of one sheet of paper with Xs where 159 First Nations persons had made their marks. Beside each mark was a name and the number of blankets that person had received. Berger learned that the conveyances for three of the properties around Victoria had been similarly executed before the correct wording had been forwarded from London, and that wording had then been inserted into the documents at a later date. Someone, however, had failed to follow suit with the Nanaimo conveyance. Where was the preamble that stated, in part, that "It is understood, however, that the land itself, with these small exceptions, becomes the entire property of the white people forever; it is also understood that we are at liberty to hunt over the unoccupied lands and to carry on our fisheries as formerly"?[620] This wording would clearly establish White and Bob's authority to hunt where they had been hunting as long as a) the west slope of Mount Benson was considered "unoccupied lands" and b) as long as Mount Benson was part of their ancestral territory.

Berger decided that, because the "hunting over the unoccupied lands" wording was extant in the other conveyances, Governor Douglas had fully intended that it would be in the Nanaimo conveyance as well. Willard Ireland assisted him by producing a letter that had been written in December 1849—before the negotiation of any of the conveyances—by Archibald Barclay, secretary of the Hudson's Bay Company in London. Barclay clearly spelled out how Douglas should proceed with the land purchases and as a condition of the transfer had recommended the continuance of fishing and hunting rights. Douglas's reply to Barclay on May 16, 1850, acknowledged his instructions, and the content of the other thirteen agreements confirms he followed them.

Now Berger had to establish that White's and Bob's ancestors had been party to that conveyance. Had their ancestors been among those persons who signed it with Douglas? As 110 years had elapsed, this seemed an almost impossible task, but again with Ireland's assistance he was able to confirm by examining census documents that White's and Bob's ancestors were indeed signatories to the Douglas "treaty." Their ancestors had been members of one of the four First Nations living in the Nanaimo area at the time, and all of the mature males had signed the Douglas conveyance. The final piece of evidence was provided by Wilson Duff, curator of anthropology at the provincial museum, who confirmed that the west slope of Mount Benson was well within the subjects' ancestral territory.

If this line of argument was to fail, Berger had a unique back-up plan. As in a previous case where he had used the Magna Carta in the defence of a local Ironworkers Union against an injunction sought by a bridge building contractor, he would advance the proposition that the Royal Proclamation of 1763, which stated that First Nations could only sell their land to the Crown, was still relevant. Since the proclamation had not been extinguished, the conveyance of the land to the Hudson's Bay Company had been in contravention of that document. He wrote that: "If the Crown did not recognize the instrument as a treaty, then the Indians could stand on their Aboriginal rights."[621] Berger filed his appeal on October 18, but since it was not scheduled to be heard in Nanaimo's County Court until 10:30 a.m. on December 11, he had a couple of months to finish preparing his case.

In mid-October, Chief George Manuel resigned his position as president of the North American Indian Brotherhood and joined the Native Brotherhood of BC "to further the aim of Indian unity in British Columbia." He said that:

> my desires have always been clear: namely, that provincial unity for the Indian people is the answer to the unsolved problems which we are facing. Without such unity, there is little we can accomplish. Without a strong, powerful organization which serves the interests of all of us, we have a severely limited bargaining ability... After giving the matter very careful and lengthy consideration, I have decided to join the ranks of those Indians who have the true desire to see provincial unity for all Indians in British Columbia.[622]

He cited the land issue and the settlement of First Nations claims as the most pressing problems. Guy Williams was also once again emphasizing unity when he spoke to a newly formed group, the Southern Vancouver Island Allied Tribes, at a meeting in Duncan to discuss raising capital to finance the White and Bob appeal. "Unity is a simple word," Williams told the gathering, "but it is very difficult to achieve."[623] Also at the meeting was Henry Castillou, legal counsel to the NAIB. He was urging support for a delegation to proceed to Ottawa to agitate for the "right kind" of Indian Claims Commission with "terms of reference that suit the Indian people."[624] But, while his plea was well meaning, he was too late.

On December 16, the federal government finally introduced Bill C-130, which would set up a five-person Indian Claims Commission, but it was a far cry from what had been envisioned or desired by the Native Brotherhood. While it provided for compensation for land that was taken "from Indians by the Crown" and "lands set apart for Indians... [that] were disposed of by the Crown," land in BC was off the agenda by virtue of the fact that all claims had to be supported by evidence in writing. Since some BC claims dated back more than a hundred years, it would be almost impossible to find the paperwork required to satisfy the commission panel because the government of the day had kept no record of transactions with any First Nations except for the fourteen land purchase agreements of the 1850s. And since BC's First Nations were never conquered, there were no treaties—with the exception of Treaty 8 in the Peace River—to provide the necessary evidence. In addition, claims would only be paid in cash, not land.

Two MPs, Frank Howard (NDP for Skeena) and Tom Barnett (NDP for Comox-Alberni), condemned Bill C-130 as being meaningless and contradictory. They criticized the ten-year time limit of the commission, the fact that there was no provision for claims to be made for land in BC that had been "taken from [the First Nations] by private individuals" and that individuals, other than as a Nation, were restricted from appearing before it. They wanted First Nations representation on the commission and asked why legal rules of evidence would not apply but the commission would instead require all evidence in writing. Howard told the *Voice*:

> This is a two-faced attempt to mislead the Indian people into thinking that they are going to get a fair deal from the Commission... Judges from the Exchequer Court of Canada may be on the Indian Claims Appeal court and thus hear an appeal against the decision they originally participated in rendering. This concept belongs to the days of Cromwell and has no place in a bill which is supposed to rectify the injustices of the past generations.[625]

As the full contents of the bill were revealed, Brotherhood president Guy Williams commented angrily that: "We are dissatisfied, to put it mildly, with the government's plans to dispose of the Indian land question."[626]

In November Maisie returned briefly to the paper to write a heartfelt editorial mourning the death of United States President John F. Kennedy, who had been assassinated on November 22. She extended her condolences to his family before going on to mourn the passing of a childhood friend, Frank Allan, about whom she wrote: "He was quick on the draw. He never touched leather. You never saw daylight between him and the saddle. Ride 'em, cowboy! RIP. Lovingly, Maisie."[627]

His death was just the latest in a year of losses for Maisie. In May her dear friend Constance Cox, court interpreter and journalist, had passed away at the age of 82. Maisie wrote that:

> Slowly the great doors of death swung open. The Ghost Drums of the North beat through the night as the soul of Chief Shim-am-a-em passed through the gates to her eternal rest.
>
> Dear, dear friend, goodbye dear Shim-am-a-em, great princess of the North, friend of the poor and afflicted. We will meet again.[628]

On New Year's Day, 1964, Heber Clifton, one of the founders of the Brotherhood, died at his home in Hartley Bay. He was 94 years old. When he was born, the great potlatch ceremony had still been practised, but he became a driving force behind transitioning his people into the new reality. The Brotherhood had been successful because, as his daughter-in-law Helen Clifton said, his role had been "to recruit the Tsimpshian part, and he went to the Gitkskan and the Naas and tried to organize them, and being a hereditary chief, he knew all the chiefs in the total area." His tremendous importance to the Brotherhood and the respect in which he was held were evident prior to his funeral when his body lay in state for four days, guarded around the clock by a four-man honour guard.

Maisie also wrote compellingly for the December *Voice* about her late husband's protégé, Tom Berger, whom she said "is genuinely shocked at the injustices suffered by Native Canadians... This young man obviously believes most sincerely and thoroughly in the aboriginal rights of the Native people of British Columbia."[629]

Meanwhile, Berger's appeal of the White and Bob case, which opened before County Court Judge A. H. J. Swencisky in Nanaimo on December 11, had been adjourned until January 8. Prior to adjournment, however, Crown Counsel Don Cunliffe had attempted "to have the appeal declared a constitutional matter, which would have to be brought to the attention of the attorney general of BC and Canada."[630] The judge, however, ruled against his argument. When the case did resume in the new year, Judge Swencisky commented that: "No matter what my verdict is in this appeal, I hope it will be further appealed to the Supreme Court of Canada for a final ruling."[631] Following Berger's and Cunliffe's arguments, the judge promised a decision by March 4.

On January 16, 1964, Maisie collapsed at her home, and since she was alone at the time, she lay semi-conscious for several hours before she could call for help. She was rushed to Vancouver General Hospital where doctors were soon able to stabilize her condition, but it was late February before she was released, and she returned home without the full use of her right arm and hand. She was thus prevented from answering her mail, prompting the Brotherhood to relocate the *Native Voice* back to the Standard Building to remove any temptation for her to get back to work, while at the same time providing her with the rest she needed. However, she did manage to thank a number of people for their good wishes including the Hon. John Diefenbaker and his wife, August Jack Khatsahlano and Brotherhood president Guy Williams.

The 1964 Native Brotherhood convention was held in Vancouver in March. High on the list of topics for discussion was Bill C-130, which was currently before the House of Commons. Before the convention Dr. Peter Kelly, still chairman of the Brotherhood's Legislative Committee and deeply discouraged by the inadequacies of Bill C-130, told the *Voice* that: "Other provinces have settled with the Indians, but BC has always refused to recognize our claims.

Our lands were ruthlessly expropriated and we are still waiting for compensation."[632] At the AGM he suggested that a "fighting fund" of $10,000 be raised to finance a campaign to establish Aboriginal title in British Columbia. "It will be costly," he said, since not "only lawyers but other men of science will have to be consulted and their fees must be met for this purpose." Then he called for unity as "there must be one voice only of the Indians of this province."[633] Alfred Adams's prophetic words had survived from the Brotherhood's inception in 1931.

Tom Berger added his voice to those condemning Bill C-130 for its deficiencies when he pointed out that the federal government's proposed commission would exclude all claims against the province of British Columbia arising between 1871, when it had become a province of Canada, and the present time. He told the *Voice* that there was a lack of knowhow as well as a lack of resources to finance the claims even if they could be established because claims going back a hundred years or more would require the assistance of anthropologists, historians and lawyers, and he was skeptical that the written evidence that the commission was requiring would even then be available. He criticized the two-year requirement for First Nations to notify the commission of their claims: "It is paradoxical that Parliament, after waiting for 97 years to establish an Indian Claims Commission, should require an Indian band with a claim to notify the Commission within two years."[634] He, Frank Calder and Guy Williams then sat down to prepare a proposal for amending the terms of the commission, as did ex-Brotherhood President William Scow, who was also troubled by the clause dealing with the requirements for evidence.

Following Berger's advice, the Brotherhood wired Prime Minister Pearson to protest the fact that the bill was "inadequate" and received a reply from the new Minister of Citizenship and Immigration, René Tremblay, that he would be pleased to receive any further representations that they wanted to submit. This was far less, however, than what Brotherhood President Williams had requested in his wire, since he had also asked for acknowledgement of Aboriginal title for the First Nations in the province. Minister Tremblay did, however, send his executive assistant, Raymond Denis, to the North American Indian Brotherhood AGM in Kamloops a couple of months later to listen to their grievances about the bill and to make the promise that the federal government would consider all suggested changes.

On March 4 County Court Judge Swencisky summarized his judgment in the White and Bob appeal:

> Briefly, to summarize the effect of my judgement, I hold that the document filed as Exhibit 8, though not signed by Governor Douglas in

his capacity as governor, is, nevertheless, a treaty and, as a result, the two accused are entitled to the benefit of the exception contained in Section 87 of the Indian Act. I also hold that the aboriginal right of the Nanaimo Indian tribes to hunt on unoccupied land, which was confirmed to them by the Proclamation of 1763, has never been abrogated or extinguished and is still in full force and effect.[635]

Berger was jubilant. White and Bob were exonerated, although only for the time being; as expected, Attorney General Robert Bonner immediately launched an appeal of the judge's decision.

In April, Maisie suffered another stroke, but it was not until Friday, June 9, that the world received news of it. And it came from an unusual source—Jack Wasserman of the *Vancouver Sun*, who reported that:

> Indomitable Maisie Hurley's last stroke put her in hospital where medics told her she was dying. To which Maisie replied, "Hell, if I'm dying, I'm going home to do it." With which she ordered an ambulance and had herself driven home. Once out of hospital, Maisie discovered that the campaign to reclaim BC for her beloved Indians was ready to go.
> And now you'd never know she'd been ill... Incidentally, everyone laughed when Maisie first said the Indians still owned BC. Now Attorney-General Bob Bonner has three lawyers working to try and save the country for our side."[636]

Home for Maisie after this hospital stay was her daughter Kitty Bell's house in North Vancouver, but she also began taking physiotherapy sessions at Vancouver's Holy Family Hospital for the extensive paralysis in her arms and legs. Among her many visitors during these months was the aging August Jack Khatsahlano and his wife, Mary. Meanwhile, staff at the *Voice* responded to the avalanche of concerned mail with a notice that:

> Neither we nor Mrs. Hurley are able to answer all her many friends and subscribers who have sent their good wishes to her and to the paper. As reported earlier, the *Native Voice* is making every effort to return to schedule. With the help of readers and advertisers, we will continue to publish regularly under the guidance of publisher Maisie Hurley.[637]

A month later the *Voice* reported that Maisie was making good progress, and she advised readers of the August issue of the *Voice* that she was looking to:

> men like Guy Williams, Frank Calder, Dr. Peter Kelly, William Scow, Alfred Scow and Tom Berger to lead the fight started many years ago

by the Allied Tribes of British Columbia... We must have an impartial Claims Commission and we must have provisions that will permit Indian claims to be settled with justice and honor and without high pressure and trickery.[638]

Although her body was slowly failing, her mind remained focussed on the task Alfred Adams had set for her so many years earlier—to give her life to his people. Maisie honoured that promise until the afternoon of October 3, 1964, when, at Lions Gate Hospital in North Vancouver, her great heart stopped beating. She was 76 years old.

Guy Williams had visited her in hospital only days earlier and after he had updated her on the latest news, including the upcoming BC Supreme Court hearing of the White and Bob case, she had said:

I am going to Victoria with you. This is what I have lived for all my life and I am going to be there.

We Indians own the whole province and don't you ever forget and give up. When I am gone, I'll be watching you. This is the beginning of our victory march... We are a proud people and we will fight for our rights... Watch that government on Bill C-130—Watch!

The Native Brotherhood is strong—remember the great men who founded the Brotherhood, and do not fail them. Use the *Native Voice*. It's yours—it will be your strength...[639]

She had been too weak to continue, but as Williams and his wife left, she called after them, "Come back soon, my darlings!"[640]

The funeral service for Maisie Hurley was held on October 6, 1964, at St. Edmunds Church, the second-oldest church in North Vancouver, with Monsignor J. L. Bradley officiating in a traditional Roman Catholic ceremony. According to the story in the October issue of the *Native Voice*, Monsignor Bradley told the crowd who filled the church that:

"The Canadian people are engaged in an unwitting destruction of the Indian people, nonetheless brutal because of the blind, ignorant process of the act." He said that everyone wants to "help the Indian become a white man" and that people think the Indian can develop no way of life on his own. "Maisie Hurley's ideal," he stated firmly, "was not that the Indian should become a sort of white man but a real Indian. Her life was devoted to helping him develop the traits and virtues of this proud race," Monsignor Bradley said.

"There were no halfway measures with Maisie," he said. "She had a deep capacity for love and an unusual understanding of the Indian.

Her idea of success was to give the Indian his rightful place in the Canadian economy.

"Be Indians," he called on the Natives present to pay their last respects. "Be proud you are Indians."

The *Voice* story continued:

Speaking for the Indians present, Chief Simon Baker expressed the sorrow of his people. "We do not appear in our tribal robes because they are reserved for more joyful occasions," he said. "But in our hearts we put everything to one side and mourn for Maisie. We have lost a leader; we have lost a dear friend."[641]

Maisie's sons, Ronald Murphy of Seattle and Terry Murphy of San Francisco, walked behind her casket as it was conveyed to her final resting place. Pallbearers on the left, from back to front, were Brotherhood President Guy Williams, Dugald McAlpine, barrister, and George North, who assisted Maisie on the *Native Voice*. On the right, from back to front, were Tom Connochie,

Maisie Hurley's great heart stopped beating. Monsignor Bradley, officiating at her funeral, said: "Maisie Hurley's ideal was not that the Indian should become a sort of white man but a real Indian. Her life was devoted to helping him develop the traits and virtues of this proud race." Photo from the family collection.

CBC producer, Ike Shulman, barrister, and Thomas Berger, barrister. At the graveside in Forest Lawn Cemetery, with a piper playing a lament and a chief making a funeral speech, she was finally laid to rest beside her late husband, Tom.

"A great splash of color has suddenly turned grey," the editors of the *Native Voice* wrote in the October issue, which was totally devoted to Maisie Hurley:

> A blazing light has grown dim. Maisie Hurley, Indian chief, warrior, member of the Native Brotherhood, is dead. Only her great heart and her indomitable will kept her alive these past few months—her limbs were almost completely paralyzed.
>
> But somehow death seemed alien to Maisie, perhaps because she was such a strong woman with an abounding enthusiasm for life, perhaps also because she fought so fiercely for the cause of the Indian people and perhaps too because her crusade was so just.[642]

And Brotherhood president Guy Williams wrote: "Maisie was all heart and a bigger Indian than any of us."[643]

Maisie had not lived long enough to learn that the attorney general's appeal of the White and Bob verdict, which was heard in the BC Supreme Court on December 15, 1964, upheld the County Court decision made by Judge Swencisky in March. Three of the five judges on the case ruled that the land conveyance agreement was indeed a treaty. However, only Justice Tom Norris, a well-respected and conservative judge, sided with Berger on the relevancy of the Royal Proclamation of 1763. The attorney general subsequently filed an appeal to the Supreme Court of Canada, which also upheld the decision of the appeal court but did not rule on the efficacy of the proclamation. (It was not until the case of *Calder v. Attorney General of British Columbia* in 1973 that it was established that "aboriginal use and possession of land from time immemorial," rather than the Royal Proclamation of 1763, was the source of Aboriginal title.) Writing about the importance of the White and Bob case, historian Ken Coates has said:

> It was an important decision... in that it demonstrated the contemporary relevance of often-ignored nineteenth century treaties, introduced social science research into British Columbia First Nations court cases, and provided a first glimpse of the important role to be played by Berger in the resolution of Aboriginal legal entitlements.[644]

In a 2012 interview, Tom Berger said as he reflected on Maisie Hurley's legacy:

I think her most important contribution was no doubt the *Native Voice*, keeping this cause... the cause is always alive, aboriginal people have never given it up... but keeping this cause alive in some measure, in the public eye or at least so that people in the legal profession and the newspaper world were conscious of it.[645]

Perhaps Monsignor Bradley, who had eulogized her in such glowing terms, said it best: "She was a great personality, the greatest woman I have known, a great Scot, a great Indian."[646]

'Tis the end of the trail.
The traveller is old.
Her body is frail, and
The evening grows cold.
The well-trodden track
She leaves with a sigh.
To sit down and rest
On a boulder nearby.
This ends this life,
When aged and frail,
And too old for work,
'Tis the end of the trail.

—Amy Ellen Chadwick Campbell-Johnston

EPILOGUE

One of Maisie Hurley's last political remarks was to the president of the Native Brotherhood of BC, Guy Williams, instructing him, among other things, to: "Watch that government on Bill C-130!" She was right to be concerned. Bill C-130, as Tom Berger had said, was "entirely inadequate," because in British Columbia it would only deal with claims prior to the province entering Confederation in 1871. He told the *Native Voice* that "it would be impossible to make a claim for land taken away after that year"[647] because of the lack of written evidence.

Having distributed the text of Bill C-130 to First Nations groups throughout the country and received their feedback, the Honourable Jack Nicholson, minister of Citizenship and Immigration, introduced an amended version, now called Bill C-123, to the House of Commons on June 21 and 22, 1965. It was then referred to a Special Joint Committee of the Senate and House of Commons for further review.

Guy Williams, still president of the Brotherhood, called this new version a "nasty piece of legislation"[648] for it was still insufficient "to begin to meet the requests put forward by the Indian people."[649] And Tom Berger, after studying it, stated that there should be "a provision in Bill C-123 acknowledging the aboriginal title of the Indian tribes of British Columbia."[650] All this effort was in vain anyway, as the bill died on the Order Paper in the fall of 1965 and was never reinstated.

In the final years of Maisie's life, she had become very worried about the future of the *Native Voice* when she was no longer there to guide it. But after she died in October 1964, her daughter, Kathleen Bell, took over as publisher for a time, and Kathleen's son, Bill Bell, recalls "assembling the paper in the living room of our house on 6th Street in North Vancouver, right down to the cutting, pasting and waxing the copy onto the layout sheets." The *Voice* carried on for many more years after Maisie's death, but where once First Nations stories had been relegated to the back pages of the mainstream newspapers, there came a time when they began to crowd the first section, and everybody read them. As a result, there was less need for the *Voice* and issues became sporadic.

As for Maisie Hurley's style of advocacy, much has been written. Today, someone like Maisie would probably be considered meddlesome, but she came on the scene when her involvement was both important and appreciated.

As columnist Jamie Lamb noted in his *Vancouver Sun* column in November 1981: "She advocated the cause of BC Indians when nobody knew there was a cause."

Were Maisie alive today, she would be encouraged by the current state of awareness and action in the world of Canada's First Peoples. For instance, the recent Supreme Court decision granting the Tsilhqot'in in BC's interior title to 1,750 square kilometres of traditional land in the remote Nemiah Valley was an incredible development in land title rights, a subject that Maisie harped upon whenever she had a podium or a pen.

Further, the recent commitment from Prime Minister Justin Trudeau's government to address the recommendations of the Truth and Reconciliation Commission is a breath of fresh air, as is the commitment to launch an inquiry into the murdered and missing women. Indigenization is the new buzzword on campuses across the nation where First Nations are being welcomed and recruited and where some institutions have made it mandatory for students to take at least one indigenous-themed course before they graduate. Buffy Sainte-Marie, singer, author and influential First Nations/Native American advocate, who once wrote for the *Voice*, as part of her advocacy is dialoguing with universities on "how to create interactive multimedia core curriculum through aboriginal perspectives." On the subject of Maisie's paper, she informed me that although she "didn't know Maisie well...*The Native Voice* was one of the few magazines of excellence around at the time..."

In short, although there are still some serious shortcomings and much work has yet to be done, there is hope on the horizon. As Chief Dr. Robert Joseph wrote in his Forward to this book, "Canadians everywhere are in a mood to seek a new way forward..."

The final words in this story belong to Maisie: "All the Indians want is what is theirs. They don't want to assimilate. They are wonderful people with magnificent traditions of their own."[651]

NOTES

Chapter 1

1. Indian Affairs Record Group 10 (RG10), *Report of the Royal Commission on Indian Affairs of the Province of British Columbia*, Queen Charlotte Island Agency Stenographic Report Index, 6.
2. *The Native Voice*, January 1953, 7.
3. *The Native Voice*, 50th Anniversary Edition, 1996, 5.
4. Letter to Hugh Dempsey, February 7, 1950.
5. *The Native Voice*, December 1946, 7.
6. Amy Ellen Chadwick Merry to William Flinders Petrie, Esq., British School of Archaeology in Egypt, March 1923, 2.
7. Imbert Orchard Records (T3279:0001), CBC (1961), BC Archives, Maisie Hurley interview track 1 and 2, 1, 2.
8. Harold Kingsmill, excerpted from The First History of Rossland, B.C. (1897); provided by the Rossland Museum.
9. Imbert Orchard Records (T3279:0001), CBC (1961), BC Archives, Maisie Hurley interview track 1 and 2, 13.
10. Maisie A. C. Armytage-Moore, "A New Side of Bill Miner's Character," Vancouver City Archives, July 8, 1943, 1.
11. Ibid., 2
12. Patrick Nagle, "Maisie Says BC Still Belongs to the Indians: A Do-or-Die Campaigner from 'way Back, She's Out to Help Them Win their Case," Vancouver Sun (weekend magazine), April 4, 1964, 16.
13. Armytage-Moore, "A New Side of Bill Miner's Character," 1.
14. Ibid., 3.
15. Ibid.
16. Ibid.
17. *The Native Voice*, August 1949, 11.
18. Peter Grauer, *Interred With Their Bones: Bill Miner in Canada, 1903–1907* (Kamloops, BC: Self -published, 2006), 337.
19. Armytage-Moore, "A New Side of Bill Miner's Character."
20. Nagle, "Maisie Says BC Still Belongs to the Indians," 16.
21. Interview with Paul St. Pierre, February 8, 2011.
22. Robert Ward, *Wealth and Notability: The Lockwood, Day and Metcalfe Families of Yorkshire and London* (2014). Ward's wife is also related to the Armytage-Moore family.
23. Nagle, "Maisie Says BC Still Belongs to the Indians," 16.
24. Interview with Maureen Woodcock.
25. Nagle, "Maisie Says BC Still Belongs to the Indians," 16.
26. Nagle, "Maisie Says BC Still Belongs to the Indians."
27. Interview with Maureen Woodcock.
28. Nagle, "Maisie Says BC Still Belongs to the Indians," 14.

29. Law Society of BC, Vancouver.

30. Bar exams taken on July 6, 1925. Law Society of BC, Vancouver.

31. Wesley Pue, *Law School: The Story of Legal Education in British Columbia* (Vancouver: UBC Faculty of Law, 1995), chapter 2: "Formal Legal Instruction Begins."

32. David Willock, "Courtroom Showman," *Weekend Picture Magazine*, October 11, 1952, 1.

33. *The Province*, December 27, 1961.

34. Nagle, "Maisie Says BC Still Belongs to the Indians," 16.

Chapter 2

35. Recollections of Michael Nicoll Yahgulanaas.

36. Ibid.

37. Philip Drucker, *The Native Brotherhoods: Modern Intertribal Organizations on the Northwest Coast*, Smithsonian Institution, Bureau of American Ethnology Bulletin 168 (Washington, DC: Smithsonian Institution, 1958), 81.

38. Ben Myers and E. D. Kohlstedt, *A Short Story of the Metlakatla Christian Mission* (Metlakatla, Alaska: William Duncan Memorial Church, 1954), 8.

39. Interview with Delores Churchill, November 1, 2013.

40. Ibid.

41. Interview with Jane Kristovich, November 7, 2013.

42. Paul Tennant, *Aboriginal Peoples and Politics: The Indian Land Question in BC* (Vancouver: UBC Press, 1990).

43. Guy Williams, *The Native Voice*, February 1960, 5.

44. Ibid.

45. Recollections of Michael Nicoll Yahgulanaas.

46. Indian Affairs RG10, Report of the Royal Commission on Indian Affairs, 4.

47. Union of BC Indian Chiefs (UBCIC), *The Lands We Lost: A History of Cut-Off Lands and Land Losses from Indian Reserves in British Columbia* (Vancouver: Author, 1974), 61; http://ubcic.bc.ca/files/PDF/McKenna_McBride/lands.pdf.

48. Section 127, Chapter 129, Revised Statutes of British Columbia, 1911.

49. UBCIC, *The Lands We Lost*, 7.

50. Tennant, *Aboriginal Peoples and Politics*.

51. UBCIC, *The Lands We Lost*, 57.

52. Section 127, Chapter 129, Revised Statutes of British Columbia, 1911.

53. Indian Affairs RG10, Report of the Royal Commission on Indian Affairs, 6.

54. Charlie Isipaymilt, testimony before the Royal Commission on Indian Affairs in the Province of British Columbia, May 27, 1913.

55. Indian Affairs RG10, *Report of the Royal Commission on Indian Affairs*, 6.

56. Ibid., 7.

57. Ibid., 4.

58. Statement of Chiefs of the Interior Tribes of British Columbia, June 5, 1914, BC Archives.

59. Drucker, *The Native Brotherhoods*, 93.

60. Alan Morely, *Roar of the Breakers* (Toronto: The Ryerson Press, 1967), 108.

61. Tennant, *Aboriginal Peoples and Politics*.

62. Morely, *Roar of the Breakers*, 8.

63. Ibid., 80.

64. Ibid., 102–103.

65. Brendan F. R. Edwards, " 'I Have Lots of Help Behind Me, Lots of Books to Convince You:' Andrew Paull and the Value of Literacy in English," *BC Studies* 164 (Winter 2009–10): 16.

66. James Roe, "Canada's Indian Conscience," *Vancouver Province*, December 27, 1956.

67. Morely, *Roar of the Breakers*, 107.

68. E. Palmer Patterson, "Andrew Paull and Canadian Indian Resistance" (Ph.D. thesis, University of Washington, 1962), 66.

69. Herbert Francis Dunlop, *Andy Paull: As I Knew Him and Understood His Times* (Vancouver: Order of the O.M.I. of St. Paul's Province, 1989), 24.

70 Edwards, "Andrew Paull," 8.

71 Morely, *Roar of the Breakers*, 107.

72 Drucker, *The Native Brotherhoods*, 97.

73. G. S. Pragnell, Inspector of Indian Agencies, to Scott, December 6, 1923. Quoted in Dana McFarland, "Indian Reserve Cut-offs in British Columbia, 1912–1924, An Examination of Federal-Provincial Negotiations and Consultation With Indians" (M.A. thesis, University of British Columbia, 1988), 93.

74. Historical Timeline from 1700s to the Present, Union of British Columbia Indian Chiefs website, http://www.ubcic.bc.ca/Resources/timeline.htm, accessed January 19, 2015.

75. Wilson Duff, *The Indian History of British Columbia*. Volume 1: *The Impact of the White Man*. Anthropology in British Columbia, Memoir No. 5. (Victoria: Provincial Museum of Natural History and Anthropology, 1964), 69.

76. Public Archives of Canada, Scott Papers, RG 10, Vol. 6810, File 473, Vol. 12, Hearings Testimony, 1921–22.

77. Morely, *Roar of the Breakers*, 113.

78. Special Joint Committee of the Senate and House of Commons appointed to Inquire into the Claims of the Allied Indian Tribes of British Columbia, as Set Forth in their Petition Submitted to Parliament in June 1926: Proceedings, Reports and the Evidence, 160. Session 1926–1927.

79. Duff, *The Indian History of British Columbia*, 69, quoted in the "Report of the Special Joint Committee on Claims of the Allied Indian Tribes," Ottawa, 1927.

80. Tennant, *Aboriginal People and Politics.*
81. An amendment to the Indian Act, SC 1926–27, c. 32, s. 149A. It became s. 141 in the 1927 consolidated statutes, RSC 1927, c. 98, and prohibited fundraising for the purpose of Aboriginal title litigation without special government leave. Raymond Frogner, Archivist, Royal BC Museum.
82. City of Vancouver Archives, Native Brotherhood of BC files.
83. *The Native Voice*, December 1953, 4.
84. Drucker, *The Native Brotherhoods*, 106.
85. Gene Joseph, *A Brief History of the Native Brotherhood of British Columbia* (Vancouver: Native Brotherhood of British Columbia, 1981), 6.
86. Ibid.
87. *The Native Voice*, November 1947, 8.
88. Letter on the letterhead of Alfred Adams & Sons (General Merchants) to W. A. Newcombe, Esq. dated September 19, 1933. BC Archives, Victoria.
89. Drucker, *The Native Brotherhoods*, 109.

Chapter 3

90. Letter from Terry Murphy to his mother, Maisie. Date unknown.
91. Letter from Maisie to her son, Michael Murphy, December 30, 1943.
92. M. Armytage-Moore, "Food for Thought," Open Forum: M. Armytage-Moore Writes. Letter to and from the Editor. Newspaper and date unknown.
93. Recollections of Bill Bell (by e-mail), February 7, 2012.
94. Nagle, "Maisie Says BC Still Belongs to the Indians," 14.
95. Interview with Judge Alfred Scow.
96. Roland Wild, "Maisie Celebrates an Indian Triumph," *Vancouver Sun* (unknown date).
97. Interview with Thomas Berger.
98. Interview with Ron Rose.
99. *The Native Voice*, November 1953, 4.
100. Wild, "Maisie Celebrates."
101. Section 27 of the Indian Act (Royal Victoria Art Gallery exhibit).
102. Indigenousfoundations.art.ubc.ca—Indian Act—The "Potlatch Law" and Section 141, Alfred Scow.
103. Chief William Scow, interviewed by Imbert Orchard, CBC Imbert Orchard Collection, Tape 2, 1967, 4.
104. Duncan C. Scott, Department of Indian Affairs Circular, Ottawa, December 15, 1921. Read to the author by the late Alvin Dixon on March 30, 2012.
105. Chief William Scow interview, 1967, 18.
106. *The Native Voice*, December 1946, 1.
107. Interview with Chief Dr. Robert Joseph, March 30, 2012.
108. Interview with Alvin Dixon, March 30, 2012.
109. *The Native Voice*, December 1946, 4.

110. Ibid., 8.
111. Ibid.
112. Nagle, "Maisie Says BC Still Belongs to the Indians," 14.
113. Letter from Maisie to Violet McNaughton, November 12, 1958.
114. J. S. Matthews, *Conversations with Khatsahlano 1932–1954: Conversations with August Jack Khatsahlano, born at Snauq, False Creek Indian Reserve, circa 1877, son of Khaytulk and grandson of Chief Khahtsahlanogh* (Vancouver: n.p., 1955) 4.
115. Matthews, *Conversations with Khatsahlano, 1932–1954*, and letter to Dr. W. Kaye Lamb, 2.
116. From an unpublished manuscript by Maureen Woodcock.
117. Letter from Maisie to Violet McNaughton, November 12, 1958.
118. Maisie Hurley, "The Mountains," newspaper article (unknown paper and date).
119. Kevin Griffin, "Rarely Seen Artworks on Display; North Vancouver Museum Exhibits Spiritually Significant Works from the Squamish First Nation," *Vancouver Sun*, January 22, 2011, D1.
120. *The Native Voice*, December 1946, 3.
121. Royal Proclamation of 1763.
122. Mapleleafweb.com, University of Lethbridge, "The Indian Act: Historical Overview."
123. Ibid.
124. Ibid.
125. Tennant, *Aboriginal Peoples and Politics*.
126. Douglas to Newcastle, March 25, 1861. Papers Connected, 19.
127. *The Native Voice*, January 1947, 2.
128. Ibid.
129. Ibid., 8.
130. *The Native Voice*, January 1947, 4.
131. Nagle, "Maisie Says BC Still Belongs to the Indians."
132. *The Native Voice*, February 1947, 1.
133. Ibid., 2.
134. *The Native Voice*, January 1947, 4.
135. Interview with Paul St. Pierre, February 8, 2011.
136. G. McKevitt, "B.C. Claims Closest Now to Settlement," *Nesika: The Voice of BC Indians* 2, no. 10, Land Claims Issue (October 1973): 9. Vancouver: Union of British Columbia Indian Chiefs, accessed via UBCIC digital collection January 19, 2015 (http://www.ubcic.bc.ca/Resources/Digital/index.htm).
137. Ibid.
138. *The Native Voice*, February 1947, 1.
139. *Vancouver Sun*, February 3, 1947.
140. *Vancouver News-Herald*, January 25, 1947.
141. *Prince Rupert Daily News*, January 27, 1947.
142. *The Native Voice*, February 1947, 8.

143. Tennant, *Aboriginal People and Politics*.

144. *The Native Voice*, March 1947, 10.

145. Ibid., 4.

146. Ibid., 14.

147. Ibid., 8.

148. *Free Press Weekly*; reprinted in *The Native Voice*, March 1947, 7.

149. Ibid., 13.

150. Interview with Alvin Dixon, March 30, 2012.

151. Chief Robert Joseph's speech upon accepting his honorary doctorate of laws degree on May 27, 2003.

152. *The Native Voice*, March 1947, 10.

153. *The Native Voice*, April 1947, p. 10

Chapter 4

154. *The Native Voice*, April 1947, 14.

155. Ibid.

156. Ibid.

157. *The Native Voice*, May 1948, 16.

158. *The Native Voice*, May 1947, 1.

159. Ibid.

160. *The Native Voice*, January 1949, 10.

161. *The Native Voice*, May 1947, 8.

162. Ibid.

163. Ibid.

164. Ibid.

165. Ruth Smith, *Vancouver Sun*, Magazine Supplement, September 11, 1948, 3.

166. *The Native Voice*, January 1949, 3.

167. *The Native Voice*, May 1947, 10.

168. Ibid., 9.

169. Interview with Jane Kristovich, November 7, 2013.

170. *The Native Voice*, May 1947, 11.

171. *The Native Voice*, November 1947, 8.

172. *The Native Voice*, June 1947, 5.

173. *The Native Voice*, October 1947, 2.

174. Ibid.

175. *The Native Voice*, March 1948, 14.

176. *The Native Voice*, November 1947, 1.

177. Interview with Darryl Stonefish.

178. *The Native Voice*, May 1948, 7.

179. *The Native Voice*, December 1947, 15.

180. *The Native Voice*, May 1948, 8.

181. *The Native Voice*, July 1948, 2.

182. Ibid.

183. Ibid., 15.
184. Ibid.
185. *The Native Voice*, August–September 1948, 15.
186. *The Native Voice*, July 1948, 8.
187. *The Native Voice*, August–September 1948, 8.
188. Correspondence from T. P. O. Menzies, Curator, Vancouver Museum (Art, Historical & Scientific Association) to Mrs. Armytage-Moore, dated September 11, 1948.
189. Hal Malone, *Vancouver Sun*, December 22, 1948.
190. David Willock, *Weekend Picture Magazine*, October 11, 1952.
191. Ibid.
192. Hal Malone, *Vancouver Sun*, December 22, 1948.
193. *Vancouver Sun*, December 30, 1948.
194. *Vancouver Sun*, December 23, 1948.
195. *The Native Voice*, January 1949, 5.
196. *The Native Voice*, February 1949, 7.
197. *The Native Voice*, March 1949, 1.
198. Ibid., 2.
199. Ibid.
200. Ibid.
201. Ibid., 10.
202. Drucker, *The Native Brotherhoods*, 139.
203. *The Native Voice*, May 1949, 2.
204. Ibid., 3.
205. Ibid.
206. *The Native Voice*, June 1949, 13.
207. *The Native Voice*, May 1949, 2.
208. *The Native Voice*, February 1950, 2.

Chapter 5

209. *The Native Voice*, June 1949, 1.
210. *The Native Voice*, November 1950, 4.
211. Ibid.
212. *The Native Voice*, June 1949, 1.
213. Ibid.
214. Ibid., 3.
215. Ibid.
216. Ibid.
217. Ibid.
218. *The Native Voice*, July 1949, 2.
219. *The Native Voice*, June 1949, 3.
220. Ibid.
221. *Omineca Express*, May 9, 2001, 3.
222. Ibid.
223. Ibid.

224. Department of National Defence (Army) Personnel Selection Report (Discharge), June 12, 1951.
225. Library and Archives Canada, File Ref. PRA-2012-01468, letter re Dick Patrick from Larry Richer, Analyst.
226. Veterans Affairs Canada, Military Medal.
227. Kitty Sparrow, *The Indian Voice*, BC Indian Homemakers' Association (BCIHA), December 1980.
228. *The Native Voice*, June 1949, 6.
229. Lisa Striegler, *Saik'uz and Settlers, A Weave of Local History*, Expanded Play Program, An Initiative of the Good Neighbours Committee (Prince George: College of New Caledonia Press, 2011), 15.
230. Earl Andersen, *A Hard Place To Do Time: The Story of Oakalla Prison, 1912–1991* (New Westminster, BC: Hillpointe Pub., c.1993), Introduction.
231. *Omineca Express*, May 9, 2003, 3.
232. Kitty Sparrow, *The Indian Voice*, December 1980.
233. *The Native Voice*, June 1949, 11.
234. *The Native Voice*, July 1949, 4.
235. Ibid.
236. Ibid., 15.
237. *The Native Voice*, March 1950, 17.
238. Ibid.
239. *The Native Voice*, August 1949, 4.
240. *The Native Voice*, November 1949, 4.
241. *The Native Voice*, August 1949, 4.
242. *The Native Voice*, September 1949, 4.
243. *The Native Voice*, January 1950, 8.
244. Masako Fukawa and Stanley Fukawa, *Spirit of the Nikkei Fleet: BC's Japanese Canadian Fishermen* (Madeira Park: Harbour Publishing, 2009), 119.
245. *The Native Voice*, March 1950, 17.
246. Ibid., 12.
247. *The Native Voice*, November 1949, 1.
248. *The Native Voice*, February 1950, 13.
249. *The Native Voice*, November 1949, 1.
250. Ibid., 2.
251. *The Native Voice*, July 1956, 8.
252. *The Native Voice*, December 1949, 4.
253. *The Native Voice*, January 1950, 3.
254. H. B. Hawthorn, C. S. Belshaw, and S. M. Jamieson, *The Indians of British Columbia: A Study of Contemporary Social Adjustment* (Toronto and Vancouver: University of Toronto Press and the University of British Columbia, c.1958), 379.
255. *The Native Voice*, October 1949, 1.
256. *The Native Voice*, January 1950, 3.

257. The Indian Act of 1927, as quoted in *The Native Voice*, January 1950, 3.
258. *The Native Voice*, June 1949, 2.
259. *The Native Voice*, March 1951, 16.
260. Ibid.
261. *The Native Voice*, January 1950, 4.
262. *The Native Voice*, April 1950, 2.
263. Ibid., 4.

Chapter 6
264. *Vancouver News-Herald*, April 13, 1950, 1.
265. Alison McLeay, *The Tobermory Treasure* (London: Conway Maritime Press, 1986), 31; a quote by William Asheby, a member of the English Embassy to the Scottish Court.
266. Royal Commission on the Ancient Historical Monuments of Scotland, Canmore, San Juan De Sicilia: Tobermory Bay, Sound of Mull, Notes and Activities; Archaeological Notes NM55NW 8013 c. 51 55 N56 37 W6 4 (specifically NM56SW 1).
267. Stanley Russell, Scottish newspaper (unknown and undated).
268. Much of the factual information about the Tobermory galleon has been gleaned from a report prepared by Wessex Archaeology entitled "Tobermory Galleon, Tobermory Bay, Sound of Mull."
269. *Vancouver News-Herald*, April 13, 1950.
270. *The Native Voice*, November 1950, 5.
271. *The Native Voice*, December 1950, 13.
272. *The Native Voice*, June 1950, 4.
273. *The Native Voice*, June 1950, 5.
274. *The Native Voice*, July 1950, 4.
275. *The Native Voice*, October 1950, 7.
276. *The Native Voice*, July 1950, 8.
277. *The Native Voice*, September 1950, 3.
278. *The Native Voice*, July 1950, 8.
279. *The Native Voice*, November 1950, 5.
280. *The Native Voice*, February 1951, 4.
281. *The Native Voice*, July 1950, 5.
282. *The Native Voice*, June 1950, 5.
283. *The Native Voice*, December 1950, 18.
284. *The Native Voice*, January 1951, 9.
285. *The Native Voice*, June 1950, 4.
286. *The Native Voice*, December 1950, 13.
287. *The Native Voice*, February 1951, 3.
288. "Indian Land Claims Debunked," *Vancouver News-Herald*, January 10, 1951.
289. "Maisie Challenges BC Historian," *Vancouver News-Herald*, January 12, 1951.
290. *The Native Voice*, February 1951, 3.

291. Ibid., 7.
292. *Vancouver Province*, January 1951; reprinted in *The Native Voice*, February 1951, 3.
293. Ibid., 16.
294. *The Native Voice*, March 1951, 3.
295. Ibid., 16.
296. Letter from Maisie to Hugh Dempsey, January 16, 1951.
297. *The Native Voice*, February 1951, 7.
298. Ibid., 8.
299. Ibid.
300. *The Native Voice*, April 1951, 3.
301. *The Native Voice*, May 1951, 9.
302. *The Native Voice*, February 1951, 16.
303. *The Native Voice*, May 1951, 9.
304. *The Native Voice*, April 1951, 14.
305. *The Native Voice*, May 1951, 3.
306. *The Native Voice*, February 1951, 4.
307. *The Native Voice*, May 1951, 9.
308. Ibid., 4
309. Ibid.
310. Ibid.
311. *The Native Voice*, January 1951, 12.
312. *The Native Voice*, August 1951, 4.
313. Interview with Phil Nuytten, July 13, 2011.
314. Interview with Chief Bill Wilson, February 29, 2012.
315. Interview with Joan Hall, September 27, 2012.
316. *The Native Voice*, August 1951, 4.
317. Ibid., 3.
318. *The Native Voice*, September 1951, 8.

Chapter 7

319. Tom Jarvis, *Vancouver Sun*, September 24, 1951; *The Native Voice*, September 1951, 4.
320. Undated letter to Hugh Dempsey.
321. Letter to Maisie from Adona Antoine (unknown date in fall 1951).
322. *The Native Voice*, December 1951, 7.
323. *The Native Voice*, October 1951, 12.
324. *The Native Voice*, November 1951, 4.
325. Ibid., 7.
326. Clipping from unknown newspaper, December 27, 1951.
327. *Vancouver Sun*, December 27, 1951, 2.
328. Ibid.
329. "Montrose Heart Here," *Vancouver Sun*, January 16, 1952.
330. Nagle, "Maisie Says BC Still Belongs to the Indians."
331. Penny Glenday, *The Scots Magazine*, 387.

332. From Maureen Woodcock's unpublished manuscript.
333. *The Native Voice*, December 1951, 4.
334. *The Native Voice*, October 1951, 4.
335. *The Native Voice*, January 1952, 2.
336. *The Native Voice*, May 1952, 11.
337. *The Native Voice*, June 1952, 11.
338. *The Native Voice*, February 1952, 3.
339. *The Native Voice*, June 1952, 11.
340. *The Native Voice*, February 1952, 3.
341. *The Native Voice*, June 1952, 2.
342. Ibid., 4.
343. *The Native Voice*, January 1952, 3.
344. *The Native Voice*, November 1952, 2, 6.
345. Ibid., 2.
346. *The Native Voice*, December 1952, 4.
347. *The Native Voice*, October 1953, 5.
348. *The Native Voice*, November 1952, 2.

Chapter 8
349. *The Native Voice*, September 1951, 3.
350. Ibid., 4.
351. *The Native Voice*, April 1955, 4.
352. *The Native Voice*, June 1955, 3.
353. *The Native Voice*, March 1956, 2.
354. *The Native Voice*, February 1953, 1, 8.
355. Ibid., 1.
356. Ibid., 8.
357. *The Native Voice*, March 1953, 8.
358. *The Native Voice*, May 1953, 3.
359. *The Native Voice*, June 1953, 4.
360. *Seattle Post-Intelligencer* (unknown date); reprinted in *The Native Voice*, June 1953, 3.
361. Ibid.
362. *The Native Voice*, June 1953, 2.
363. Ibid.
364. The *Native Voice*, October 1953, 2.
365. *The Native Voice*, August 1954, 3.
366. *The Native Voice*, December 1953, 6.
367. *The Native Voice*, January 1954, 7.
368. Ibid., 1.
369. Ibid.
370. Ibid., 4.
371. Ibid., 3.
372. Ibid., 1.
373. *The Native Voice*, May 1954, 5.

374. *The Native Voice*, June 1954, 2.
375. *The Native Voice*, April 1954, 5.
376. *The Native Voice*, April 1955, 5.
377. *The Native Voice*, September 1954, 4.
378. Ibid., 8.
379. *The Native Voice*, May 1954, 3.
380. Ibid.
381. Ibid.
382. Ibid.
383. Ibid.
384. *The Native Voice*, March 1955, 2.
385. Ibid., 3.
386. Ibid., 4.
387. Ibid., 1.
388. *The Native Voice*, July 1954, 5.
389. Ibid., 4.
390. Ibid.
391. Ibid., 5.
392. *The Native Voice*, February 1955, 1.
393. *The Native Voice*, November 1954, 5.
394. *The Native Voice*, December 1954, 2.
395. Ibid., 3.
396. Ibid., 2.
397. Ibid.
398. *The Native Voice*, January 1955, 4.
399. *The Native Voice*, April 1955, 4.
400. *The Native Voice*, May 1955, 3.
401. Ibid., 4.
402. *The Native Voice*, May 1955, 3.

Chapter 9

403. *The Native Voice*, July 1955, 1.
404. Ibid.
405. Ibid., 3.
406. Ibid., 3, 7.
407. *The Native Voice*, February 1955, 3.
408. *The Native Voice*, August 1955, 2.
409. Ibid., 3.
410. Ibid., 2.
411. *The Native Voice*, September 1955, 3.
412. Ibid., 2.
413. *The Native Voice*, November 1955, 1.
414. *The Native Voice*, December 1955, 3.
415. Ibid., 7.
416. Ibid., 4.

417. *The Native Voice*, January 1956, 1, 8.
418. Ibid., 4.
419. *Calgary Herald*, date unknown; reprinted in *The Native Voice*, July 1956, 4.
420. *The Native Voice*, April 1954, 5.
421. *The Native Voice*, January 1956, 3.
422. *The Native Voice*, February 1956, 3.
423. *The Native Voice*, December 1956, 3.
424. *The Native Voice*, May 1956, 7.
425. Ibid., 11.
426. Ibid.
427. *The Native Voice*, July 1956, 5, 7.
428. *The Native Voice*, September 1956, 8.
429. Ibid., 3.
430. Ibid.
431. *Indian Missionary Record*; reprinted in *The Native Voice*, July 1956, 7.
432. *The Native Voice*, September 1956, 1.
433. *The Native Voice*, October 1956, 3.
434. Ibid., 1, 3.
435. Ibid., 3.
436. *The Native Voice*, November 1956, 8.
437. *The Native Voice*, January 1957, 4.
438. Ibid.
439. Ibid.
440. *The Native Voice*, March 1957, 7.
441. *The Native Voice*, February 1957, 4.
442. Ibid.
443. J. W. Pickersgill, *Seeing Canada Whole* (Markham, Ontario: Fitzhenry & Whiteside, 1994).
444. *The Native Voice*, March 1957, 4.
445. *The Native Voice*, February 1957, 1.
446. Ibid.
447. *The Native Voice*, March 1957, 1.
448. Ibid., 4.
449. *The Native Voice*, April 1957, 5.
450. Ibid
451. *The Native Voice*, May 1957, 1.
452. Discussion with Andy Everson via telephone on May 24, 2012.
453. *The Native Voice*, July 1957, 4.

Chapter 10

454. *Calgary Albertan*, August 7, 1957; reprinted in *The Native Voice*, September 1957, 4.
455. *The Native Voice*, October 1957, 4.
456. *Prince Rupert Daily News*, September 11, 1957; reprinted in *The Native Voice*, November 1957, 2.

457. Ibid., 3.
458. *The Native Voice*, December 1957, 3.
459. Ibid.
460. *The Native Voice*, February 1958, 1, 4.
461. John G. Diefenbaker, *One Canada: Memoirs of the Right Honourable John G. Diefenbaker, The Crusading Years 1895–1956* (Toronto: MacMillan, 1976), 29–30.
462. *The Native Voice*, November 1958, 7.
463. *The Native Voice*, April 1958, 4.
464. *The Native Voice*, May 1958, 5.
465. *The Native Voice*, June 1958, 1.
466. Letter #342139, June 30, 1958, University of Saskatchewan Archives, Diefenbaker Collection.
467. *The Native Voice*, July 1958, 4.
468. Ibid., 7.
469. *The Native Voice*, Special Centennial Edition, 1.
470. Ibid., 3.
471. Ibid., 7.
472. *The Native Voice*, September 1958, 4
473. *The Native Voice*, October 1958, 4.
474. Ibid., 8.
475. *The Native Voice*, January 1959, 8.
476. Ibid., 5.
477. *The Native Voice*, July 1959, 7.
478. *The Native Voice*, January 1959, 1.
479. Ibid.
480. Ibid., 5.
481. *The Native Voice*, December 1958, 4.
482. Ibid.
483. *The Native Voice*, February 1959, 5.
484. Ibid.
485. *The Native Voice*, May 1959, 1.
486. *Vancouver Sun*, April 28, 1959; reprinted in *The Native Voice*, May 1959, 2.
487. *The Native Voice*, June 1959, 1.
488. *The Native Voice*, July 1959, 1.
489. *The Native Voice*, August 1959, 1.
490. *The Native Voice*, July 1959, 2.
491. Drucker, *The Native Brotherhoods*, 139.
492. *The Native Voice*, August 1959, 3.
493. *Toronto Telegram*, December 1959; reprinted in *The Native Voice*, December 1959, 4.
494. *The Native Voice*, Special Edition, February 1960, 1.
495. Ibid., 1.
496. Ibid., 4.

497. Ibid., 3.

498. Ibid.

499. Interview with Chief Bill Wilson on February 29, 2012.

500. Roland Wild, "Woman in the News," *Vancouver Province*, September 6, 1960.

Chapter 11

501. *The Native Voice*, April 1960, 6.

502. Ibid., 4.

503. Ibid., 5.

504. *The Native Voice*, May 1960, 4.

505. *The Native Voice,* Special Edition, February 1960, 7.

506. Ibid., 5.

507. *The Native Voice*, March 1960, 1.

508. Ibid., 7.

509. *The Native Voice*, April 1960, 3.

510. *The Native Voice*, October 1960, 3.

511. *The Native Voice*, October 1961, 4.

512. *The Sheridan Press*, Sheridan, Wyoming; reprinted in *The Native Voice*, October 1960, 4.

513. *The Native Voice*, June 1960, 6.

514. *The Native Voice*, July 1960, 7.

515. Ibid.

516. *The Native Voice*, August 1960, 7.

517. *The Native Voice*, October 1960, 1.

518. *The Native Voice*, July 1960, 7.

519. Ibid.

520. *The Native Voice*, June 1960, 1.

521. Ibid.

522. Tennant, *Aboriginal Peoples and Politics*, 122.

523. The Native Voice, June 1960, 4.

524. *The Native Voice,* August 1960, 2.

525. *The Native Voice*, October 1960, 1, 4.

526. Ibid.

527. *Vancouver Province*, October 14, 1960, 19; reprinted in *The Native Voice*, November 1960, 1.

528. Ibid., 1, 8.

529. Ibid., 8.

530. *The Native Voice*, December 1960, 4.

531. Ibid.

532. *The Native Voice*, January 1961, 1.

533. Ibid., 1, 5.

534. *The Native Voice*, February 1961, 2.

535. *The Native Voice*, March 1961, 1.

536. Ibid.

537. *The Native Voice*, April 1961, 1.
538. *The Native Voice*, May 1961, 1.
539. Ibid., 6.
540. *The Native Voice*, June 1961, 1.
541. Ibid., 6.
542. Ibid., 2.
543. *The Native Voice*, December 1960, 1.
544. Ibid., 11.
545. *The Native Voice*, April 1961, 3.
546. *The Native Voice*, August 1961, 6.
547. Ibid., 7.
548. *The Native Voice*, November-December 1961, 4.
549. Ibid., 1, 9.
550. *The Native Voice*, December 1960, 12.
551. *The Native Voice*, April 1961, 3.
552. Ibid., 4.
553. Ibid.
554. *The Native Voice*, August 1961, 3.
555. *The Native Voice*, May 1961, 1.
556. *The Native Voice*, June 1961, 3.
557. Ibid., 2.
558. *Vancouver Sun*, July 14, 1961; reprinted in *The Native Voice*, August
     1961, 4.
559. *The Native Voice*, August 1961, 1, 5.
560. Ibid., 5.
561. *The Native Voice*, September 1961, 4.
562. Ibid., 1.
563. *The Native Voice*, November-December 1961, 6.
564. Ibid.
565. *The Native Voice*, October 1961, 1.
566. *The Native Voice*, November-December 1961, 4.
567. Ibid., 4.
568. Ibid., 12.
569. Ibid., 15.
570. Letter to Prime Minister John G. Diefenbaker, December 29, 1961.
     Letter #343757, University of Saskatchewan Archives, Diefenbaker
     Collection.

Chapter 12

571. *Vancouver Sun*, December 26, 1961.
572. *The Native Voice*, January 1962, 1, 2, 4.
573. Ibid., 4.
574. Ibid., 1.
575. Ibid.
576. *The Native Voice*, March 1962, 2.

577. *The Native Voice*, July 1962, 3.
578. Ibid.
579. *The Native Voice*, October 1962, 2.
580. *The Native Voice*, May 1962, 2.
581. *The Native Voice*, March 1962, 4.
582. Ibid., 1.
583. *The Native Voice*, April 1962, 6.
584. *The Native Voice*, March 1962, 8.
585. *The Native Voice*, May 1962, 5.
586. Ibid.
587. *The Native Voice*, October 1962, 5.
588. *The Native Voice*, March 1962, 2.
589. Letter to Ian Drost from J. A. Macaulay dated May 30, 1962, regarding Maisie's concern. University of Saskatchewan Archives, Diefenbaker Collection.
590. Ibid.
591. Ibid.
592. *The Native Voice*, June 1962, 3; letter from Prime Minister Diefenbaker to Maisie.
593. *The Native Voice*, June 1962, 4.
594. *The Native Voice*, September 1962, 4.
595. Ibid., 1.
596. Interview with Judge Alfred Scow on March 5, 2012.
597. *The Native Voice*, December 1962, 10.
598. Ibid., 1, 6.
599. Ibid., 9.
600. Ibid., 11.
601. *The Native Voice*, January 1963, 1.
602. *The Native Voice*, December 1962, 4.
603. Maisie Hurley, "The Mountains," newspaper article (unknown paper and date); reprinted in *The Native Voice*, December 1962, 4.
604. *The Native Voice*, January 1963, 2.
605. *The Native Voice*, December 1962, 4.
606. *The Native Voice*, January 1963, 2.
607. Ibid., 4.
608. *The Native Voice*, April 1963, 1.
609. *The Native Voice*, July 1963, 1.
610. Ibid.
611. Ibid.
612. Ibid.
613. Bill Morriss, *Winnipeg Free Press*, August 15, 1963; reprinted in The Native Voice, August 1963, 1.
614. Ibid., 1.
615. Ibid., 4.

616. Thomas R. Berger, *One Man's Justice: A Life in the Law* (Vancouver and Toronto: Douglas & McIntyre, 2002), 87.
617. Ibid.
618. *UBCIC News*, "A Chronology," February 1979, 17. Vancouver: Union of British Columbia Indian Chiefs, accessed via UBCIC digital collection, January 19, 2015, http://www.ubcic.bc.ca/Resources/Digital/index.htm.
619. Berger, *One Man's Justice*, 89.
620. The Douglas Treaties: 1850–1854. Executive Council of British Columbia, BC Archives.
621. Berger, *One Man's Justice*, 101.
622. *The Native Voice*, November 1963, 1.
623. Ibid., 3.
624. Ibid.
625. *The Native Voice*, January 1964, 4.
626. *The Native Voice*, February 1964, 1.
627. *The Native Voice*, November 1963, 2.
628. *The Native Voice*, May 1963, 1.
629. *The Native Voice*, December 1963, 4.
630. Ibid., 1.
631. *The Native Voice*, January 1964, 1.
632. *The Native Voice*, February 1964, 1.
633. *The Native Voice*, March 1964, 1, 5.
634. Ibid., 3.
635. Court of Appeal summary: *R. v. White and Bob*.
636. Jack Wasserman, *Vancouver Sun*, June 9, 1964; reprinted in *The Native Voice*, June 1964, 1.
637. *The Native Voice*, April 1964, 1.
638. *The Native Voice*, August 1964, 6.
639. *The Native Voice*, October 1964, 2.
640. Ibid.
641. Ibid., 4.
642. Ibid., 1.
643. Ibid., 2.
644. Ken Coates, *The Marshall Decision and Native Rights* (Montreal and Kingston: McGill-Queen's University Press, 2000), 84.
645. Interview with Thomas Berger, January 20, 2012.
646. *The Native Voice*, October 1964, 4.

Epilogue
647. *The Native Voice*, November 1964, 4.
648. *The Native Voice*, June 1965, 1.
649. Ibid.
650. *The Native Voice*, July 1965, 1.
651. *Vancouver Sun*, Weekend Magazine, April 4, 1964.

BIBLIOGRAPHY

Andersen, Earl. *A Hard Place To Do Time: The Story of Oakalla Prison, 1912–1991*. New Westminster, BC: Hillpointe Publishing, c.1993.

Berger, Thomas R. *One Man's Justice: A Life In The Law*. Vancouver and Toronto: Douglas & McIntyre, 2002.

Davis, Chuck. *The Chuck Davis History of Metropolitan Vancouver*. Madeira Park: Harbour Publishing, 2011.

Diefenbaker, John G. *One Canada: Memoirs of the Right Honourable John G. Diefenbaker, The Years of Achievement 1956–1962* and *The Crusading Years 1895–1956*. Toronto: MacMillan, 1976.

Drucker, Philip. *The Native Brotherhoods: Modern Intertribal Organizations on the Northwest Coast*. Washington, DC: Smithsonian Institution, Bureau of American Ethnology Bulletin 168, 1958.

Duff, Wilson. *The Indian History of British Columbia*. Volume 1: *The Impact of the White Man*. Anthropology in British Columbia Memoir No. 5 Victoria: Provincial Museum of Natural History and Anthropology, 1964.

Dunlop, Herbert Francis. *Andy Paull: As I knew Him and Understood His Times*. Vancouver: Order of the O.M.I. of St. Paul's Province, 1989.

Edwards, Brendan F. R. "'I Have Lots of Help Behind Me, Lots of Books to Convince You': Andrew Paull and the Value of Literacy in English." BC Studies 164 (Winter 2009–10).

Fortney, Dr. Sharon. "Entwined Histories: The Creation of the Maisie Hurley Collection of Native Art." BC Studies 167 (Autumn 2010).

Grauer, Peter. *Interred With Their Bones: Bill Miner in Canada, 1903–1907*. Kamloops, BC: Self-published, 2006.

Hawthorn, H. B., C. S. Belshaw, and S. M. Jamieson. *The Indians of British Columbia: A Study of Contemporary Social Adjustment*. Toronto and Vancouver: University of Toronto Press and the University of British Columbia, c.1958.

Introduction to RG10 Indian Affairs, Royal Commission on Indian Affairs of the Province of British Columbia, Queen Charlotte Islands Agency, Queen Charlotte Agency, 1913. Excerpted from *Haida Laas*, originally published September 2001, reissued September 2010.

Joseph, Gene. *A Brief History of the Native Brotherhood of British Columbia*. Vancouver: Native Brotherhood of British Columbia, 1981.

Matthews, J. S. *Conversations with Khatsahlano 1932–1954: Conversations with August Jack Khatsahlano, born at Snauq, False Creek Indian Reserve, circa 1877, son of Khaytulk and grandson of Chief Khahtsahlanogh* Compiled by Major J. S. Matthews, city archivist, and typed by Mrs. Alera Way, City Hall. Vancouver: n.p., 1955.

Morely, Alan. *Roar of the Breakers.* Toronto: The Ryerson Press Toronto, 1967.

Orchard, Imbert. *Maisie Hurley, Interview Tracks 1 and 2.* Vancouver: CBC, 1961.

_____*Chief William Scow Interview.* Vancouver: CBC, 1967.

Patterson, E. Palmer. "Andrew Paull and Canadian Indian Resistance." Ph.D. thesis, University of Washington, 1962.

Pickersgill, J. W. *Seeing Canada Whole.* Markham, Ontario: Fitzhenry & Whiteside, 1994.

Public Archives of Canada, Scott Papers, RG 10, Vol. 6810, File 473, Vol. 12, Hearings Testimony, 1921–22.

Pue, Wesley. *Law School: The Story of Legal Education in British Columbia.* Vancouver: University of British Columbia Faculty of Law, 1995.

Royal Proclamation of 1763.

Striegler, Lisa. *Saik'uz and Settlers, A Weave of Local History.* Expanded Play Program. An Initiative of the Good Neighbours Committee. Prince George: College of New Caledonia Press, 2011.

Tennant, Paul. *Aboriginal Peoples and Politics: The Indian Land Question in BC.* Vancouver: UBC Press, 1990.

Union of British Columbia Indian Chiefs. *The Lands We Lost: A History of Cut-Off Lands and Land Losses from Indian Reserves in British Columbia,* http://ubcic.bc.ca/files/PDF/McKenna_McBride/lands.pdf, 1974.

Ward, Robert. *Wealth and Notability: The Lockwood, Day and Metcalfe Families of Yorkshire and London.* Huddersfield, UK: Self-published, 2014.

INDEX

C

D

H

I

J

K

Miner, Bill (see Edwards, George)
Minute 1036 — 202, 215
Montrose, First Marquis (aka James Graham) —18, 139-141, 145
Murphy, Martin Joseph — 27-31, 33

N

National Covenant of 1638 — 139
National Harbours Board — 224-225
National Indian Council (NIC; later known as the Assembly of First Nations)
— 226, 237, 244
Native Brotherhood of British Columbia (NBBC) — 36-37, 43, 49-52, 58, 60-
63, 68-71, 73-75, 77-82, 84, 87, 90, 95-99, 107-110, 114, 117, 120-121, 126-130,
135, 145, 151-152, 154, 156-158, 162-165, 167-168, 170-174, 177, 186-188, 194-
195, 197-198, 201-202, 205, 208, 213-214, 217, 219, 226-228, 237-242, 246,
249-252, 254-256, 258
Native Sisterhood of British Columbia (NSBC) — 62-63, 99, 114, 134, 156, 167,
174, 197
Newcombe, W. A. — 50
Nielsen, Erik (Progressive Conservative for Yukon) — 193
Nisga'a Land Committee — 40, 51
Nisga'a Petition — 42
Nisga'a Tribal Council — 210, 217-218, 240-241, 244
Norris, Justice Tom — 256
North American Indian Brotherhood (NAIB) — 73, 80, 88, 128, 154, 202, 227,
237-238, 240-241, 243, 249, 252
North Island (Langara Island) — 34
North, George — 132, 255
Nuytten, Phil — 132-133

O

Oakalla Prison Farm — 104, 111, 123, 130, 134, 196-197, 246
Oliver, Premier John — 46
Oppenheimer, Mayor David (children, Rena and Flora) — 21

P

Pacific Coast Native Fishing Association (PCNFA) — 51
Patrick, Dick — 101-105, 123, 163
Paull, Andrew — 42-48, 51, 73, 79-81, 96, 124, 128-129, 154, 160, 171, 189, 197,
202, 223, 225
Paull, Cliff — 225
Paull, Percy — 225, 227, 234

St. Laurent, Prime Minister Louis — 111, 120, 171, 180-182
St. Pierre, Paul — 26, 70-71
Stewart, Charles (Federal Minister of the Interior) — 45-46
Swencisky, Justice A. H. J. — 251-252, 256

T

Tecumseh — 148
Teit, Alexander — 45-46
Tremblay, Minister of Citizenship and Immigration René — 252
Tysoe, Appellate Justice C. W. — 231

U

United Fishermen and Allied Workers (UFAWU) — 107-108, 196
United Nations Declaration of Human Rights — 110, 121

V

Vancouver, Captain George — 152, 154

W

Weir, Harold — 161-162
Wheatley-Crowe, Captain Henry Stuart — 141
White, Clifford (see White and Bob case) — 245-246
White and Bob case — 246-249, 251-254, 256
Wicks, Labour Minister Lyle — 169, 175, 202, 208
Williams, Guy — 37, 49, 73, 77, 79-81, 95, 125, 127, 139, 145, 152, 173, 188, 192, 211, 214, 219, 226, 228, 239-240, 249-256, 258
Wilson, Chief Bill (Hemads-Kla-Lee-Lee-Kla) — 133-134, 205
Winch, Harold (CCF Leader) — 61, 105
Wismer, Attorney General Gordon — 95, 97, 104, 108, 119, 144
Woodcock, Maureen — 29

ERIC JAMIESON is the author of *Tragedy at Second Narrows: The Story of the Ironworkers Memorial Bridge* (Harbour Publishing, 2008), co-author of *South Pole: 900 Miles on Foot* (Horsdal and Schubart, 1996), and has contributed articles on outdoor living and history to a variety of newspapers and magazines. In 2009, he was awarded the Lieutenant-Governor's Medal for History Writing.